A History of

WOKING

Emmets Mill

Sandpit Hill

Bourn Brook

Straught

Youngs F.

Mill BR. Almansley E.

Com

Coxhill Green

Woodham Heath

Byfleet Corner

Sheer Water E.

Wes Lo

Horsell Birch

Pottas Corner

Basingstoke Canal

The Anch

Kettlewell

Horsell

Woking Heath

Tirford Green

Tirford

Whistley Warren

Hardland Worthy

Royal Oak Green

Oaks

Heath Side

Grassland

Monu.

Round Br. E.

Ruins of Newark Abbey

Belmond

Kingsland Green

Hoe Br.

Hoebridge Place

Woking Park

Newark Mill

Barnsbury

Woking

Dunsboro House

Egley

Homewood E.

Woking Mill

Wey River

Ripley

Mayford Green

Loampit

Beach Hill

Westfield Rundley Wood

Fisher

Tan Yard

Paperstock F.

marts Heath

Lee Place

24

Pile Ho.

Cricket Hill

Send Marsh

Brick Kilns

Whitemoor Pond

Fry lane F.

Sutton Green

Westram

Send Barn Fethill

Send

Sundrish F.

Panoma

Grove

Send E.

25

Whitemoor Common

Luvgrove

Three Fords

Hazelhu F.

Jacobs Well

Lutton Hay

26

Burpham Oil Mill

Gasding Hill

Ea.

Tenement F.

Place

Fortunes

A History of
WOKING

ALAN CROSBY

 PHILLIMORE

2003

Published by
PHILLIMORE & CO. LTD
Shopwyke Manor Barn, Chichester, West Sussex, England

ISBN 1 86077 262 5

Printed and bound in Great Britain by
BUTLER & TANNER LTD
London and Frome

The frontispiece is an enlarged extract from the first edition Ordnance Survey one-inch to one-mile map of Surrey, published in 1816. The most remarkable aspect of the landscape shown is the almost complete lack of any habitation in the entire area between Hoe Bridge, Kingfield, Horsell and what is now West Byfleet. Town Square, the focal point of early 21st-century Woking, is close to the crossing of the rough tracks shown in the middle of the empty expanses of Woking Heath.

This book is dedicated to the memory of my father, George Hugh Sinclair Crosby, who died in 1978. I should like to add a further dedication to Douglas Butterworth, my geography master at the Boys' Grammar School from 1966 to 1973, and for the last thirty years a friend and correspondent. He taught me a great deal.

CONTENTS

Acknowledgements   xi
Illustration Acknowledgements   xii
Introduction   xiii

Before the Railways Came   1

  1. The geographical background   2
  2. The archaeological record   3
  3. The Saxon settlement   5
  4. Woking Minster   6
  5. The manor and palace of Woking   8
  6. Other manors in Woking parish   11
  7. Manors in Byfleet, Horsell and Pyrford   14
  8. Landscape, society and economy in medieval Woking   16
  9. Churches, religion and piety   19
 10. The villages before the railways came   23
 11. The waste   30
 12. Managing the waste   31
 13. The piecemeal enclosure of the waste   32
 14. The squatter settlements   33
 15. Open fields, meadows and greens   35
 16. The Wey Navigation   38
 17. Population change in the 18th century   40
 18. Occupations and employment in the early 18th century 41
 19. Agriculture and industry in the 18th century   42
 20. Crime and misdemeanour   47
 21. Isolation or integration: the evidence for mobility 48
 22. The Basingstoke Canal   50
 23. Nurserying   53
 24. Parliamentary enclosure   55
 25. The landscape of enclosure and its fate   58
 26. Dealing with poverty in early 19th-century Woking   61
 27. Unemployment, distress and unrest   63

A New Town Grows   65

 28. The coming of the railway   66
 29. The railway network 1840-1910   68
 30. The impact of the railways   69
 31. The London Necropolis and National Mausoleum Company 70

32. The London Necropolis Company Act of 1852   71
33. Acquiring the land and the 1854 Act   72
34. Later amending Acts: 1855, 1864 and 1869   73
35. Brookwood Cemetery   74
36. The role and importance of the Necropolis Company   77
37. The new town centre   78
38. The first land sales   79
39. The town centre takes shape   80
40. Walton Road and Goldsworth   82
41. The Royal Dramatic College and Oriental Institute   85
42. South of the railway   88
43. Hook Heath   92
44. The institutions   93
45. The convict prison and barracks   93
46. Brookwood Hospital   96
47. Knaphill and St Johns   98
48. The crematorium   100
49. Horsell   101
50. Byfleet   103
51. West Byfleet   105
52. The southern borders: Pyrford to Mayford   107
53. Images and reflections   109

People and Government   **113**

54. The population in the 19th century   114
55. Where they came from   115
56. Governing the growing town   117
57. The introduction of urban government   118
58. Further changes, 1900-1933   119
59. Water supplies   120
60. Roads, bridges and their repair   121
61. Sewers and drains   123
62. Gas and electricity   126
63. Street lighting   127
64. Fire services and wartime emergencies   128
65. Employment in the 19th century   130
66. The pattern of agricultural change   131
67. Brickmaking in the 19th and 20th centuries   133
68. Paper and printing   134
69. Railways   136
70. Rural industries in the 19th century   136
71. Religion in the growing town   137
72. Religious faith in the mid-19th century   139
73. Education   140
74. The school boards   142
75. Secondary education   143
76. Public health and medical care   143

Between the Wars   **145**

   77. Overview   146
   78. Town planning questions   146
   79. The geography of growth, 1918-1939   147
   80. Public housing between the wars   149
   81. Higher density private building   151
   82. The exclusive estates   155
   83. Local government since 1920   157
   84. Unworthy meeting places   158
   85. Councillors and officials   160
   86. Streets and roads   162
   87. Leisure and recreation   165
   88. Population in the inter-war years   168
   89. Shops and traders, 1840-1940   169
   90. Industry, employment and commuting   174

Yesterday, Today and Tomorrow   **177**

   91. The post-war context   178
   92. Overspill   178
   93. The green belt   180
   94. Council housing   183
   95. Mount Hermon and Goldsworth Park   185
   96. Population changes since 1945   188
   97. Employment in Woking since 1945   190
   98. Roads, traffic and railways   192
   99. Redeveloping the town centre   193
  100. Planning, environment and conservation   198
      Endnote   202

      Sources and Bibliography   203
      Index   205

ACKNOWLEDGEMENTS

When I researched and wrote the first edition of this book I was helped by many people, and it is a pleasure to be able to repeat the thanks which I expressed to them in 1982. The staff of what were then the Surrey Record Office in Kingston and the Guildford Muniment Room; Woking Library, Guildford Library and Guildford Museum; the Public Record Office; Woking Borough Council; Brookwood Cemetery Office; and the *Woking News and Mail* all gave invaluable assistance and it is true to say that neither the first edition nor this second edition could have been written without their patient and generous help back in 1980-81. I also thanked individuals who contributed to my work: David Chapman, Howard Cook, John Wetton, Barry Lynch, Dawn Chinnery, Mrs P. Fosberry of Warminster, and Mr T.G. Fuller, and it is sad to record that some have since died. I would like to express my special regret that among them was Dawn Chinnery, a much-loved friend for forty years, Woking born and bred and an entertaining expert on the unofficial (sometimes *very* unofficial!) history of the town and its people. My mother Elsie Crosby and my sister Alison gave extensive help with the first edition and a lot with the second, including putting me up and putting up with me on my frequent visits to Woking.

For this second edition I have received invaluable help from the West Surrey Family History Society and its chairman, Phillip Arnold. Their excellent transcripts of parish registers, will calendars and other documentary material, and Phillip's work on Woking Palace, have made the task of research far simpler than it would otherwise have been. The Society has generously allowed me to make use of its material in this way and I am very grateful. Above all, in this edition, I have been assisted by the staff of the Surrey History Centre in Goldsworth Road. During the past twenty-five years I have worked as a researcher and historian in over forty record offices and archive repositories across the length and breadth of England (and a couple in Scotland and Wales) and I can truthfully say that the Surrey History Centre is one of the top three for quality of service, helpfulness of staff, and excellence of working environment. Woking is indeed fortunate to have such a superb resource in its midst. I am grateful to all the staff, but would like to mention in particular Julian Pooley who has arranged for the reproduction of many of the illustrations and given general encouragement. Thank you, too, to Nicola Willmot and Phillimore for producing such an attractive and well-designed book.

ALAN CROSBY

ILLUSTRATION ACKNOWLEDGEMENTS

I should like to give my particular thanks to all the owners and custodians of photographs and other images which have been used for illustrations in this book. The specific acknowledgements are as follows. The two aerial photographs, on pages 195 and 197, are from the Surrey History Centre Woking photographs box and are reproduced by kind permission of Aerofilms Limited. The illustrations on pages 29 (top), 61, 95 (top), 104 (both), 108 and 130 are from the collection of David Chapman. Those on pages 20 (bottom), 26, 95 (bottom), and 102 are from the collections of Guildford Museum and have been used by courtesy of Guildford Borough Council. The pictures on pages 81 (photograph), 87 (medallion), 89, 99, 108 (top), 136 and 171 are from the collection of the late John Wetton. Those on pages 25 (both), 138 and 170 (top) were made available by the *Woking News and Mail*. Unwins provided the picture on page 135. The pictures on pages 52, 90 and 172 are from private collections. The picture on page 38 belongs to Noel Osborne of Phillimore, a native of Woking, who commissioned this book – and its predecessor in 1982.

The Surrey History Centre provided the majority of the other photographs and pictures, and gave invaluable assistance with the selection and reproduction of this material. The following are from collections held in the Surrey History Centre: pages 22 (brass), 28 (mill) Byfleet Photographs Box; page 200 Pyrford Photographs Box; pages 10 (beacon), 27 (Sutton Green), 39 (lock), 42, 44, 46, 55, 80, 117 (bottom), 154 Woking Photographs Boxes; pages 12 (drawing), 13, 67, 71, 75, 86, 88, 101, 111, 136, 167, and 201 from collection reference PX 160; pages 121 (both) from collection PX 121; page 20 (middle) from PX 25; pages 8, 20 (top), 23, 24, 103, 153 from the Barclay collection of illustrations reference 4348; pages 24, 31, 45, 52, 83, 84 (bottom), 107, 108, 121 (both), 122, 125, 133, 138, 150, 152, 159 (both), 163 (both), 164 (both), 165, 166, 172, 173 (both), 175, 176, 184, 186, 192, 196, 198 (both) from the photographic collections of Woking Borough Council (reference 6198/5).

The Ordnance Survey extracts reproduced in the book are from the 25-inch to 1-mile series, using the editions published in 1871, 1896, 1912-1916, and 1934-1936. All the maps used are from the collections held at the Surrey History Centre. The copies of older pre-Ordnance Survey maps including Speed (1610), Sellers (1690), Rocque (1762), and Lindley and Chapman (1793) are also from the collections of the Surrey History Centre. The maps, graphs and document transcripts on the following pages were drawn by or created by the author. They are the copyright of Alan Crosby and may not be reproduced without permission: 6, 7, 9, 10, 21, 22, 23, 29, 32, 34, 35, 36, 47, 49, 58, 59, 60, 62, 66, 68, 69, 73, 79, 81, 84, 91, 102, 115 (both), 118, 119, 139, 146, 148, 157, 179, 181, 182, 186, 188, 189, 199, and 202. The sources of the transcribed extracts are: p. 21 J.R. Daniel-Tysson (1869); p.22 original will of John Ynwood; p.47 QS2/6/1790/Mid 47; p.49 QS2/6/1799/Mid 38; and p.139 QS2/6/1777/Mic 35a-b.

INTRODUCTION

The first edition of this book was published in 1982. Woking seemed then to be settling down to a period of relative calm after two decades of upheaval and expansion. Appearances were deceptive. In the last twenty years even more dramatic changes have taken place and there is another chapter in the story of the town. My book was the first-ever full history of Woking and since then other local historians have used it extensively (and occasionally without acknowledgment!) as a source and background text for their own work. That is what I intended, for one of my hopes was that it would make readers more conscious of the history of their town and encourage better levels of protection for the heritage of the borough. Over twenty years later it is especially gratifying that Woking will soon have a museum, but it is also a matter of major satisfaction that Woking Borough Council has become so active and progressive in its policies towards building conservation, the designation of conservation areas, the protection of the rural environments of the area, and environmental issues in the wider sense. At last it is possible to say that in the future Woking's history will be properly cared for. Nor should we forget the valiant efforts of those volunteers in local history, conservation and environmental organisations who have campaigned over the years towards these ends and have been instrumental in keeping up the pressure for enlightened policies and real action. Their dedication of time, money and effort has been to the greater good of the community as a whole.

My 1982 book has long been out of print and I felt that it was appropriate to produce a new edition which would reflect not only the changes which had taken place in Woking over that time, but would also draw upon my own continuing development as a professional local and regional historian working in different parts of England. It is inevitable that what I wrote in my early 20s is not always what I would write now, though the book has stood the test of time very well. But there were aspects of the town's history which I did not then cover in detail but which in this edition receive more attention, and vice versa. I could also take advantage of the dramatic changes in technology since 1980 when I wrote the first edition. Then my mum sat at home typing out my longhand manuscript ... now of course it is all done on the computer. Photographs were expensive and few. Now the book can be much better illustrated.

The largest town in Surrey is the least appreciated. It merits only a few lines in published histories of the county and is usually dismissed as uninteresting, a dull dormitory town with no redeeming features. To others it is a railway station, or the place from where the coach to Heathrow goes. That, of course, is very far from the truth. Woking not only has a remarkable and extraordinary history, but also it is a complex and in some ways contradictory place. One of the themes which I identified twenty years ago and which is more prominent in this edition of my book is that 'other' Woking, of poor housing, social problems, inadequate infrastructure and an absence of planning, rural poverty in the past, housing crises in the present. While these are not desirable attributes for any town, their existence emphasises that the uniformly bland place of the outside image is not a reality now and never has been. Another theme is Woking's struggle to find itself, to grow up and take its proper place among the leading towns of south-east England. It took 150 years for this to happen, but now it is for the first time a place which has the status, confidence and positive character which its large population merits. That process has now been completed by the news that Woking will soon become the administrative capital of the county, when Surrey County Council moves from Kingston in 2007. In a few years' time it might even be known as the county town. How that would have amazed the people who watched the first train steam into the little station on the empty heath in May 1838!

In revising and extending my text all sorts of memories came back. For me it was partly a nostalgic journey into a Woking childhood forty years ago. I used to lie awake on clear frosty nights when strange atmospherics meant that down in Kingfield you could hear every single sound and movement as the steam engines shunted through the night in Woking yard. I remembered the most wonderful smell in all of Woking, as the haze of blue smoke emerged from the pavement-level grille outside Carwardine's door when the coffee was being roasted. I recalled going into the fields off Mill Moor in Old Woking on sunny summer afternoons to catch sticklebacks and minnows in nets, and walking back from school through the park on winter afternoons as the chilly mist was rising from the Hoe Stream. There were other memories … the floods of 1968; the sound of the air-raid sirens being tested (that must have been about 1960); watching the orange glow in the eastern sky as Newark Mill burned down in 1966; Aldershot & District Traction Company buses; snow over my wellington tops in the bitter winter of 1962-63; going to the scruffy old market next to Victoria Arch on Saturday mornings and always being given an apple by the lady on the fruit stall. In part, therefore, this book is a reminder of a Woking which has gone, but it is also a history which comes up to the present day, because history does not come to an end. When I am quite a lot older, and the third edition is being written, what new events and changes will I describe? I do not know, for I have learned not to make predictions. However, writing this second edition has been even more enjoyable and rewarding than writing its predecessor, so I look forward to doing the next one with great interest.

ALAN CROSBY

August 2003

BEFORE THE RAILWAYS CAME

1. The geographical background

The four ancient parishes of Woking, Horsell, Pyrford and Byfleet, which today form the borough of Woking, lay across the watershed between the basins of the Wey and the Bourne (also known as Windle Brook and the Hale Bourne), a short tributary of the Thames which it reaches at Chertsey. Below Old Woking the Wey is joined by one of its larger tributaries, the Hoe Stream (or Stanford Brook) which drains the heaths and damp meadows of Worplesdon, Pirbright and Wanborough. There are other minor streams, such as the Rive Ditch, which rises in the vicinity of Goldsworth Park and flows east to the Wey at Brooklands, through a shallow valley which in the past was notably boggy, and feeding a large shallow lake, the Sheerwater, which was drained (not very successfully) in 1820. *Rive* is an Old English word meaning 'ditch' – this anonymous and largely forgotten watercourse had no proper name. The stream which rises on Sheets Heath and flows south, through another watery valley, via Brookwood to Crastock and the Hoe Stream was once called Corsebrook, a name derived, appropriately enough, from the Celtic word *cors*, a bog.

Separating the shallow damp valleys and basins is a series of low ridges, which give the area its topographical identity and help to provide visual and physical variety. Travelling through Woking it is still very clear that they are the three-dimensional frame across which the town was stretched. Go from Horsell Birch, down Horsell High Street, into the town centre, and the rise and fall of the land is subtle but clear. Carry on down Guildford Road and the steep slope which runs along the whole of the northern edge of the Wey valley is very obvious – less than a hundred feet vertical difference but making a sharp descent with distant views across the valley to the North Downs. The drop of Anchor Hill at Knaphill, the hill on which Pyrford church stands, the sudden descent from Hook Heath to Mayford, the long line of the scarp east of Old Woking Road – these are the underlying landforms. This was a crucial factor in shaping Woking for, small though these features are, the early development of the district was extremely sensitive to minor differences. Damper ground was avoided, while steeper slopes delineated the edge of the heaths and the boundary of cultivation. No less important, for the affluent newcomer in the 1890s the slopes and ridge edges with wide views were the ideal place to live. It is noticeable how many of the most expensive housing developments of the half-century from 1880 were to be found in such locations.

The Woking area, as shown on John Speed's map of Surrey 1610: the map shows the Wey, the Hoe Stream and the Bourne, and marks the four main parks at Sutton, Woking, Pyrford and Byfleet. Most prominent, however, is the great wood of Brookwood, a major landscape feature of which the woodlands south of Brookwood Hospital along Brookwood Lye are the last surviving remnants.

Geographers also identify other key landscape features. The river terraces are long belts of flat gravel-covered ground, the result of erosion processes. Two are recognised in the area: one, at about 15-18 metres above the present level of the river Wey, extends from Pyrford through West Byfleet to New Haw, and is also identified at Sutton Green and Pyle Hill. The other, at only three to five metres above river level, is better developed and stretches in a discontinuous line along the Wey from Sutton Place through Old Woking to Pyrford and Byfleet, and along the Hoe Stream through Mayford, Westfield and Kingfield. If you stand at Hipley Bridge, Old Woking, you can see how the terrace on the north bank is raised a couple of metres above the level of the river, while on the south bank the floodplain is close to river level. This terrace is of major importance in the history of the area because it was a choice location for early settlement, close to the river yet relatively dry, above the level of most floods (but, as we know in our time, not all of them) and easily worked for agriculture.

2. The archaeological record

This area of Surrey has never had a high priority for archaeological investigation and few sites have been systematically excavated. Although over the decades small pieces in the jigsaw have been put in place, and some important evidence has emerged, there is still a great deal to be discovered and an even larger amount which has been lost forever during the course of development over the past two centuries. It used to be considered that the sandy ridges and heaths of west Surrey were always largely barren and never had any substantial level of occupation, but recently a more sophisticated analysis of past environments has demonstrated a higher level of settlement and economic exploitation than previously realised. Such reassessments involve not only a greater understanding of the extent of human activity but also upward revision of population estimates. They are found very widely across the British Isles and have allowed gaps in knowledge and spaces on the map to be filled, particularly for the prehistoric and Roman periods.

In the Woking area, as elsewhere in Surrey, the heaths and commons, with their characteristically scrubby vegetation and thin soils, are now known to be largely the creation of man himself. Four or five thousand years ago these areas were used for farming and agriculture. Aerial photography and field surveys have revealed, for example, the faint remains of Bronze-Age field boundaries on Whitmoor Common, Smarts Heath and Horsell Common, barely detectable from a casual view but clear enough from the air or during meticulous field-work to be identified with confidence. Thus, the heathlands were agricultural land five millennia ago. Why, then, did the heaths develop? The answer is probably quite simple. The thin sandy soils were relatively infertile and can never have supported intense farming, but they were also vulnerable to ecological and environmental damage. The arable areas were overworked and under-fertilised, while the grasslands (where domesticated herds and flocks roamed) were overgrazed. Soil quality fell sharply, the grasslands became impoverished, the woodland areas were cleared by deliberate felling or by animal grazing and could not regenerate. Farmland had to be abandoned and throughout west Surrey and east Hampshire was invaded by heather, gorse, bracken and coarse moorland grasses. By the Roman period the typical ecology and landscape character of the west Surrey heaths were well established. This process of heath and moor development is now known from many parts of southern England, such as Exmoor, the Dorset heaths and the fringes of Dartmoor. It was an early, and dramatic, illustration of man's impact upon the environment, and was not destined to be reversed for several thousand years. We know little of the people whose farming activities were responsible for this change, but a few long familiar monuments, unspectacular but archaeologically significant, do survive. The most notable are three Bronze-Age tumuli, or burial mounds, on Horsell Common near the Six Crossroads. Elsewhere, Mesolithic (Old Stone Age), Neolithic (New Stone Age) and Bronze-Age occupation has been confirmed at a variety of locations, including the Mizen's Farm site near Dunford Bridge, excavated in 1996-99; in the vicinity of Byfleet mill and Newark Priory on the terraces of the Wey; and at Woking Park Farm and Derry's Field, Old Woking. We cannot draw a proper picture of settlement or human activity over these long centuries and millennia, but what we do know is striking in itself – that man's presence was already the main determinant of landscape change.

The geography of settlement and landscape in the Roman era is almost as unclear, though more is known about this period elsewhere in Surrey. Here, too, more is being discovered and reappraisals of former views are in progress. The Romans came to a landscape which was settled and everywhere showed the hand of man. There is some definite evidence for occupation during the Roman period – thus, coins and pottery have been found at Coldharbour in Pyrford, while at Old Woking there are Roman tiles in the fabric of the church – but much remains obscure and there is potential for more archaeological and landscape history investigation. It has long been known that a Roman road headed north-west from Rowhook near Horsham to the Romano-Celtic temple at Farley Heath near Shere. It must have carried on towards the Thames valley, perhaps destined for the Maidenhead area (though Silchester is another possibility). In 1972 the line of the road was apparently confirmed when it was found during the building of the M3 at Lightwater, so it now seems likely that it passed through Bisley and somewhere in the vicinity of Knaphill or Bridley before heading towards Merrow and Newlands Corner. More recently, another road, running east towards Ewell from the small Roman town at Neatham near Alton, has also been postulated. This, too, probably passed through the Woking area. There is, as yet, little indication of fully-Romanised settlement in Woking itself but there is abundant evidence of such occupation nearby, including villas in the Guildford area and the spectacular temple complex at Wanborough which has been excavated (and plundered by treasure-seekers) in the past twenty years. Archaeological work has, however, revealed the remains of semi-Romanised native farmsteads, most notably beside the river at Woking Park Farm below Old Woking, and at Mizen's Farm where the site was intermittently occupied during the Roman period (as well as for two thousand years before and a thousand years after).

3. The Saxon settlement

Most major place-names in the Woking area are topographical – that is, they relate to landscape features – and are of Anglo-Saxon origin. Byfleet means 'the place by the stream' (*fleot*, as in Fleet in Hampshire), though why this location rather than any other in this watery land should have been singled out is unclear. Pyrford means 'the ford by the pear tree' (*pyrige*) (a word also found in Pirbright, 'the wood with the pear tree'): it indicates the wild pear, a distinctive and beautiful species. Mayford means 'the ford with the mayweed'. Numerous names relate to woodland and trees, such as Brookwood (the straightforward 'the wood with the brook') and Woodham ('the wooded place'), and this frequency undoubtedly reflects the above average proportion of woodland in the local landscape a millennium and a half ago. Horsell is more of a problem because the name is not recorded until the 13th century, much later than the others. It is probably derived from *horig scylf*, which means 'muddy slope or shelf on a hillside'.

The most significant name, though, is that of Woking itself. Until the mid-1960s it was believed that places with names ending in *–ing* represented settlements founded in the earliest phase of the Anglo-Saxon occupation. According to this theory, these were the primary places from which colonisation spread outward to secondary communities, which themselves eventually emerged as fully-fledged villages. More recently the theory has been discredited. It was observed that pagan burial grounds, dating from the century and a half before the conversion to Christianity in 597-610, are almost invariably remote from the places with *–ing* names. So, it was argued, the *-ing* places were more likely to be settlements founded in the *later* phases of colonisation. This view had a certain logic, for it suggested that in Surrey the initial colonisation was along the belt of drier land north of the North Downs, from London towards Guildford (where there are virtually no *–ing* names) and settlement then spread northwards into the less attractive heaths and marshy valleys of the Woking area and southwards along the upper Wey, where *–ing* names are comparatively frequent. Thus, according to the 1960s' idea, the Woking area was possibly first settled by the Saxons in the years around 600. It is, however, important to recognise that the Saxons came not to virgin territory, as also used to be thought, but to farming communities in which man had been active in modifying and reshaping the landscape for several thousand years. It now seems likely that there were already settlements at places such as Woking and that these were simply renamed by the newcomers.

More recently, though, historical research on the early territorial arrangements of Surrey has given renewed weight to the notion that places such as Woking and Godalming were of major importance at a very early stage in the Saxon colonisation. The name Woking means 'the place of Wocc's (or Wocca's) people' and there is an obvious similarity with Wokingham and Wokefield in Berkshire, in which the same personal name presumably appears. This perhaps indicates that Wocc/Wocca was a leading figure (a 'chieftain' in the old romantic terminology) whose tribe or group colonised a wide area of the heathlands of north-west Surrey and south-east Berkshire – though it is also of course possible that there was more than one person with the same

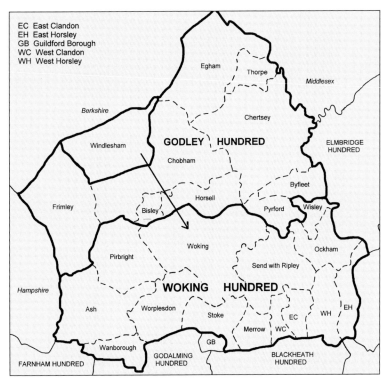

EC East Clandon
EH East Horsley
GB Guildford Borough
WC West Clandon
WH West Horsley

Egham

Thorpe

Middlesex

Berkshire

Chertsey

GODLEY HUNDRED

ELMBRIDGE HUNDRED

Windlesham

Chobham

Byfleet

Horsell

Pyrford

Wisley

Frimley

Bisley

Woking

Ockham

Pirbright

Send with Ripley

WOKING HUNDRED

Hampshire

Ash

Worplesdon

Stoke

EC

WH

EH

WC

Merrow

GB

Wanborough

GODALMING HUNDRED

BLACKHEATH HUNDRED

FARNHAM HUNDRED

The two hundreds of Woking and Godley, which together formed the territory of the Wocchingas in the period immediately after the Anglo-Saxon colonisation in the 6th century. The map shows the late medieval parish boundaries.

name. We will never know. It is, however, certain that the county boundary roughly follows the line of a major territorial division dating back to the early Saxon period when Surrey was a sub-kingdom in its own right, and that throughout recorded history there has been no connection – administrative, political or ecclesiastical – between the Woking area and Wokingham. They were in different kingdoms, dioceses and counties.

Woking was the centre of a medieval hundred (the main sub-county administrative divisions) extending from the Hampshire border at Ash, as far as East Horsley, and including Stoke next Guildford. However, Windlesham, though detached geographically, was also associated with Woking and was in the hundred throughout the Middle Ages. The hundred of Godley, based on Chertsey, included Byfleet, Horsell and Pyrford, and the documentary evidence makes it clear that this hundred was created later than that of Woking, sometime before the Norman Conquest, so that the lands and estates of the powerful monastery of Chertsey would be within its administrative jurisdiction – in other words, the hundred of Godley was carved out of what was once a much larger administrative unit based on Woking. The historian John Blair proposes that Woking, an important royal manor at the time of the Domesday Survey in 1086, was therefore one of the *regiones* of Surrey. These were very early Saxon territorial divisions based on royal estates. He argues that Woking hundred and Godley hundred together formed a district which must be the original tribal territory of the Woccingas, the people of Wocc/Wocca. Its boundaries are described in a charter of about 672 by which lands were granted to Chertsey Abbey. It lay between the Thames, the lands of the Sunninges (the tribe whose territory covered the Sonning and Sunningdale area of Berkshire), and an ancient ditch called the *Fullingadic* which is traceable on St George's Hill, Wisley Common and Ockham Common. The unit thus defined was logical in geographical terms, a neat rectangle with the Downs and Hogs Back to the south, the Blackwater valley to the west, the wide heaths to the north-west, the Thames to the north-east and the watershed between the Wey and the Mole to the east. This was the original *regione* of Woking, from which the two later hundreds emerged sometime in the pre-Conquest period.

4. Woking Minster

The earliest written reference to Woking appears – remarkably enough – in a letter from Pope Constantine to the monastery at *Medeshamstede* (now

Peterborough) in about 710. It related to two other monasteries, daughter houses or dependents of Peterborough and both dedicated to St Peter, at *Vermundesei* (Bermondsey) and *Wocchingas* (Woking). This fascinating reference is reinforced by a charter dated sometime around 780 and issued by the celebrated King Offa of Mercia (the overlord of Surrey) in which he confirms a grant of 20 hides of land to the church at Woking 'in which place the monastery is situated'. The charter, which gave proper legal title to an existing grant, was issued at the request of Abbot Pusa of Peterborough and a nobleman, Brordar. Slightly earlier in origin was the great monastery at Chertsey, founded in about

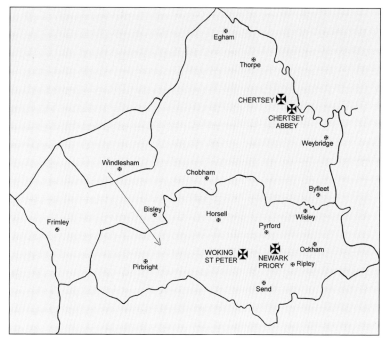

The parochiae *(large ancient parishes) of Woking and Chertsey in the pre-Conquest period. These were the territories served by the ancient minster churches and in each an early Saxon monastery was situated. Both parishes included a number of dependent chapels which eventually became fully-fledged parish churches in their own right.*

666 and destined to be one of the wealthiest religious houses in the medieval south-east. In his masterly account of the political, administrative and ecclesiastical organisation of Surrey in the period 500-1300, John Blair analyses the implications of these two very early monasteries for the territorial arrangements of the north-west of the county, and for the history of the churches and parishes in the Woking area.

Using early charters and deeds he demonstrates that the church and monastery of St Peter at Woking was the 'mother church' or minster for a parish (or *parochia*) which extended in a broad sweep from the ridge west of Pirbright, through Horsell and Woking to the Ripley area, and included not only the minster church of Woking but also dependent chapelries at Pirbright, Bisley, Pyrford, Wisley, Send and Ripley, together with Windlesham as a detached outlier to the north-west. Similarly, he argues, Chertsey parish originally embraced Byfleet, Weybridge, Chertsey, Thorpe and Egham, Chobham and Frimley. These huge parishes formed the framework for ecclesiastical administration and also reflected the landholdings of the monasteries, whose endowed estates were located within these bounds. Their significance was temporal as well as spiritual. Comparable minster churches, with very large early parishes, can be identified at, among other places, Godalming, Farnham and Leatherhead. The monastery at Woking was almost certainly on the site of the present St Peter's church, the dedication of which is derived from that of its monastic predecessor. It lay at the very edge of the later Woking parish, but, if the original boundaries which Blair postulates are accepted, it stood at the centre.

There is another important theme in Blair's analysis. In the mid-1190s Newark Priory, a house of Augustinian canons, was founded by Ruald de Calne, a local landowner, and Beatrix his wife. The founding charter specifically states that the new monastery was to be given to an existing body of canons, and Blair suggests convincingly that these were the secular canons

A south-east view of the ruins of Newark Priory, engraved by Samuel and Nathaniel Buck in 1728: the priory was the direct successor to the ancient monastery of St Peter at Woking, and it remained a central element in the religious life of the district until its dissolution by Henry VIII in 1538. Its romantic remains, in the watery meadows by the Wey, are the best-preserved monastic site in Surrey, although they are not open to the public.

still living at Woking. This implies that the Saxon monastery had ceased to function as a religious house in the later sense, but that the parish church retained its high status and was served by a group of canons rather than a single parish priest – a hangover from a much earlier monastic arrangement. Thus, the canons of Woking simply moved a couple of miles down the river to their new buildings on the water meadows of the Wey at Newark Priory ('the new work' or 'the new place') and their successors remained there until the Dissolution of the monastery in 1538, giving a historical continuity over almost a thousand years. The territorial assets of Newark Priory reinforce this explanation, for in the 13th and 14th centuries these included rights over the churches and chapels at Woking, Horsell, Pyrford, Send and Ripley, all part of the ancient *parochia* of Woking. As a result of the expansionist activities of Chertsey Abbey, the creation of Newark Priory and its endowments, and the elevation of dependent chapels into fully-fledged parish churches, the parish of Woking was gradually reduced in extent. Pyrford, Horsell, Pirbright, Bisley and Windlesham retained tenuous connections with Woking until the 14th century, but by 1400 each of these had been formally separated. Horsell was closely linked with Pyrford, and they constituted a joint parish in the later Middle Ages, though Pyrford's closest links after 1550 were with the equally small and under-populated chapelry of Wisley.

5. The manor and palace of Woking

Parallel with the pattern of parishes and hundreds was the manorial system which developed by the time of the Norman Conquest. Manors were private property and could be bought, sold, confiscated and regained, so they usually have a complex history inextricably associated with the genealogies of leading families and the fortunes of individuals. They did not necessarily coincide with the boundaries of other administrative units, so the pattern of their geography can also be confusing. The manor of Woking eventually covered 6,830 acres (roughly 70 per cent of the parish) but originally it was somewhat smaller. As an important royal possession before the Norman Conquest, in 1066 it automatically passed to the new king, William I. It was formerly believed that there were two manors of Woking, the other being the property of the bishop of Exeter, but it is now known that this arose from an error in Domesday Book – the bishop's manor of East Horsley was erroneously listed under the heading of Woking. In 1200 King John granted Woking manor to a leading supporter, Alan Bassett, and it remained with his family until 1260 when it passed by marriage to Hugh le Despenser. In 1326 Hugh's grandson, one of the favourites of Edward II, was executed and the next king, Edward III, granted Woking to his uncle, Edmund Holland, Earl of Kent. In the mid-15th century the manor and its estates were inherited by the Margaret Beaufort, Duchess of Somerset, whose husband was the grandson of John of Gaunt and whose only daughter was Lady Margaret Beaufort.

This was of major importance for the district, because the substantial manor house beside the river just below Woking village was now associated with royalty. Lady Margaret was a central figure in the turbulent and violent politics of later 15th-century England, playing a prominent part in the conspiracies by which her son eventually seized the throne at Bosworth Field in 1485 and succeeded as Henry VII. Woking was her home for most of her later life and it was also one of the houses frequently visited by the king and by her grandson, Henry VIII, to whom she bequeathed it on her death in 1509. The house had been described in a survey of 1327 as comprising a hall, chapel, two chambers, pantry, buttery, kitchen, larder, bakehouse, brewhouse, poultry house and laundry, with moats, a gatehouse, outbuildings and gardens. Under the early Tudors, as one of their series of major houses in the area beyond but easily accessible from London, it was extensively rebuilt and improved, as befitted a royal palace. Henry VIII undertook major construction work here in the latter part of his reign between 1532 and 1542, and archaeological investigation during the past twenty years has revealed important information about the scale and grandeur of the complex which Henry created. The accounts of building work, and contemporary surveys, list over 57 rooms, apartments and domestic buildings, many of them specifically named for individual members of the royal family and household. Though we know virtually nothing of the furnishings of rooms such as 'The King's chamber of presence', the 'Great Chamber', the Lady Mary's lodgings, the 'King's holiday closet' and the 'King's privy jakes' (though we can guess at the latter) there is no doubt that by 1540 Woking was an exceptionally luxurious and well appointed residence, palatial and splendid, and set amid fine gardens, orchards, ponds and moats, beside the slowly flowing waters of the Wey.

There are numerous references to the house in royal correspondence and official documents of the reigns of Henry VII and Henry VIII. Historians use the places

The Tudor royal palace at Woking, redrawn from Norden's map of 1609: prominent in this view are the moats and bridges, together with the residential and state buildings arranged around three sides of a great courtyard. This is the only reasonably reliable image of the great house which we have, since most of it was demolished by Sir Edward Zouch twenty years later. Today only fragments remain of what was, in its heyday, one of the greatest buildings in southern England.

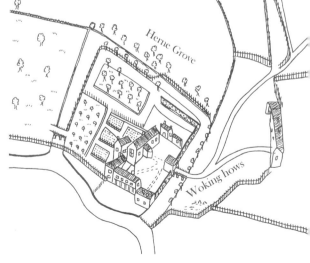

where correspondence was dated (thus, 'given at our house of Okyng' at such and such a date) to identify the travels of kings, queens and leading courtiers and ministers, and this evidence confirms that Woking was a regular holiday home, meeting place and venue for great events. Famously, it was here in 1497 that Henry VII signed a friendship and non-aggression pact with the Emperor Maximilian of Austria, a document known to history as the treaty of Woking. Thomas Wolsey is said to have been staying at Woking with Henry VIII when the formal confirmation was received that the pope had made him a cardinal, and Henry spent several weeks here every summer. Archaeological research has shown that there were wharves or a quay on the riverside, suggesting that the king might well have arrived and departed by water.

Mary I and Elizabeth I viewed Woking Palace with less favour, staying only intermittently and – typically of Elizabeth – spending little on repairs and maintenance. The house began to deteriorate and by the end of the 16th century was regarded as old-fashioned. It stood largely empty and in 1618 James I, always desperate to raise some cash, sold the house, estate and manor to one of his favourites, Sir Edward Zouch, granting him leave to demolish as many of the buildings as he wished. Zouch pulled down most of the palace and used the materials for the construction of Hoe Place, for extensions and improvements to what became Woking Park Farm, and for other buildings in the area. He also built the tower or beacon (said to be a lighthouse to guide travellers across the wild heaths) which stood on the hilltop above Hoe Place. The

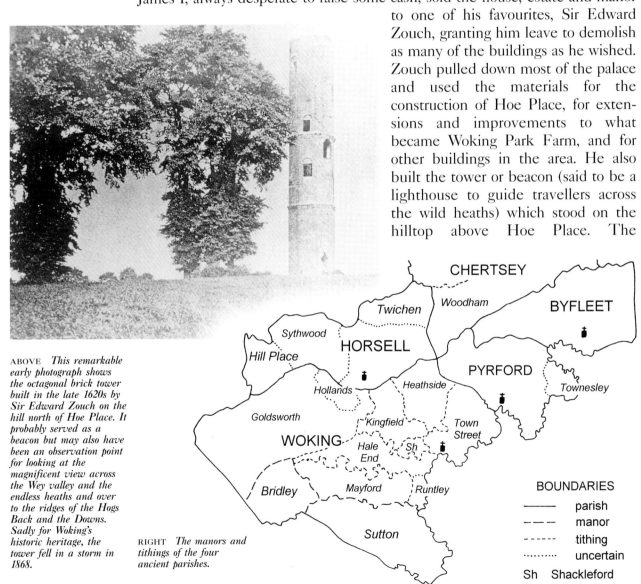

ABOVE *This remarkable early photograph shows the octagonal brick tower built in the late 1620s by Sir Edward Zouch on the hill north of Hoe Place. It probably served as a beacon but may also have been an observation point for looking at the magnificent view across the Wey valley and the endless heaths and over to the ridges of the Hogs Back and the Downs. Sadly for Woking's historic heritage, the tower fell in a storm in 1868.*

RIGHT *The manors and tithings of the four ancient parishes.*

CHERTSEY

Twichen   Woodham

BYFLEET

Sythwood

HORSELL

Hill Place

PYRFORD

Hollands   Heathside

Townesley

Goldsworth   Kingfield   Town Street

WOKING   Hale End   Sh

Bridley   Mayford   Runtley

BOUNDARIES

——— parish
– – – manor
- - - - tithing
·········· uncertain
Sh   Shackleford

Sutton

Jacobean tower, octagonal and 60 feet high, gave its name to Monument Hill and remained a landmark, ruinous and unsafe, until it collapsed during a great storm in 1868.

The site of the palace was largely abandoned after 1630. The moats became silted and overgrown, the gardens disappeared under scrub, and only some sections of walling and one fine red-brick Tudor barn now survive, though there is still much of great interest on the site. The surrounding deer park, at one time over five miles in circumference and extending along the meadows of the Wey and up the slopes towards Old Woking Road and Pyrford church, reverted to agriculture and field hedges were laid out across the open grassland during the 1620s. The destruction of the palace was probably inevitable, for the royal family had too many large houses, and fashions and tastes had changed, but we may lament its loss, for this would surely have been a building of national architectural and historical importance. Had it remained in royal hands and royal use it would have dramatically affected the way that Woking developed in more recent centuries. But that was not to be. The male line of the Zouch family became extinct in 1671 and though the manor reverted to the Crown, Charles II (following well established tradition) granted it to one of his many mistresses, Barbara, Duchess of Cleveland. In 1715 it was bought by John Walter and in 1752 his son sold the entire estate and lordship to the Earl of Onslow, the leading Surrey nobleman and an avid collector of lordships and estates.

6. Other manors in Woking parish

The other major manor in Woking parish was Sutton, 'the south hamlet' (referring to its position within the parish). In 1070 it was given by William the Conqueror to Robert Malet, one of his companions in arms, and it was probably he who built the first manor house on a site close to the later Sutton Place. In 1100, during the bitter dispute between Robert, Duke of Normandy, and his younger brother, Henry I of England, Malet backed the losing side. His properties were confiscated by Henry I and Sutton was a Crown possession until 1200 when King John gave it, with Woking, to Alan Bassett. From then until 1521 it was held jointly with its larger neighbour, but in that year Henry VIII separated it once more and gave it to a favoured courtier, Sir Richard Weston. Thereafter the Weston family and their descendants were lords of the manor of Sutton until the early 20th century. After a period in the ownership of the dukes of Sutherland, who lived there as their 'just outside London' residence in the 1930s-50s, it was bought by John Paul Getty, the oil magnate, as his English home and since then has had a succession of opulently wealthy owners.

The manor house of Sutton, described as ruinous in 1329, had been demolished long before the manor was separated from that of Woking in 1521. In the intervening two centuries there had been no need for another large house, as the two manors were administered as one unit. But after Sir Richard Weston had been given the lordship and estate he set about building a grand house for himself, to reflect the high status and leading public position of a newly rich and very influential gentleman of the court. The site was at the top of a low hill with fine views across the Wey valley, and the great house was designed in the most fashionable style. It is the finest building by far in Woking and one of the greatest early Tudor houses in England.

Sutton Place also has an important position in architectural history, because it was one of the earliest all-brick houses and among the first in the country designed entirely for domestic comfort and architectural splendour. Unlike the previous generation of country houses there was not even a pretence at defence or military design – no moats, no battlements, no hint of castle architecture. Woking Palace, a couple of miles away, had the full panoply of moats and a very traditional layout, but Sutton, just ten years later, marked the advent of a new age. Simple in conception, as a two-storey quadrangle around a courtyard (one side of which was demolished in the 18th century), it was elaborated by the use of exquisite architectural details, such as prefabricated Italian terracotta panels (the earliest important instance of such a device in England), while its symmetrical plan around a central

Sutton Place: this drawing, of which the original is now lost, is probably the earliest surviving image of the house, the finest building in Woking and one of the most important buildings of the early 16th century. The drawing was made in the 17th century, and its delightful representations of horses, cattle, pigs, hares and hounds draw attention – whether deliberately or not – to the fact that the house was the centre of a large agricultural estate. Note also the four-storey central gatehouse tower, and compare with the next illustration.

great hall was also innovative and trend-setting. The estate dominated Sutton and its manorial lords ruled a semi-feudal fiefdom well into the 19th century. Almost all the land in the manor was owned by the Westons and they provided most of the employment, either directly in the house, gardens and home farm, or indirectly through the tenancies of farms and smallholdings. Nobody lived in Sutton unless the lords allowed them to do so, and they controlled very strictly the lives and the business of all the inhabitants. Though part of Woking parish, Sutton was quite distinct and set apart, physically relatively remote though close to Woking and Guildford. It is still, in the early 21st century, a surprisingly separate community, away from the very well-beaten track of the A320 with its incessant streams of traffic.

In the south-west of Woking parish was a third, much smaller, manor, usually known as Bridley (though the alternative name, Crastock, was widely used). Until the 12th century this was part of the manor of Pirbright, but in the mid-1240s it was acquired by Fulk Bassett, bishop of London and lord of Woking. Thereafter it was firmly attached to Woking parish and, though not united with Woking manor, was usually held under the overlordship of the latter. The manor was sub-let to a long succession of tenants and the history of its leasing and possession is extremely complex. Mayford was also considered as a distinct entity, separate from Woking, Sutton and Bridley, until the middle of the 13th century. It was not, however, a manor in its own right and when, in the 1240s, Fulk Bassett bought it from the trustees of Henry Kinton he amalgamated it with Woking manor and its semi-separate existence ended. The manor of Runtley or Emley was another shadowy division, marked

on maps in the 16th and 17th centuries, extending across the flat meadows between Sutton and Woking. Locke, in the early 20th century, suggested that it might have been a property held by the monks of the Saxon monastery of Woking, while it is also possible that it was associated with Newark Priory. The sub-manor of Rudehall or Hollands lay across the damp basin of what was a thousand years later to become Goldsworth Park. It is improbable that the name was derived from the Holland family, earls of Kent, a theory popular in the 19th century, and the name is more likely to derive from the Old English *healh*, 'a wide shallow basin'. Both Hollands and Emley were fully absorbed into Woking manor by the mid-17th century.

The manor of Woking was divided into seven tithings at least as early as the 14th century. Tithings were the smallest administrative unit, below the level of the manor and parish. Each tithing chose representatives (known as 'tithingmen') to attend parish meetings and to perform other minor local government duties. In Woking these divisions were still generally recognised and formed the framework of local administration as late as the 19th century. Town Street tithing covered Woking village; Shackleford, the smallest, included the land which is now built over by Gloster Road, Shackleford Road and Vicarage Road; Kingfield tithing extended almost to the present town centre along the Hoe valley and its northern slopes, as well as around Kingfield Green; Heath Side included Maybury, Heathside Road and the Walton Road district; Hale End stretched in a narrow belt from Blackhorse Road via Hook Heath to the river near Woking village; Mayford included Smarts Heath, Mayford Green and much of Westfield; and the very large tithing of

A sketch of Sutton Place published in the Gentleman's Magazine in 1789. It shows the house at the nadir of its fortunes, after many decades of serious neglect and in a partly ruinous state. The decay of the gatehouse is particularly obvious: how much real help did the frail timber supports actually give?! In the years after 1790 John Webb Weston, the inheritor of the estate, undertook major restoration works.

Goldsworth included all the rest of the manor, from Brookwood and Knaphill through Goldsworth itself. From the 17th century onwards Sutton and Bridley or Crastock were also recognised as tithings, making a total of nine.

7. Manors in Byfleet, Horsell and Pyrford

The boundaries of the manor of Byfleet coincided with those of the parish. At the time of the Domesday Survey it was held by Ulwin, a tenant of Chertsey Abbey, and it had been among the estates granted to the abbey on its foundation in the middle of the seventh century. Other lands granted to Chertsey at that time included the manor of Woodham in Chertsey parish. The manor of Byfleet had 'members', detached portions of land in other parishes which were jointly administered with the main manor. Thus, it had members in the parish of Effingham and also in Bisley – joint sessions of the manor court between Byfleet and Bisley were held as late as the 17th century. Although it had been an ecclesiastical manor, Byfleet passed into royal hands in the early 14th century and was granted by Edward II to his lover, Piers Gaveston, suggesting that it was deliberately confiscated in order to enrich the king's favourite. After Gaveston's downfall and execution it became part of the estates of the Duchy of Cornwall, though Chertsey Abbey retained a residual interest, and passed from king to eldest son and back again for the next two centuries. In 1533 it was given to Catherine of Aragon as a small recompense for being divorced by Henry VIII, but she died in 1536 and the abbey was dissolved in 1537, so royal control was swiftly resumed. Henry VIII treated the manor as an endowment for the great palace of Hampton Court and it was so administered, always sub-let to private tenants, until 1650 when the Commonwealth government sold it. In 1660 Charles II granted it to his mother, Henrietta Maria, and it remained in royal hands, still sub-let to bring in useful income, until in 1804 a private Act of Parliament allowed Frederick, Duke of York to acquire the manorial rights, lands and titles of Byfleet, Weybridge and Walton Leigh.

He died in 1820 and in 1829 the property and title were sold yet again, to Lord King of Ockham, already lord of the manor of Pyrford. On his death it passed to his relatives, the Locke King family, who remained lords of the manor until just before the Second World War. Alone among its long succession of owners and tenants, the

An extract from John Rocque's map of Surrey (1762) shows, but does not name, Byfleet Park, south-east of the village on the banks of the River Wey. In contrast 'Purford Lodge' is labelled. It occupies a not dissimilar location, just above the beautiful riverside and well distant from the rest of the populace. The house was demolished shortly afterwards and Pyrford Place built in its stead.

Locke Kings took a genuine interest in Byfleet, making a real effort to improve the conditions of their tenants and the welfare of the village and acting as leading patrons of local good causes. The manor house of Byfleet, often known as Byfleet Park, was at the southern end of the parish in the long loop of the Wey. The medieval house (of which almost nothing is known) was pulled down in the 1540s by Sir Anthony Browne, the courtier who was at that time lessee of the manor from the Crown. He is said to have built a new mansion, but a survey of the park at Byfleet, made in about 1568, described the house as 'decayed', which suggests that the work was either much less ambitious or had remained unfinished. The same survey stated that the park covered 200 acres of ground, half of which was given over to arable farming, and that it had about a hundred deer. In 1615, when the estate was temporarily in the tenancy of Anne of Denmark, wife of James I, extensive building work began, to be completed by Sir Thomas Fullerton in 1620. Yet more reconstruction was carried out in 1685-90, leaving only a magnificent pair of gateposts (designed by the German architect Wendel Detterlein) from the earlier house. More remodelling in the 1730s and the late 19th century left the basic late 17th-century design relatively unscathed and, despite this long list of changes and improvements, the house was described by Ian Nairn in the 1960s as one of the best of its date in the county ... but which date!

Pyrford and Horsell manors were held jointly throughout the medieval period, and early boundary charters of Chertsey Abbey indicate that a portion of Woodham, in the angle between Horsell and Pyrford, was also included and was held as such during the Middle Ages. Horsell was always the junior partner and as a result it is the only one of the six main manors in the Woking area which never had a large house. Although both parishes had early associations with Chertsey Abbey, and came within the hundred of Godley, the joint manor was owned by Edward the Confessor in 1042 and from the mid-1050s was leased to Earl Harold. After his brief reign as Harold II, and death at Hastings, it was seized by William I. In 1069 the new king granted it to Westminster Abbey and it remained their property until the Dissolution in 1540, when it was taken by the Crown. In 1574 Elizabeth granted it to Edward Clinton, Earl of Lincoln, and from him it passed through a succession of different owners until 1677 when the Earl of Onslow bought it. In 1805 an Act of Parliament authorised the enclosure of Pyrford and Woodham, which were then sold as a separate lordship to Lord King of Ockham, but Horsell was not enclosed and the manor of Horsell was held by the earls of Onslow into the 20th century.

A small manor of Townsley or Toundesley, recorded in 1297, lay beside the Wey in the south-east corner of Pyrford parish, extending north almost as far as Pyrford Green. In 1366 it was acquired by Westminster Abbey and united with Pyrford manor, but its name survived as Townsley Meadows, the former common meadows of Pyrford. In Horsell there were two sub-manors. Twichen, a name first recorded in 956, was on the northern edge of the parish along the Bourne between Dunford Bridge and Mimbridge. This small area had only two farms but was always regarded as distinct from Horsell proper. The unusual name is derived from the Old English *twicene*, 'a meeting of the ways', referring to the junction of several tracks across the heathland near Bonsey's

Farm. Hill Place, at the extreme western end of the parish, was recorded as a separate manor in 1332 but never became completely separate from Horsell. It occupied the hilly wooded land north of Knaphill and east of Bisley Church, around the large house and farm which is called Hill Place to this day. For administrative purposes the joint manor was divided into three tithings – Horsell, Pyrford and Sithwood – each with its own constable and aletaster. Sithwood lay around Littlewick and Lower Knaphill, and the name was in current parlance until the late 18th century when it fell into almost complete disuse. It was revived more recently for part of the Goldsworth Park estate.

The manor house of Pyrford stood on the riverside east of Pyrford church, surrounded by a large moat fed from the Wey. In 1568 the park was said to cover 80 acres of mixed arable, pasture and waste ground, but 'there ys no dere within the same parke nor hath not bene of longe tyme' while the manor house was 'very sore in Ruyne & decaye for want of Reparacions that xxv[li] [£25] will not suffycyently repayre the same'. Shortly after this the house was demolished and replaced by a large new half-timbered house further up the slope to the north-west. Built by the Earl of Lincoln, it enjoyed a fine setting with views southwards across the water meadows and river towards the North Downs. It was surrounded by a large park, described by Daniel Defoe in the early 1720s as 'exceeding pleasant, especially for the most beautiful intermingling of wood, and water, in the park, and gardens, and grounds adjoining'. Unfortunately this building, which would have been a notable addition to the architectural and historical heritage of the Woking area, was demolished half a century later and replaced by the present Pyrford Place.

8. Landscape, society and economy in medieval Woking

In the medieval period agriculture was the mainstay of the local economy, the only significant source of employment, and the means by which the landscape of the four parishes was shaped. The Domesday Survey provides our first important information about the economy and its organisation, though statistical conclusions drawn from this source must be tentative and treated with caution. In north-west Surrey – the hundreds of Woking and Godley – the population density was much lower than in north-east Surrey, where the influence of London and the better soils and farming in the Thames-side parishes boosted numbers. Densities were broadly similar to those of the Surrey Hills and Weald, but the least populated part of the county was, not unexpectedly, the high ground around Hindhead. The numbers of plough-teams, the best measure of the intensity of agricultural exploitation, were lower in Godley hundred than any other part of Surrey, and the prevailing impression is of a thinly populated territory with large areas of waste (that is, heathland and woods). A key factor in this was undoubtedly the poor soils. While the sands are easy to work, especially compared with the heavy clays in some of the Surrey vales, they are thin, infertile and (as later observers described them) 'hungry'. Without heavy applications of fertiliser and loam to enrich the soil, the sandy areas of the Woking district could not support a more intensive agriculture or a large population. Apart from the riverside areas of the south bank of the Thames and the Wey valley much of the area was hardly settled until the mid-12th century. John Blair has supplemented the generalised evidence of Domesday Book with detailed assessment of the surviving local documentary sources and concludes that parts of north-west Surrey were virtually uninhabited before then.

The early 12th century marked the beginning of rapid population growth and economic expansion across north-west Europe. The population of England began to increase at a much faster rate and pressure upon agricultural resources – the land itself and the food supplies which were produced – meant that colonisation outwards from existing settlements became a widespread and very important phenomenon. There was an urgent need to bring new land into productive farming use, to grow more crops and support more livestock. In north-west Surrey this process of land colonisation was not easy or straightforward. Not only was the land itself very poor and much investment of labour and fertiliser was needed to improve it, but also the whole area was placed under forest law by Henry II in the late 1150s, so that restrictions were imposed upon the private exploitation of the land. The forest law, designed to protect game (and especially deer) as a royal prerogative for hunting purposes, limited agricultural development because that interfered with the ability of the deer to roam and feed freely. It also enforced draconian penalties upon those who infringed the law. Henry II's afforestation of the area included most of Woking parish and Pyrford as part of a massive extension of the existing Windsor Forest. The laws were not rigorously implemented, but under Richard I the boundaries were extended to embrace substantial parts of Horsell and Byfleet as well. Henry III's government reversed the process in 1226, taking the Woking area out of the forest boundaries, but in 1280 Edward I in turn re-established the forest and thenceforth, nominally at least, the wastes of the Woking area were under forest law until the 17th century.

On this extract from Rocque's 1762 map of Surrey the small village of Hoswell is shown almost encircled by heathland and commons. On the map the field boundaries and patterns, though apparently accurate, are in fact merely representational and do not show the actual layout. Even so the large open arable fields around Horsell itself contrast clearly with the smaller piecemeal enclosures of meadows and pastures along the Bourne valley to the north.

Given that this area was peripheral to the vast Windsor Great Forest, and because there was intense pressure for land colonisation as a result of population growth, in the Woking area (in contrast to, for example, the situation around Bracknell) the Crown reluctantly tolerated a substantial number of enclosures from the waste, whereby local people created new fields and smallholdings. Documentary sources record the clearance of woodland (a process known as *assarting*) and the extension of farmland into heaths and commons. Many of these were tiny plots, few being more than a couple of

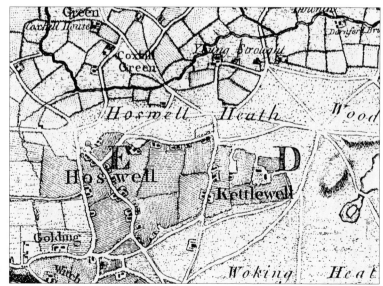

acres (for that was all a peasant farmer could normally manage to clear and fence in). John Blair's analysis of surveys of encroachments onto the waste, made in 1256 and 1269, suggests that in the mid-13th century the average size of *assart* (clearance for fields) was about five acres in Horsell and two acres in Woking, and that of *purprestures* (tiny plots for non-arable use) only a few square yards. The place-names of the Woking area give other evidence for this phase of woodland clearance and colonisation of the waste in the 13th and early 14th centuries. There are certain distinctive terms incorporated in the names of farms and fields which are excellent indicators of the process. Thus, *leah* (modernised as 'ley' or 'lee') and *sceat* (modernised as 'shot') refer to woodland clearance: local examples include Bridley, Hipley, Runtley, Burdenshot and Wapshott.

The woodland in 1086 was substantial – it was valued in Domesday Book as equivalent in value to 133 pigs – but the area shrank slowly but steadily over the next two hundred years. Painstaking enclosure of small parcels of land from the heaths, and the laborious clearance of damp woodland along the valley sides, increased during the 13th century and carried on until the 1320s, when the economic expansion came to an end and the population growth slackened as human epidemics took an increasing toll and animal plagues and bad weather disrupted agriculture and food

Knaphill (shown here on Rocque's 1762 map) was a squatter settlement on the edge of the common immediately beside the parish boundary between Woking, Horsell and Bisley. Many of the small fields which are shown in stylised form on this map were carved out of the waste in the 13th and 14th centuries as illegal enclosures. Note the great wood of Brookwood and the brick kiln at what later became Kiln Bridge, St Johns.

supplies. Nonetheless, the extent of woodland in the Woking area remained considerable. A map of 1630, for example, shows large areas of woodland in the area between St Johns, Knaphill and Hermitage, while another of 1709 states that the Brook Wood even then covered 684 acres. This high rate of woodland survival, and existence of expanses of heathland, meant that the proportion of land in 'regular' agricultural use was among the lowest in the county. But we should appreciate that the woods themselves were of considerable economic value, not only for timber but also as grazing areas for pigs (of which there were large herds at Brookwood in the 1230s), while the heaths and commons played a major though under-recognised role in the agricultural economy as grazing lands, sources of brushwood and thatching materials and, especially, for digging the peat which was the main local fuel.

Woking was a relatively poor area throughout the medieval period and its general level of prosperity only began to increase in the 16th century. The 1334 Lay Subsidy, a taxation return, lumps Woking together with Horsell and Sutton and jointly taxed them at £10 13s. 7d., while Byfleet paid £3 11s. 1¼d. and Pyrford £2 12s. 0½d. In comparison, Guildford town was worth £15 2s. 9½d. and Godalming town £16 9s. 10¾d., both these places being wealthy as a result of their important cloth trade. In 1636, when Guildford was assessed for ship money at £58, Reigate at £60 and Walton on Thames at £38, Woking with Sutton had to pay £56 10s., Horsell £28, Byfleet £11 and Pyrford £14. Thus suggests that the area had become somewhat more prosperous, but these figures must be treated with a certain caution.

9. Churches, religion and piety

Religion was a central element to the life of any medieval community, the influence of the Church extending far beyond the simple matter of attending services. The four ancient churches of the district were focal points in the daily existence and annual calendar of individual parishioners and were the most important and substantial buildings. Despite the pervasive impact of Victorian improvements and rebuildings, much remains of the medieval fabric of two local churches. Pyrford St Nicholas is one of the finest and least-spoiled early country churches in the region, typifying the architecturally unambitious and simple churches which once were characteristic of much of Surrey. Its plan is very straightforward, with a rectangular nave, smaller chancel, and neither aisles nor side-chapels, and it dates almost entirely from the years 1140-60 when it was completely rebuilt, under the auspices of Westminster Abbey which had acquired the rights to the church and manor. Such rebuilding is also known from other churches held by Westminster Abbey, including Horsell, but there, as in most other cases, later reconstruction means that no 12th-century fabric survives. Pyrford is therefore particularly precious, and its importance is greatly increased by the miraculous survival of sections of the wall-paintings which formed part of the original decorative scheme. They were whitewashed over by Protestant zealots in the reign of Edward VI (1547-53) but, because the restoration scheme undertaken in 1868-70 was unusually delicate and sensitive to the character of the late Norman building, the paintings were rediscovered.

This attractive drawing of St Nicholas church, Pyrford, was produced in 1909 by Jenny Wylie, the talented artist and engraver employed to illustrate the volumes of the Victoria County History of England. *Her view clearly shows the late Norman chancel which is almost as large as the nave.*

The wall paintings discovered in Pyrford church during restoration work in the 1870s are of outstanding historical and artistic interest. There are two sets, one painted over the other and both later covered with whitewash. The first series dates from about 1140 and shows scenes from Christ's passion: on the left, he is tied to a pillar and is being scourged by a figure wielding a flail; on the right he is dressed in a diamond-patterned robe and standing in a pillared building. The second series of paintings (from the years around 1220) is known as a psychomachia, a battle between virtues and vices. The details are not very clear, but this painting is represented by the mysterious procession of armed men and a group of horsemen.

The diaries of Arthur Munby of Wheelers Farm, who described the work in progress, reveal how close even this church came to over-drastic improvement:

> **"** The interior was a heap of rubbish; all the old pews and seats gone or waiting rearrangement. A few scraps of rude old fresco, scraped bare, showed on the walls. Outside, the ivy is gone from tower and gable and wall; and within the ancient porch … barrels of mortar were standing a-row. In the churchyard … the ivy torn from the church lay about in heaps. **"**

Horsell St Mary (a chapel in the joint parish of Pyrford with Horsell throughout the medieval period) and Byfleet St Mary were both heavily restored in the middle years of the 19th century, though both had already been extensively altered and enlarged in a piecemeal fashion over the centuries. As the villages grew the early medieval churches were seen as inadequate and insufficient – the very smallness of Pyrford's population, and the physical isolation of the church, helped to save it from a similar fate. Woking St Peter, much the most important of the four, was substantially altered in the 17th and early 18th centuries and, uncharacteristically, the Victorian improvers left some of the internal fittings from this period. This means that St Peter's is not only an important medieval church but also has considerable historic interest because it includes elements of the 17th-century reshaping, a period poorly represented in English parish

MIDDLE *This very attractive pen and ink sketch of Byfleet church, undated but c.1800, shows the characteristically simple early medieval plan, without transepts and with a chancel which is only slightly smaller than the nave, which is found in many West Surrey churches. The shingled spire is also typical. Like its neighbour at Horsell, Byfleet church was drastically rebuilt in the mid-19th century during 'improvements' and 'restorations', and lost much of its medieval character and authenticity.*

BOTTOM *St Peter's church and Woking village from the south, 1820. This was the largest of the parish churches and stands on the site of the early Saxon monastery of St Peter. The engraving conveys well the riverside location of the church and the semi-urban air of the street to its west. The tower or beacon above Hoe Place is shown (out of scale) at the right-hand edge of the picture.*

church architecture as a whole. Its most important single treasure, the remarkable Norman west door (one of the oldest doors in any English church), was mercifully left untouched.

The close emotional attachment between local people and their parish church is demonstrated – as it is elsewhere in the south and east of England – by the evidence of the bequests made in wills. It was customary for testators to leave small sums to their church, often for a specific purpose, and historians can use this to illuminate attitudes to religion before and after the Reformation. The wills of people in the Woking area, dating back to the middle of the 15th century, provide many examples. Thus, Horsell and Woking residents of the 1480s left a steady stream of donations and bequests relating to 'lights', the candles kept burning before altars dedicated to particular saints or before statues of those saints. A whole series of wills made in 1485 illustrate the point. Thomas Rooke of Horsell left twopence to the high altar, a sheep to the light of St Mary the Virgin (the sheep would be sold and the money used for funding the light), and another sheep to the light of Corpus Christi. John Hillier the younger of Sythwood left two tapers weighing one pound each to burn before the altars of St James the Apostle and St Mary. Several of these wills refer to Horsell church as dedicated to St James, probably because the cult of that saint was a particular local favourite. Richard Page of Woking left money to the high altar at St Peter's and also gave a sheep each to the lights of the Cross and St Mary of Pity, while Thomas Trevet gave fourpence to the high altar of Woking and another fourpence to the light of the Rood. John Gaddiston was notably generous, bequeathing 20 pence each to the lights of the Cross, St Christopher and St Mildred.

These gifts by ordinary people reflect the piety prevailing in late medieval 'grassroots' Catholicism, revealing genuine affection for the Church and a personal attachment to certain saints and their special places within the building. That adherence continued until after the Reformation. There is no evidence that enthusiasm waned

The goods of Woking parish church 1553

a pix of silver – viiij oz
four chalices parcell gilte thirti ownces
iij corporax clothes and their cases
iij alter clothes of velat and silke
iij aulter clothes of lynnen
ix vestimentes
ij coopes of velatt
a surplice and four rochettes
a desk cloth
ij canype clothes
ij crosse clothes
a cros staffe
v towells
a red silk cloth quilted

a canype of silke
iiij tunacles and iiij albes
a crose of coper
a senser
ij water pootes
v candelstyckes
a latten bason and an ewere
a crosse cloth
viij stremars and banners
a font cloth
ij braunches of yron for taperes
v gret bells in the stepull
iiij littell small bells
a saunce bell
a paire of orgaynes

The goods of Pyrford parish church 1553

j challice of tynn
j pyx of lattyn
ij corporis with ij casis of silke
ij krewittes of tyn
ij candillstickes of brasse
iij aulter clothes of lockeram
iij towelles of lockeram

j surplus ij sackring belles
ij belles in the steple …
j vestement
ij crossis of brasse with one banner clothe
ij cloothes to kever the font
j coope of silke

In 1553 commissioners appointed by the king visited every English church and made a complete inventory of all the movable furnishings, plate, liturgical vessels, vestments and other treasures (unless these had been concealed or spirited away in advance). The lists give a unique insight into the possessions, and the visual quality, of these churches at a point when all was about to be destroyed (the purpose of the visitations was to eradicate all traces of Catholic worship). Here the relative wealth of Woking church and the poverty of Pyrford is revealed, though neither was as rich as, for example, Farnham or Guildford Holy Trinity, and nowhere in Surrey could compare with the glorious splendour of the East Anglian wool churches.

alb   a long white tight-sleeved vestment
copes   the sleeveless hooded vestment worn by the priest
corporax   [corporis] the cloth on which the bread and wine of the eucharist were laid out
latten   brass-type alloy
lockram   a coarse linen fabric
parcel   partly
pyx   box in which the host was kept after consecration
rochette   a close-fitting surplice worn by the priest
sackring   sacral [rung during the service]
tunicle   [little tunic] a short wide-sleeved vestment

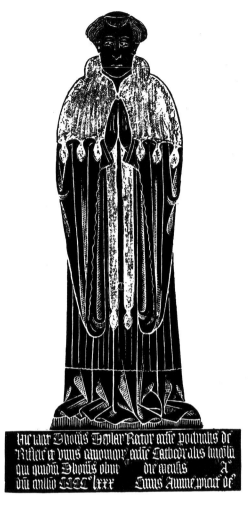

or that overtly Protestant views were demonstrated. The break with Rome was in 1534, but its impact even so close to London was far from immediate. Many clung to the old faith as long as they could. In 1536 Robert Hone of Horsell gave a sheep to the high altar at St Mary's, a bullock to the light of the Rood, and a sheep to the light of St James. In the same year his neighbour Joan, the wife of Robert Walden of Horsell, left not only twopence to the high altar, a sheep to the Rood light, and a sheep to the light of devotion, but also her old ring and another ring to the light of Our Lady. A year later, Thomas Norwood of Horsell, in a particularly detailed set of bequests, gave a sheep to the high altar, 20 pence each to the lights of Our Lady and the Rood, a hearse cloth to cover coffins on the bier, five shillings each to buy torches for the churches of Horsell, Woking and Bisley, and money for one mass for his soul each day for a month after his burial, culminating in a special 'month's mind' mass at the end of that period.

Comparable devotion to religious houses is also apparent. In the Woking area there were several local monasteries to be favoured, for Chertsey Abbey, Newark Priory and the friary at Guildford each owned land in and close to the four parishes. This is typical of late medieval England, where ordinary testators gave small sums to local favourites. Newark, a major landowner, had very close ties with Woking, Horsell and Pyrford and it was especially popular. The bequests continued to the very end and no indication of disenchantment is traceable. Edward Gybbs of Byfleet (1532) left 3s. 4d. to the monastery of Our Lady and St Thomas of Newark, while four years later, in the last full year of its life and at the end of his, Hugh Dydlesdon of Pyrford, a wealthy yeoman farmer, left it the huge

I comend my Soule to allmyghty god our blessed ladye saynt marie and to all the holye companye of heven and my bodye to be Buryed withine the churche yarde of the parishe of Wocking … I do geve and bequethe to the mother churche of Wynchester iiij^d I do geve and bequethe towarde the reparations of my parishe churche of Wocking ij^s Item wyll that myne executors under wrytten see my bodye Buryed and at my buriall my wyll is to have fyve masses and xx^s of monye geven to pore Folkes and in the lyke mind to have done at my moneth Tyde (that is to say Fyve masses with xx^s to be destribute among pore Folkes to pray for my Soule and all Crystyane Soules …)

sum of £1 as well as substantial sums to Pyrford church. Some people clearly disregarded the upheavals in the world of religion. As late as 1546 William Wheeler of Byfleet left money for masses and altar lights, but Catholicism in Surrey was doomed and, despite Mary's concerted attempt at restoration between 1553 and 1558, it would never return in any strength. But perhaps, in the wills of Elizabeth's reign, we can see a residual element of this type of piety and religious feeling. There are significant numbers of bequests to 'the mother church' (that is, Winchester Cathedral which, in the absence of monasteries, must have seemed the next best thing) and to general purposes such as church repairs – thus, Robert Purdam of Horsell (1558) gave fourpence to the cathedral, 3s. 4d. to Horsell St Mary and 6s. 8d. to Woking St Peter. The church still mattered, even if it had changed in so many important ways.

10. The villages before the railways came

Woking, the largest of the villages, was technically a tiny market town. In 1452 Henry VI had granted the lord of the manor, Edmund, Duke of Somerset, a charter to hold an annual fair on the Tuesday after Whitsunday. This, which by the 18th century was known as the 'Toy Fair', continued to be held until the 1870s. It is likely that from the 15th century, if not earlier, there was also an informal or customary market held at the widening of the road where Church Street joins High Street. In 1665 Sir James Zouch obtained a charter from Charles II

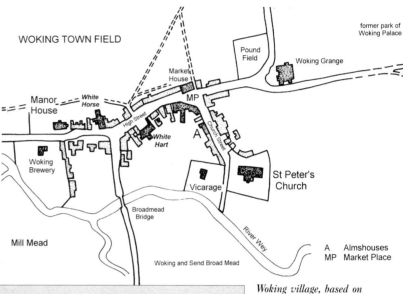

Woking village, based on the Ordnance Survey 25-inch map of 1874.

John Hassell's 1823 watercolour of the Market House, Woking village. As with other paintings by this artist, the setting is exaggerated, for the open area in front, the junction of High Street and Church Street, was never as wide as implied here. The building itself is presumably shown with reasonable accuracy, and there is a strong impression of a dusty, sleepy village with not much happening.

authorising a weekly market at Woking, suggesting that an existing informal arrangement was being regularised (so that Zouch could make money out of market tolls and fines). It is possible that the increase in trade brought by the Wey Navigation was another factor in the scheme. A market house was built on the north side of High Street opposite Church Street. In 1813 it was described as 'out of repair [and] ruinous and dangerous' to passers-by, and orders were given for its repair. In 1824 John Hassell painted a watercolour of the building, and it survived into the early 20th century for in 1908 Woking Urban District Council gave planning permission for its conversion into a row of eight cottages, nos.193-197 High Street. When in the late 1970s restoration work was undertaken on these properties no certain trace of 17th-century work was found and it may be that the 1908 conversion amounted to a total rebuilding.

The village was close to the Wey and to the east lay the site of the Tudor palace and the deer park, occupying the angle between the Wey and its tributary, the Hoe Stream. The main road from Woking to Byfleet makes a very sharp left-hand bend beside Woking Grange at the end of the village but the ancient road ran due east

ABOVE *The parsonage of Woking, painted by Hassell in the mid-1820s; it is just west of St Peter's church and this view shows the house from the south.*

BELOW *The manor house, Woking village, in about 1900, with the prominent and very fine Dutch gable not yet concealed by the trees. The telegraph has arrived, but otherwise the village street had not changed much for a century or more. Send Corner had not yet had its heart torn out.*

towards the palace, Newark Priory and Pyrford. The narrow lane on the south side of The Grange marks the beginning of the old route, which must have been diverted around the perimeter of the great deer park when the latter was created in the late 15th or early 16th centuries. The nucleus of the village was the road junction at Church Street, with the oldest surviving properties those in Church Street itself: 'Wey' and 'Lea' cottages include 15th-century work, and this short street also had the 17th-century parish almshouses.

Old Woking High Street looking west, 1931: this and the previous view can be dated by the newly-erected electric lamp standards. The conversion from gas to electric lighting took place in the previous year.

Old Woking High Street looking east, 1931: in essence the scene remains the same today ... apart, that is, from road surfacing, white lines, yellow lines, an incessant stream of cars, TV aerials and dishes, and the disappearance of the local shops.

At the west end of the village was the Old Brew House of 1715 and the delightful red-brick manor house, with its prominent Dutch-style gable, built in the 17th century. Today its position, so close to an extremely busy main road, means that it is difficult to appreciate its qualities and its setting is marred, but in the past it provided a worthy terminating feature in views along to the village street. Woking village was ill-served by the 20th century. The charming and picturesque townscape, with its varied gables, small cottages and larger properties, old church and irregular streetline, all edged by the peaceful waters of the Wey, was ravaged by development and rendered gap-toothed and incoherent by demolition. The junction with the Send road, next to the bridge at the start of the long causeway across the Wey meadows, had as its focus the *White Horse* inn, one of the oldest in the area. It was built in the 16th century but incorporated medieval fabric, and survived as one of the best half-timbered properties in the Woking area until the 1920s, when it was wantonly razed to the ground for road widening and the construction of a bypass which has never materialised. Its disappearance, and the simultaneous destruction of old cottages on the other corner of the road junction, destroyed the heart of the village and left an ugly hole, now filled by traffic and a small roundabout. Photographs from before the First World War indicate what was lost and show how this delightful scene was wrecked.

Beyond the manor house a discontinuous line of farms and cottages was strung out along the road to Kingfield. To the south were the flat floodlands of the Wey, to the north the open fields stretching across to Hoe Stream. The street was originally known as Town Street, but the name High Street came

The White Horse *and* Send Corner, Woking *village, in about 1900: the* White Horse, *one of the most attractive and historic buildings in the village, was wantonly demolished in the 1920s (together with the 15th-century jettied timber-framed house on the opposite corner, and other nearby buildings) to make way for road-widening which has never materialised.*

into regular use in the 19th century. Shackleford was a small but distinct settlement in its own right, with scattered dwellings in the fields to the north at Sundridge and along what is now Vicarage Road towards Westfield. Some of the older buildings of Shackleford also remain, notably the half-timbered Old Cottage, but here too the 20th century brought unattractive infill, garish garages and intrusive shopping parades, while the quiet street is now thronged with incessant traffic.

Kingfield and Westfield were separate hamlets, in an irregular scatter around the Green and the Common respectively. Kingfield tithing was a poor area in the 18th and early 19th centuries, though it had some larger farms of which one, the very attractive and partly half-timbered Howards Farm, survives tucked away and almost unnoticed between the Green and Kingfield Gardens. Sutton and Mayford, the most rural parts of south Woking to this day, were clusters of cottages and farms but, because of their distance from the village, they had a wider range of local services. Each had a public house and a smithy. In 1841 Bray described Mayford Green as 'a fine open space, surrounded by detached cottages … the hills clothed with verdure, the fields cultivated, the banks and hedgerows gay with violets and other spring flowers', and he contrasted this idyllic scene with the adjacent black and inhospitable heaths. At the far south-

ABOVE *Mayford in 1874: the 25-inch OS map emphasises the wide strips of roadside waste along Egley Road and towards Smarts Heath, which widened to form the green. The entirely rural community had two smithies, a public house, and a few farms and cottages.*

RIGHT *Sutton Green: the muddy village pond, then still used for watering cattle, and the post and telegraph office (now the Old Post Office, a very fine 16th-century timber-framed house on a solid brick plinth and with a brick infill between the framing) photographed in 1901.*

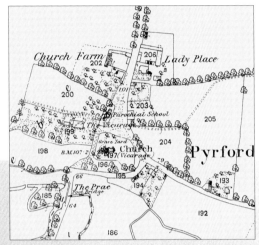

Pyrford church and its surroundings, 1874: the least-altered of the four ancient churches of the present borough, St Nicholas also has the least changed setting. There has been almost no residential development around the church since the map was produced. At the bottom of the hill was a wide ford, shown here with the footbridge alongside. It was replaced in the 1920s when road improvements were undertaken, removing a picturesque scene particularly favoured by local artists. The word Prae means 'meadow' and marks the site of one of the erstwhile common meadows of Pyrford parish.

west corner of the parish of Woking was Bridley, which in the late 18th century comprised little more than a row of cottages along Crastock Street, a few dwellings elsewhere, and Bridley Manor.

Goldsworth and Knaphill were similarly remote from the rest of the parish, separated from it by the ridge of Hook Heath. Goldsworth was on the better-drained land south of Parley Brook and just above the very damp lowlands between Knaphill and Horsell. The canal was built through the area in the early 1790s and encouraged the development of a few small brickfields, while by 1800 nurserying was becoming a major activity in the district. Knaphill, in contrast, was a more substantial community, which had evolved at the farthest point of the parish as an untidy assortment of cottages and squatters' dwellings on the edge of the common and around a network of rough tracks which spilled over the slope of Anchor Hill. It had little connection with Woking village, over three miles away, and much more in common with the western end of Horsell parish and with Bisley, for which it acted as a small local centre with shops and tradesmen. Many Knaphill people attended Bisley church, which was far

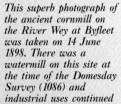

This superb photograph of the ancient cornmill on the River Wey at Byfleet was taken on 14 June 1898. There was a watermill on this site at the time of the Domesday Survey (1086) and industrial uses continued for over 80 years, though it was not always a cornmill – in the 17th and 18th centuries the mill was variously used for papermaking and iron-working.

ABOVE *Plough Bridge, across the Wey at Byfleet, photographed in about 1905. On the left is the old ford, which was still in use in the early 20th century for driving animals and larger farm vehicles because, as can be seen, the old bridge was very narrow. It was rebuilt in 1906-7 by Chertsey Rural District Council. The wooded slopes of St George's Hill in the distance were in the parish of Byfleet until 1933.*

more convenient than their own parish church of Woking St Peter.

Horsell, a small and poor village, was largely overlooked by antiquarians and other writers of the 18th and 19th centuries. There was not even a manor house in the parish and Manning and Bray, the greatest Surrey historians, dismissed it as 'some few farms and scattered tenements'. Pyrford was a

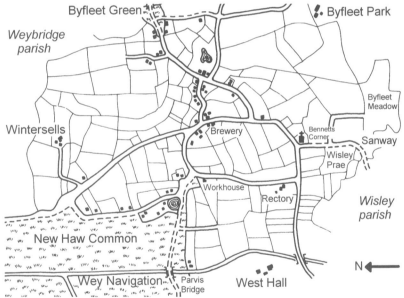

Byfleet village in 1800, after the opening of the Basingstoke Canal and before the enclosure of the village greens and commons. Wintersells, one of the finest medieval farm hamlets in the Wey valley, was demolished in 1906 to make way for Brooklands racetrack.

parish without a village and at the beginning of the 19th century had the smallest population of the four, divided between two settlements – one, a few farms and their attendant cottages, was grouped around the church while the other was on the fringes of Pyrford Green almost a mile to the north-east. The village pound, where stray animals were put until their owners paid a small fine for their release, was on the north side of the green next to Lock Lane, and the tiny parish workhouse was behind the cottages which still survive on the west side. In 1908 Eric Parker, in typically romantic vein, described 'a cluster of red-brick farm-buildings, a footpath over meadows of buttercups, a score of arching elms, and a little shingle-spired Norman church … Pyrford is one of the smallest and sweetest of Weyside villages'. Even today the area around the church, uniquely in the Woking district, is still a scarcely altered rural community though the rural lifestyles have gone for ever.

Byfleet, the second of the villages in size and importance, stood on the terrace of the River Wey just above normal flood levels, though the whole area was damp and lowlying and the village was intersected with drainage ditches and channels. The church stands well to the south beside the river and here, as at Pyrford and many other places in Surrey, the small community near the church was quite distinct. East of the church was Byfleet Park with its large manor house, while Byfleet Mill was just above the ancient Plough Bridge. The green extended from both ends of the bridge, for until 1933 the western slopes of St George's Hill were in Byfleet parish. At the opposite end of the village was another green, an extension of New Haw Common, forming a tongue of roadside waste along High Road and Rectory Lane. The large village pond was on this green in the angle formed by Chertsey Road and Parvis Road. Byfleet had no obvious focus but there was a cluster of cottages and small farmsteads along the twisting main street (now High Road), with a smithy in Rectory Lane and a brewery at the junction of Oyster Lane and High Road next to the present *Plough Inn*.

11. *The waste*

To outsiders at the end of the 18th century the great expanses of heathland so characteristic of west Surrey were particularly repellent (not too strong a word, given their exaggerated reactions). No contemporary writers found these areas, known as 'the waste', anything but bleak, forbidding and frightening, dangerous to cross, the haunt of bandits, and agriculturally worthless. Defoe's celebrated comment of the early 1720s, that Bagshot Heath was 'not only poor, but even steril … horrid and frightful to look on … much of it is a sandy desert, and one may frequently be put in mind here of Arabia Deserta', was echoed seventy years later by the agricultural writers William James and Jacob Malcolm, who described 'cold and exposed wastes'. In 1809 William Stevenson, another agriculturalist, expressed loathing of the 'wild and desolate heaths' with their 'heathy or moorish soil … dreary and almost irreclaimable', and with a fine string of abusive adjectives claimed that 'it is difficult to conceive a character of soil worse than that of the heaths of Surrey: it is a barren sand, soft, deaf and duffy, mixed with a poor hungry gravel'.

Two hundred years later the remaining expanses of these landscapes are protected for their beauty, their international ecological importance and their recreational value, but they have changed very considerably in the past century. Most of the surviving heaths have been invaded by scrub and many smaller patches have succumbed to the development of full woodland. This is solely because of the end of agricultural activity for, despite the prejudices of older writers, the heaths were a major asset for local farming communities. They were a source of brushwood, thatching materials and peat for fuel, but they were also vital for grazing sheep, cattle and geese. The animals prevented the regeneration of woodland and ensured that the distinctive heathland vegetation and the bare appearance were maintained. The ending of grazing in the early 20th century meant that encroachment of scrub became possible for the first time in a thousand years and within a couple of generations the west Surrey heaths were disappearing under a cover of birch, willow and pine.

12. Managing the waste

The commons and heaths belonged to the lord of the manor, but manorial tenants and freeholders had the right to use them and their resources. Each manor regulated the exploitation of the waste, and offenders who disobeyed the rules were brought before manor courts and fined for their transgressions. The regulations were designed to give a specific allocation of resources to each individual, though this did not mean 'equal', since most rights were determined at least in part by the status of the tenant or freeholder. The term 'common', so widely used in west Surrey, derives from the crucial fact that these resources were exploited communally. In Woking manor, for example, common rights included grazing livestock; cutting peat; taking furze (gorse) which was used for fuel in ovens; cutting brushwood for hurdles; heather and reeds for thatching; and digging sand and gravel.

St Johns Lye in 1928: this photograph was taken as part of the prosecution evidence in a case brought by Woking Council against a local man who allowed his pigs to roam on the common contrary to the byelaws. It shows damage resulting from the pigs foraging for roots, and illustrates why in earlier centuries it was essential to have strict controls on the numbers of animals put to graze on the common.

These commodities could be taken in limited quantities – usually, as much as a man could carry on his back – and the regulations sought to prevent over-use of finite resources. Only a certain number of animals could be grazed, and within strictly limited periods. Nobody who exercised common rights could sell manorial resources for profit, or hand them on to other people – they were solely for the use of the individual and his or her immediate family. Offenders who sold such materials commercially were viewed with particular disfavour by the courts. In 1813, for example, even as significant a figure as Robert Donald, the nurseryman of Goldsworth, was fined by Woking manor court because he had 'lately cut Turf, Sods and Mould from the waste of this Manor and carried the same off this Manor to the injury of the said Lord and tenants thereof'. Even minor uses of the waste could be essential to the well-being of the poor. The 18th-century name 'Candlerush

Grove', for the part of Woking Common near what is now Maybury Arch, reveals a typical use – the pith from rushes growing on the wetland was used as the wick for tallow candles and rushlights, the only source of artificial light available to most cottagers.

Digging peat, or turf, was essential because there was no local coal and wood was scarce – as noted above, its present-day abundance is the result of landscape change in the last 150 years. The peatbogs which dotted the heaths were a prized resource until, in the early 19th century, the use of coal (brought by water from the Midlands) began to reduce the need for turf as a fuel. Edward Ryde of Woking village, writing in the 1880s, recalled how in the reign of George III 'a very large number of turves were cut annually by the poor for fuel, turf being at that time about the only fuel burnt by the cottagers. The custom used to be for the cottagers to cut their own turves with an instrument called a Turfing Iron, and for each farmer to send a wagon and horses to cut the turf for his own labourers'. The turf would be cut in the summer and dried ready for winter, stored in a hut or under a lean-to roof: thus, Richard West of Byfleet specified in his will of 1704 that his wife should be able to use 'a room in the turf house for her fuel'.

13. The piecemeal enclosure of the waste

Small-scale medieval encroachments into the waste have already been noted, but despite this nibbling away at the fringes of the commons about 35 per cent of the area of the present borough, a total of just under 5,500 acres, was still occupied by heath in 1800. The precise proportion varied from 76 per cent in Woodham to 24 per cent in the manor of Sutton. As the map shows, the great stretches of empty sandy commons around Knaphill, between Woking and Horsell, and north of Pyrford extended into neighbouring parishes and seemed

The wastes of Woking: commons and heaths in 1800.

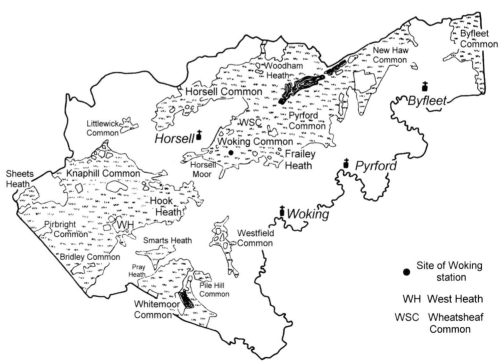

limitless, but the 17th and 18th centuries had seen acceleration in the rate of enclosure as new land was brought into cultivation. Individual tenants and freeholders obtained permission from the lord of the manor to fence in sections of heath. The process was discontinuous and fragmented, but numerous examples appear in manor court records: for example, in January 1652 John Palmer of Crastock was allowed to enclose a parcel of waste on Bridley Common for the payment to the lord of 8d. a year and 2s. 6d. or 'one fatt capon' on Christmas Day.

During the 18th century, as population growth and new technologies in drainage and land improvement offered incentives for change, larger bites were taken out of the commons in the vicinity of what is now West Byfleet; Havering Farm was carved out of the boggy heath of Whitmoor Common in Sutton; and on Pirbright Heath enclosure was beginning in the area of the later Brookwood Cemetery. There were also many illegal encroachments by individuals who pushed fences a few yards into the heath, or took sufficient land in a remote corner of the common to build a small shack and start a garden plot. These encroachments were often unsuccessful, for manorial stewards were vigilant, and the court books contain numerous examples of proceedings against the people involved. The usual course was to levy a hefty fine and then retrospectively authorise the enclosure. In April 1802, for example, 23 such cases were brought before the Woking manor court, involving areas of between two acres and five square yards. On other occasions the court was more determined and insisted that the illegal encroachments be destroyed: in April 1825 Woking manor court heard that 'several incroachments made in the previous year have all been thrown open, as then ordered, but that the same have been all again inclosed without Leave or Licence of the Lord or Tenants of the Manor – whereupon the Bailiff is commanded to throw the same open again'.

But the most important point about all this is that whereas in many parts of southern England the half century from 1780 saw large-scale enclosure of heaths and commons by means of Acts of Parliament, which authorised wholesale reallocation of land and remodelling of the landscape with new fields, roads and farms, in the Woking area such formal large-scale enclosure was very limited. The heaths were so extensive, the ground so poor, and the agricultural potential so limited (unless massive financial outlay was involved) that landowners saw little incentive for major change. Small-scale changes continued to nibble away at the waste, and there was some parliamentary enclosure, but the bulk of the commons remained into the early Victorian period. This led, indirectly, to the growth of a new town.

14. The squatter settlements

A consequence of the illegal encroachment upon the waste was the creation of new communities on the edges of the heaths. These became characteristic of parts of the Woking area during the 18th century and their imprint upon the landscape is clear even today, 250 years later. Many of the encroachments were eventually accepted as legal even if they had never been formally approved by the manor courts. Their occupants became, to all intents and purposes, 'commoners' – those exercising common rights – in the same way as the legal

A detailed map of Knaphill in 1800, showing the numerous very small enclosures carved out of the waste, each with a 'squatter' cottage, clustering along the parish boundary and the edge of the great heath. Note, too, the very sharp contrast between the landscapes of Woking and Horsell parishes, and the network of irregular tracks which extended across the heathland.

tenants of the manor and when in 1854 the common rights were extinguished they received compensation just as the 'proper' manorial tenants did. The people who constructed the new dwellings, initially no more than huts and hovels, were known as 'squatters'. George Bourne, writing at the beginning of the 20th century about the Farnham area seventy years before, describes these settlements accurately: 'hardly anywhere are there to be seen three cottages in a row, but … the little mean dwellings are scattered in disorder … wanting in restfulness to the eyes and much disfigured by shabby detail.' Such places tended to be in the remoter corners of the waste, close to parish and manorial boundaries and well away from centres of authority and respectability. Their haphazard plan of cottages, gardens, tiny fields, tracks and remnants of the commons gave a chaotic and confused landscape.

Thus Knaphill, on the border between Woking, Horsell and Bisley, was almost entirely composed of such habitations: in the 17th century it was no more than a few scattered farms, but by 1830 it comprised a large number of cottages, smallholdings and little enclosures strung out along what became Anchor Hill and High Street. These hugged the parish boundary – they were on the furthest edge of Woking parish – and spilled over into an equally remote corner of Horsell. At Frailey Heath, on the boundary between Woking and Pyrford, another community of squatters grew up. It was notorious for the rough and poor people who lived there and was colloquially named Bunker's Hill (possibly after the battle of Bunker Hill in the American War of Independence, which may date its origins). In Horsell, Cheapside was a squatter settlement forming a tattered fringe to the common, distant from the village and parish church. It took its name from Cheapside in London, but here the title referred, in a sardonic fashion, to the cheapness and poverty of the area, with its makeshift cottages. Another such community, renowned for its poverty in an area now celebrated for its wealth, was the Coldharbour district of Pyrford. In all these places the first detailed maps, in the early 19th century, show how the commons were being eroded and fragmented by enclosure. In Westfield a similar process gave rise to the landscape which we still see today – south of the *Cricketers* and along Westfield Road patches of common land, now heavily wooded, are interspersed with groups of houses and individual older cottages. Even the infilling and housing estate development of the 20th century has not disguised the untidy informality of the 18th-century pattern of enclosures.

15. *Open fields, meadows and greens*

In the Middle Ages most manors in the area had open arable fields, divided into long strips and farmed on a communal basis subject to regulation by the manorial courts. According to agricultural writers of the 1790s and early 1800s the typical pattern of farming in the Woking area had been the three-field system, whereby each year one of the great open fields was left fallow to regenerate and recover its fertility, but there is little reliable evidence for its use. Gradual enclosure of the open strips to form hedged fields greatly reduced their extent between 1500 and 1800 and, because most vanished before the first maps were made, we have only limited evidence as to their extent and layout. At Byfleet, which was largely enclosed by the end of the 16th century, Bennets Corner, an 11½-acre field of open arable strips, survived in 1800 immediately south of the church. Map and documentary evidence suggests that other open fields formerly occupied the land between the church and Eden Grove, and south from Winern Glebe towards the Wey: in 1704, for example, Richard West of Byfleet referred in his will to his four acres of land in Byfleet Common Field.

Pyrford's open fields lay across the slopes west of the Green and north of the church, and in the early 19th century some long narrow enclosed fields in this area marked the 'fossilised' pattern of the older strips. Two small remnants

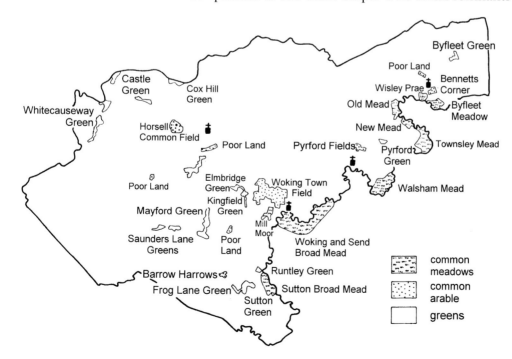

The greens, roadside wastes, common meadows, and open arable fields of Woking in 1800.

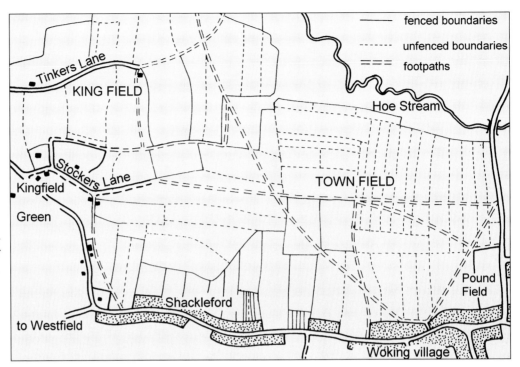

Woking Town Field, as shown on the tithe map of 1840: the large numbers of long narrow strips are very clear. In Shackleford and Kingfield there are wider fields which resulted from the consolidation and amalgamation of strips before 1800.

of the common fields still survived, on either side of Sandy Lane north of Stone Farm and retaining the names of their once-extensive predecessors: Pyrford Upper Field and Pyrford Lower Field. In Horsell there was an open arable field north-east of the village between Parley Brook, Horsell Birch and Bullbeggars Lane, in an area still known as Common Field in 1854, and another around Grove Barrs, east of the village. There the land was open and unfenced even at the beginning of the 20th century. At Sutton there were medieval open fields but these were reduced by enclosure (and by the creation of the great park in the 1520s) so that in 1800 all that was left was 3½ acres called Barrow Harrows, on the eastern slope of Pyle Hill. The tithe map of 1848 implies that Pile Hill Field and Whitemoor Field may have been the names of open fields in previous centuries.

In Woking the open fields lasted much longer and were still functioning in the 20th century, though it is not entirely clear why this was so. Woking Town Field had extended from Kingfield Green to Hoe Bridge and the tithe map of 1841 showed that 51½ acres north of High Street were still 'Common Fields', divided into 30 strips and plots, some as small as ¼ acre. There were six different landowners and 13 occupiers, though only one owner, Robert Hodd, actually worked his own strips – the others let out theirs to tenants. Consolidation had been in progress, for James Fladgate had a block of eight adjacent strips and Robert Hodd six, but the classic strip field layout still survived remarkably intact. Until Rydens Way was built between the wars this area remained unenclosed, with something of its medieval character, though it was not by then farmed communally. Even in the early 1960s, when my father had an allotment on Derrys Field north of Rydens Way, the land still retained its openness.

Woking manor had other open fields. The Lower West Field was on the east bank of Hoe Stream from the site of the football ground southwards towards Bonsey Lane, while Upper West Field adjoined this and extended along Westfield Road towards the common, where the Westfield schools were later built. In 1800 a few long narrow fields near Elmbridge still preserved the shape of medieval strips. The third field, Kingfield, was smaller than the other two and vanished well before 1800. It extended from Elmbridge Green near the football ground across the site of the Elmbridge estate and north of Kingfield Green, to the edge of Town Field behind Stockers Lane. In the heyday of the system, therefore, a continuous sequence of open arable strips extended from Westfield Common along the southern side of the Hoe Stream as far as Hoe Bridge.

The flat riverside tracts along the Wey were unsuitable for arable farming but ideal for hay meadows and grazing. Each of the southern manors – Byfleet, Pyrford, Woking and Sutton – had substantial areas of meadow, though by 1800 they had been considerably reduced by enclosure. Management of the meadows was strictly regulated by manorial courts. They were apportioned among the tenants in unenclosed strips, as with the arable fields, and the hay was cropped from them during the summer, after which the manorial tenants and freeholders were entitled to turn animals out to graze (and thus to manure the meadows) during autumn and winter. In Pyrford manor, where Walsham, Townsley, New and Old Meads formed an almost continuous line of meadows along the riverside, tenants and freeholders could graze livestock from 15 August to 12 January, each being allowed to put one horse, two cows and five sheep onto the meadows for every acre of land owned or rented elsewhere in the manor. The manor paid a herdsman to supervise the grazing, funding this from a levy of 6d. per animal imposed upon the users of the meadow.

Woking and Send Broad Mead was on the Send side of the Wey but was common to both parishes. It covered 365 acres and in 1794 there were about 50 owners. The hay was harvested in early June, after which the grass was allowed to grow again and a second cropping was taken in early September. On 18 September the meadow was opened to cattle and sheep. Over the centuries

it had become the custom for the animals not only of any parishioner in Woking and Send but also 'of more distant places' to graze there – the latter paid for the privilege and this represented profit for the meadow proprietors. William James and Jacob Malcolm, the agricultural writers of the 1790s, deplored this practice and urged that the Broad Mead be enclosed. Their advice was not heeded and fortunately much of the area remains open to this day.

Greens are still characteristic of the Woking townscape. Most did not resemble the classic English village green, but were areas of rough grassland and rushes (usually with at least one pond) edged with scattered cot-

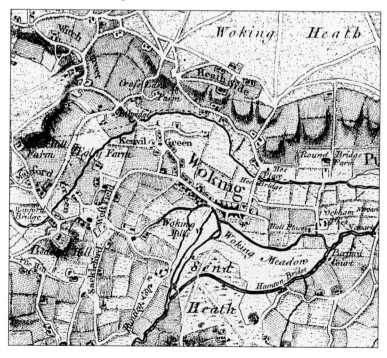

tages. The largest, Goldsworth Green, survives (though reduced by road widening) as the expanse of grass and trees extending from Triggs Lane roundabout along Goldsworth Road. Elmbridge Green is the open area at the entrances to Woking Park and the football ground: it formerly extended along Kingfield Road to join up with Kingfield Green (which still has its pond, now restored to full glory after many years of neglect) and then along Loop Road where there was a chain of four splashes or shallow ponds. The greens at Pyrford, Sutton and Byfleet were eliminated by enclosure Acts which parcelled them out among private owners, though the first two remained in unofficial use for public grazing into the late 19th century. Of Byfleet Green there is no trace, but the others at least survive as place-names. Other greens were simply elongated stretches of roadside waste, used for grazing animals (including geese). Excellent examples surviving today are the extension of Mayford Green (which itself has been badly damaged by the construction of the roundabout) along either side of the main Guildford road northwards to Barnsbury, and the belt of wooded grassland along the Knaphill-Chobham road from Barley Mow Lane to Barrs Lane. Roadside greens have been particularly vulnerable to road-widening, for as more-or-less public land they have been all too easily swallowed up by the highway authorities – they may now be detectable only by a slightly wider verge, as in some stretches of Saunders Lane in Mayford.

16. The Wey Navigation

The project to make the Wey fully navigable from the Thames to Guildford encouraged modest economic development in the Woking area and introduced a new element into the local landscape. The river was always used for transport

This primitive 19th-century painting of Old Woking church shows, as foreground interest, a traditional West Surrey punt in use on the river. Though barely documented, such craft were numerous on the Wey and its tributaries, as they were on other waterways in the Thames basin. They were used for transporting reeds and thatching materials, animals and goods, and were also suitable for line fishing. Thus, these rivers and brooks were in one sense always navigable, even if formal navigation works were not undertaken until the 17th century.

to a limited and undocumented extent. There was a late medieval wharf at Woking Palace, implying use of the river for freight and maybe even passenger traffic in the early Tudor period, while recent archaeological work on the riverside in Guildford, which suggests that there were wharves there in the Middle Ages, implies that there may have been a more intensive trade than hitherto supposed. A 1566 reference to 'a certen locke … between Woodham lande and Brooke lande upon the water of Weye' is exactly contemporary with the Exeter Canal, usually regarded as the first artificial navigation in Britain since the Roman period, so pioneering navigation works may have been implemented in the mid-16th century. By the reign of James I, though, there was a belief among Guildford merchants that better links with London were needed to revive the failing commercial prosperity of the town, which was suffering the decline of the important cloth trade. Unsuccessful navigation bills were submitted to parliament in 1621 and 1624.

In the late 1640s the idea was revived by Sir Richard Weston of Sutton Place. He had his own motives for promoting the river navigation, seeing the scheme as a useful means of improving his own estates by allowing flood control and drainage works. Weston had observed canals being employed for navigation and land drainage in the Netherlands and was an enthusiast for Dutch innovation in the technology and science of agriculture and land management. In 1651, under his sponsorship, parliament passed an Act which authorised the improvement of the river from Weybridge to Guildford, including the construction of locks and also of long stretches of completely

Trigg's Lock on the Wey Navigation (1651-2), photographed in 1902: the lock stands on the boundary between Woking and Send parishes at Sutton Green. In this view a Wey skiff is moored at the bank. By the early 20th century these were also being used for leisure, with summer evenings spent drifting gently down the river.

new channel to cut out bends. This was the first navigation in Britain to involve such extensive new work, and the first in the country to use the now-standard pound lock with double gates. Work began in August 1651 and was completed only a year later. Weston spent a great deal of his own money on the project, the total cost of which was £15,000, and he went bankrupt in consequence. The hastily executed scheme had been poorly built and by 1670 this, and the precarious financial circumstances of the Weston family, meant that the undertaking was almost moribund. However, major repairs were undertaken in the late 1670s and the river settled down to a profitable and largely uneventful existence, as a key element in Guildford's reviving fortunes and a modest catalyst to business activity in the villages along its banks – most notably, Woking and Send, where at Cartbridge a small waterside community with warehouses and wharves developed during the 18th century. For 150 years after the opening of the navigation its presence was clearly felt in the Woking area. The local sense of remoteness was reduced and commercial links with London – via, for example, the flour trade from Woking mills – helped to tie the district more closely into the expanding regional economic system.

17. Population change in the 18th century

Across England as a whole the 18th century was a time of continued and accelerating population growth, but the first national census, which gives accurate population figures for individual parishes, was not taken until 1801. Before that time we must rely on less complete sources, more prone to error and miscalculation. Using the data from the parish registers, which record baptisms and burials, it is possible to produce approximate figures for population size. For the Woking area, the early 18th-century registers were well kept so we can use them with some confidence. Furthermore, the registers of Woking St Peter regularly record the tithing in which a family lived, allowing the calculation of figures for different parts of that large parish. Calculating population statistics from baptisms is based on a well-tried formula stating that there were 30-40 baptisms per year for every 1,000 people. This gives a large margin of error and provides a general, not an exact, figure, but is very useful for assessing the relative sizes of different places. Applying this formula to the Woking area, and taking the median of the range (35 baptisms per 1,000 people) gives the population levels shown in the table below.

Each of these figures relates to an administrative unit, not to a specific built-up area or village. Thus, Goldsworth tithing includes Brookwood, Knaphill and Goldsworth, as well as many scattered farms and cottages. However, it is possible to use these estimates to suggest that even the main village in the district, Woking (with its physical extension, Shackleford) only had a population of perhaps 225. The small size of communities such as Mayford, Sutton Green and Pyrford is immediately apparent.

How did these figures change during the 18th century? The parish figures from the 1801 census are given, as well as rough percentage growth rates for the century. The increase over the Woking area (51 per cent), though not inconsiderable, was appreciably less than the national average (71 per cent). A rising birth-rate and higher levels of fertility across the country as a whole

Parish	Tithing	Approx. population in early 18th century	Population 1801	Approx. % change
Byfleet		277	362	+ 30
Horsell		298	493	+ 65
Pyrford		117	230	+ 96
	Crastock	28		
	Goldsworth	192		
	Hale End	104		
	Heathside	50		
	Kingfield	87		
	Mayford	89		
	Shackleford	73		
	Sutton	111		
	Town Street	176		
Woking		910	1340	+ 47

meant that increase in population was typical of the time, but the relatively low growth in west Surrey is a reflection of the obvious fact that it did not share the rapid industrialisation and urban growth which affected much of the north, midlands, and London area. Locally, population grew most rapidly in Pyrford, though the numbers involved are small and the percentages can mislead, but the largest increase in absolute terms was in Woking parish. Here the 18th century saw significant expansion in the Knaphill area, where a new village was emerging, as well as in Woking village itself.

18. Occupations and employment in the early 18th century

Agriculture remained by far the most important element in the local economy throughout the 18th century, as it always had been, but we can identify differences between and within the parishes. In Woking village the employment structure was notably less dependent on farming and more concerned with crafts, trades, and commerce. We may reasonably suppose that it resembled a very small town rather than an agricultural village. The most reliable information is found in the baptism entries which note the occupation of the father. We do not have such evidence for Horsell, and for Byfleet only for the years 1701-06, but for Pyrford the parish registers give occupation details for 1703-28 and for Woking the coverage is 1698-1726. Additionally, in most cases the Woking register records the tithing in which the father lived, so the clear differences between the different parts of the parish are highlighted. For Byfleet the analysis is complicated by the presence of a wiremill, in which six of the 29 identified fathers were employed (either as wire-drawers or 'melters'). It is impossible to say whether any of the 18 men listed only as 'labourer' worked in the wiremill or on the land. In the case of Pyrford, where the record is complete for a quarter of a century, 28 of the 36 fathers (78 per cent) were engaged in agriculture, and another four were landowners or estate workers – an overall figure of 89 per cent working on, or owning, land.

But in Woking parish a very different picture emerges. Here 263 individuals were identified by occupation and place of residence, and a further 38 only by

A magnificent photograph of the smithy and wheelwright's shop at Whitmoor in Sutton Green, 1900. In the doorway stands the proprietor, William West. The photographer, John Bulbeck, took this and many other superb images of the Woking area in the years around 1900. Although he cannot have realised it, the picture has a special historical interest because of the excellent collection of farm wagons which are visible – the great haywain on the right, the lighter two-wheelers, the individual cartwheels, the wooden shafts ... all betoken a world which had disappeared a generation later.

occupation. For the parish as a whole, two-thirds were employed in agriculture or were listed as yeomen farmers or husbandmen (smallholders). But the proportion varied very significantly between tithings. In Crastock, the most rural part of the entire district, 91 per cent were engaged in agriculture, and in Hale End and Mayford tithings over 80 per cent. In contrast, 62 per cent in Kingfield and only 33 per cent in Shackleford worked on or owned land, while in the Town Street tithing the proportion was only 17 per cent. In other words, Woking village (and its geographical extension, Shackleford) were indeed very distinctive. The largest single category of employment in Woking village was crafts and domestic trades (such as cordwainers, carpenters, blacksmiths and wheelwrights), closely followed by those engaged in retailing and commerce, or as watermen on the Wey Navigation. Together these groups accounted for 56 per cent of the working population in Woking village and 52 per cent in Shackleford. The numbers involved are small, but the implication is clear and important. These two tithings, which together formed the main built-up area in the district, had an employment structure which resembled that of contemporary urban communities and was quite different from that of the remainder of the four parishes. It was indeed the case that Woking was a miniature town, not a conventional country village.

19. *Agriculture and industry in the 18th century*

Figures compiled for the year 1800, based on map and documentary evidence, reveal how, in the last period when agriculture was pre-eminent in the Woking area, the waste remained the largest single category of land use:

parish	waste	cereals	other arable	grass	other inc. woods, buildings
Byfleet	36	21	16	23	4
Horsell	30	16	11	37	6
Pyrford	40	14	8	35	3
Woking	34	18	10	29	9

Estimated land use by parish 1800 (percentage of total area)

We can analyse some of these categories in more detail. In 1801 the parish clergy were instructed by the government to submit returns of the acreages under different crops. These statistics, together with contemporary descriptions, give a picture of agricultural patterns at a time when, because of the severe food shortages and economic disruption caused by the Napoleonic Wars, the subject was a matter of special importance. The table below shows the 1801 crop acreages for the area (returns for Horsell are missing and those for Chertsey include Woodham tithing):

parish	wheat	barley	oats	rye	potatoes	peas	beans	turnips
Byfleet	141	131	84	25	17	26	18	80
Chertsey	26	19	11	1	½	8	9	0
Pyrford	101	115	32	12	12	6	10	60
Woking	469	449	131	60	14	111	19	399

These returns emphasise the preponderance of wheat and barley which writers of the time also note. However, the precise acreages are questionable because farmers may well have understated them (they paid tithes to the clergy, so were probably reluctant to give too much away) and, more importantly, they give no evidence for the pastoral side of farming, which was certainly important at the time, or for the orchards, market gardens and nurseries which were of major significance in the Woking area. The agricultural writers James and Malcolm referred in 1794 to the cultivation of root crops in the district, especially where the sands of the heathland met the loams of the valley and combined to produce an ideal deep light soil. Potatoes, carrots and parsnips were produced in considerable quantities for the London market and also for seed which was sold across the south-east, but turnips (of which a substantial acreage is noted in the 1801 crop returns) were used mainly for cattle fodder. This was particularly appropriate since Sir Richard Weston of Sutton Place was popularly credited with the introduction of turnips to England for this purpose, having seen them used in this way in the Netherlands in the 1630s. Carrots were a local speciality. In 1800 another agricultural commentator, William Stevenson, noted that 'the culture of carrots is followed with ... considerable spirit, skill and success, and to a considerable extent, in the parishes of Chobham, Horsell, Pyrford [and] Byfleet' and that in Pyrford and Woking the growers 'used formerly to select and transplant some of the most vigorous and healthy roots, but as the price of carrot seed is now so low, they are seldom at that trouble'.

The same writer devotes much attention to the rotation of crops, indicating that the usual sequence was turnips, followed successively by wheat, clover and peas, the last being favoured because (though this was known by experience rather than scientific understanding) they return very large quantities of nitrogen to the soil and are especially effective in increasing fertility. Edward Ryde noted that by the middle of the 19th century artificial or imported fertilisers had rendered rotation largely unnecessary. Before that time the soil was improved by turning animals onto the arable fields after harvesting or cropping so that their dung provided a natural fertiliser, and this pattern (which also included grazing on the meadows after the second hay crop was cut) was part of a carefully balanced system of exploitation which had existed 'since time immemorial'. It was also essential. Most of the soils of the Woking area lacked naturally high levels of fertility or were difficult to work. Edward Ryde considered the riverside meadows 'exceedingly low and damp, and where they are not very well looked after they soon become rushy and of very inferior quality'. Nevertheless, when well-dressed and manured they could be productive and the use of the slightly chalky clay known locally as 'loam' (that is, marl) for top-dressing sandy soils was widely practised in the Woking area. Names such as Loampits Farm (Westfield) and Loampits (Pyrford Green) recall this activity.

The importance of livestock in the farming economy is easily underestimated, because during the 19th century it gradually waned, and local writers gave it relatively little attention. However, the wills and probate inventories of people in the area in the 16th and 17th centuries include frequent references to cattle and sheep. Even a small farmer such as John Cooke of Woking, who died in 1560, left a total of 18 sheep as bequests (he

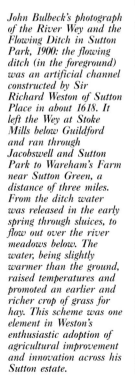

John Bulbeck's photograph of the River Wey and the Flowing Ditch in Sutton Park, 1900: the flowing ditch (in the foreground) was an artificial channel constructed by Sir Richard Weston of Sutton Place in about 1618. It left the Wey at Stoke Mills below Guildford and ran through Jacobswell and Sutton Park to Wareham's Farm near Sutton Green, a distance of three miles. From the ditch water was released in the early spring through sluices, to flow out over the river meadows below. The water, being slightly warmer than the ground, raised temperatures and promoted an earlier and richer crop of grass for hay. This scheme was one element in Weston's enthusiastic adoption of agricultural improvement and innovation across his Sutton estate.

also had an acre of rye and an acre of oats) while a substantial yeoman, John Chylde of Kingfield, left an impressive flock of at least 46 sheep as well as cattle in 1522. In this period sheep were, by a considerable measure, the most important animal, and as late as 1854 the manor of Woking (that is, the parish excluding Sutton) had at least 6,900 sheep and 34 sheepowners. Sheep could be grazed on the scanty vegetation and thin grass of the heaths and so offered a means of turning poorer ground to good use, while until it collapsed in the 17th century the very important textile industry of Guildford and Godalming offered a major local market for the wool. Indeed, there were a few weavers in Woking itself – five are listed in the early 18th-century parish registers.

Blackness Farmhouse, 1908: this photograph shows the characteristic architecture of more substantial houses built in the Woking area in the 16th century, with a comparatively straightforward timber frame and infill of small handmade bricks. Here, as in many others, the brickwork was then limewashed. Blackness Farm stood roughly where the bowling green in Woking Park is today. Derelict in 1908, it was demolished shortly afterwards as part of the scheme (completed in 1911) to lay out the recreation ground.

Cattle were grazed mainly on the riverside meadows and pastures, though cottagers were entitled to put them on the commons as well. In the 16th century oxen and bullocks were still used as draught beasts to pull carts and ploughs – in 1558 for example William Atlee of Woking left his two sons four working bullocks with yokes and chains, while in 1562 John Hathewell of Horsell had 'horsshows', with a yoke and harness, confirming the use of a plough-horse, but he also left 'an ox-harrow'. Cottagers usually kept only a pig or two and these animals were an important element in the local peasant economy in the early 19th century (when the manor court records include many prosecutions of people who let their swine roam unringed in the streets and lanes) just as they had been eight hundred years before. The enclosure of the heaths and the sale of land for building put an end to extensive livestock farming and by the end of the 19th century those animals that *were* kept no longer grazed on the commons. The result was that the ecological balance of these areas, dependent upon intensive grazing to prevent woodland regeneration, began to alter.

The industries of the area were mainly those which processed agricultural products and were of purely local importance. The Domesday Survey of 1086 had recorded mills at Woking, Byfleet and Sutton, and two at Pyrford, and 750 years later some of the same sites were still in active use – for example, the great and beautiful wooden mill at Newark, destroyed by fire in 1966 when the night skies for miles around were lit up by the glow of the flames. Woking Mill, on its ancient site south of Town Street, was one of the largest on the Wey. In the early 19th century it was described as 'a water corn mill, the flour manufactured there being chiefly sent to London by road, the horses employed in drawing it there making the journey three times a week'. Water transport was also used, since the Wey Navigation passed close by and flour from Woking was one of the main products handled at Cartbridge Wharf in Send. The corn was grown in Woking and Send, supplemented by supplies purchased on Guildford market, but in 1835, after over 800 years, it was

converted to paper production. The competition from the new industrial mills on the Thames had proved too strong.

Byfleet Mill, on a 14-acre island between two arms of the Wey, had a more chequered career. In the mid-17th century it was converted into a papermill and operated, with Downside Mill at Cobham, by the Company of White Paper Makers. At the end of the century this business was abandoned and the mill was then used for smelting iron and the production of wire and other iron goods. A small local iron industry flourished for about a hundred years in the triangle formed by Byfleet, Weybridge and Cobham, as a distant outpost of the great Wealden iron industry. The ore, with about 23 per cent metal content, was dug in shallow trenches and pits from the sandstones on St George's Hill, Wisley Common and Weybridge Heath. Byfleet mill closed in 1815, put out of business by the end of the Napoleonic Wars, the exhaustion of easily accessible local ore, and fierce competition from new iron industries in south Wales and the Midlands.

Other industries were small and served purely local markets. Limekilns were operated in several places, burning chalk from the North Downs or, after 1793 when the canal opened, brought by water from Hampshire. The lime was used for dressing the acid peaty soils. Traces are few but older field names recall their existence: examples include Kiln Field, between Oyster Lane and High Road in Byfleet, and Great Limekilns, at the junction of Smarts Heath Lane and Saunders Lane in Mayford. Brick kilns and small brickyards were

A particularly evocative photograph taken by John Bulbeck in 1900 shows the woodman and his boy coppicing in the woodland beside the River Wey at Sutton Park. Coppicing involved regular felling of trees to promote the growth of numerous smaller shoots rather than a single stem. These grew long and straight and were ideal for fencing, tool handles, roofing work and many other agricultural and domestic requirements. In this picture the piles of long coppiced stems (including the neat stacks at the right of the picture) contrast with the bundles of brushwood along the riverbank and the smaller pile of larger trunks which will be cut for firewood. Such activities had been going on for a thousand years: within thirty years they would more or less have ended.

more numerous, exploiting local deposits of clay and sand. Sutton Place estate had its own kilns in woodland overlooking the Wey at the southern extremity of the parish. A 1709 manuscript map of Brookwood shows brick kilns east of The Hermitage in what later became St Johns and also just south of Knaphill. The kilns in this area were expanded when the Basingstoke Canal was under construction in the early 1790s and in 1812, for example, the Earl of Onslow leased to William Woods of Knaphill 'all those edifices and Buildings with their Apurtenances called Brookwood Brickkilns and the adjacent New Coppice': the coppice, which is marked on the 1709 map, provided the wood for firing the kilns.

20. Crime and misdemeanour

The records of the quarter sessions courts tell us about the darker side of life in an agricultural community, recounting petty crimes and revealing much about daily life and the activities of ordinary people. There is nothing remarkable about the poaching, petty theft and minor affray, but in the Woking area some accounts point to the existence of much more serious levels of organised crime. Accounts of the theft of fish and geese are quite frequent. In 1783, for example, Samuel Wells of Woking, in league with James Wells of Pyrford and William Hammerton of Papercourt in Send, went on a poaching expedition to Little Whitmoor Pond in Sutton. There John Boughton of Send saw them take three of four pairs of carp belonging to John Webb Weston of Sutton Place, throw them into a sack, and run away. Later that year Abraham Fenn of Woking, labourer, watched two men in Runtley Wood near Mayford follow some geese belonging to Richard Bonsey of Westfield. The birds were feeding in the wood, and the men (one a well-known criminal named James Davis 'otherwise Sooty') killed two of them with sticks. Three years before, Daniel Wells, a labourer of Woking, had offered some hats for sale at a shilling each in the garden of the *White Hart* public house in Woking village. The hats had been stolen from James and Hannah Hart, who ran the grocer's shop in the village, but Wells denied this and said – implausibly – that he had bought them from Mr Fawkes of Guildford. There were also the usual acts of violence and physical assault when individuals got into fights. In 1776 Thomas Baker of Woking, yeoman, claimed that James Fledger (Fladgate) had assaulted him in the street by

The full transcript of a statement made in a case of goose-stealing, 1790: such sources not only reveal much of historical significance, but also tell a vivid human tale. We can picture the events of that April day very clearly in our mind's eye, and a tiny episode in Woking's more distant past comes to life.

Surrey: The Information and Complaint of James Williams of the Parish of Woking in the said County Wharfinger [21 April 1790]

'Who on his Oath saith that he has at several different Times missed his young Geese and not knowing what were become of them He suspected that somebody had stolen them which made him watch early & late in order that He might find out the Person who came to the place where he kept his said Geese That on Tuesday Evening now last past he went into a Wood called Runtley Wood in the said Parish of Woking between six and seven o' Clock and there He saw Henry Turner of Westfield in the Parish of Woking aforesaid Labourer running after this Informant's Geese one of which he took up and tucked under his arm & soon afterwards he catched another and put that also under his arm & afterwards another which he also concealed under his arm and carried them away with him That upon the said Henry Turner's going away with the said Geese He this Informant went close to him and then the said Henry Turner threwed the said Geese upon the Ground two of which ran away and the said Hy. Turner took up the other which this Informant examined before the said Henry Turner and saw was the Property of him this Informant That the said Henry Turner then shook his Fist at this Informant and very much abused him and that when the said Henry Turner so shook his Fist at this Informant he this Informant knocked the said Henry Turner down and after the said Henry Turner got up from the Ground a Scuffle ensued between him And this Informant' 'striking & scratching him in the Face', while in 1786 Marcy, wife of James Farley, labourer, accused Mary Harland of Woking of attacking her, scratching her lip and tearing her handkerchief.

None of this was in any way remarkable: every community had such incidents. But in the mid-18th century another dimension to local criminal activity began to emerge. The relative remoteness of the Woking area, and its extensive tracts of wild common and woodland, meant that it was an attractive hideaway for criminal gangs as a base for thieving expeditions to nearby towns and country houses. In 1769 it was claimed (with considerable exaggeration as to the numbers involved) that

> 66 There are not less than five hundred gypsies, vagrants and smugglers who have taken sanctuary in a wood between Guildford and Naphill. All the farmers and inhabitants thereabouts have suffered more or less from these rapacious vagabonds, who subsist chiefly by plundering people of their geese, fowls, ducks, or whatever may come their way. Fourteen pieces of cannon, mounted upon carriages, set out on Saturday, by order of Lord Albemarle who, together with the neighbouring gentlemen, are determined to dispossess, by force, this nest of thieves from preying upon the honest farmers. 99

Whether or not that particular retaliation was a success is unclear, but in a series of highly publicised and well documented cases almost a century later the lawless reputation of the Woking area as a place of sanctuary for criminals was still very much apparent. The historian Roger Wells investigated 'a network of itinerant and principally unskilled workers, nomadic hawkers and general dealers, and criminal gangs' responsible for many spectacular and violent robberies in Sussex and rural Surrey in the decade up to 1851. They were led by James 'Butcher' Hamilton, a 29-year-old who dealt in horses and was also a travelling broom-seller. He and his wife and daughter lived in a small cottage on a remote part of Woking Common, 'the heart of a notorious resort for Gypsies, Vagabonds and other indifferent persons [where] scarcely three days elapse without the Commission of greater or less depredations'. The gang met at events such as Farnham Fair to plan their robberies, and several of the key members lived in wooden huts and tents on the commons of Hook Heath and Brookwood. A contemporary described the area as 'a notorious centre for criminals active in the adjacent unpoliced and wild countryside … which embraced a great quantity of waste land'. The enclosure of the commons by the Necropolis Company in the mid-1850s thus put an end to a genuinely serious threat to law and order in west Surrey. It is intriguing to think that Hook Heath, now so exclusive and expensive, was 150 years ago the haunt of feckless and criminally-minded rogues.

21. Isolation or integration – the evidence for mobility

Defoe's comment about Woking, that it was 'a private country market-town, so out of all road, or thorough-fare, as we call it, that 'tis very little heard of in England', is often quoted … but was it true or did the famous novelist exaggerate? Woking was a small place, much in the shadow of Guildford and Chertsey, but isolation can easily be overstated. From the 1650s the area had been crossed by one of the busiest waterways in southern England and, despite Defoe's statement, the main London-Portsmouth road was only a couple of miles away, while the road from Guildford through Mayford to Chertsey was an important local route. Many people moved around looking for work or wandered more or less aimlessly as vagrants and travellers. These people were largely invisible to the likes of Defoe, with his interest in commercial expansion and fine buildings, but they were by no means insignificant in the 'community of the ordinary folk'. Writers in the years around 1800 were tempted to contrast the tiny town and its extremely modest market with the vigorous and thriving community which they supposed had existed in the 16th century when it was the seat of royalty. Their perspective was based on past glories, but the reality was that in 1800 the area had more people and a more active commercial life than ever before, even if kings and queens no longer came up the river to their palace.

The remoteness was thus exaggerated. London, after all, was only 25 miles away and Guildford a mere six. The compilers of *Patterson's Roads*, a volume

The main road from Guildford to Chertsey passed through Mayford: the Woking area was much less isolated than some writers, then and now, like to suggest. But travel was not necessarily straightforward, as this petition to the magistrates complained – though we may suspect that nothing was lost in the telling of this tale, for complaining about the state of the roads has been an English national pastime for many centuries!

It would have been inadvisable for any traveller to rely on John Seller's map of Surrey, published in 1690. Knob Hill [Knaphill] is shown south of Brookwood near Pirbright; Wisley is placed approximately where Maybury is situated; Kettlewell is, oddly, between Mayford and Woking village; and – strangest of all – the Wey is named as the Loddon River, which actually flows from Basingstoke to the Thames at Reading!

of itineraries for travellers which appeared in 1822, deemed it worthwhile to give a separate account of the route from London to Woking, and they place Byfleet (somewhat improbably) on the cross-country road from Windsor to Brighton. By the 1830s there was a twice-weekly scheduled stagecoach service from Woking to London. The *Emerald* left the *White Hart* in Woking village at 6 a.m. on Mondays and Fridays and travelled to Blossom's Inn near the Monument via Byfleet, Cobham and Esher. It was operated by a local man, Joseph Chitty, and was very expensive (8s. 0d. inside and 5s. 0d. outside single fares, with a reduction of a shilling for Byfleet passengers) but the fact that it ran demonstrates that Woking was clearly not 'out of all road'.

There is another way of showing that the isolation was overstated. Woking parish has a good collection of 18th-century Poor Law papers, among them settlement certificates (issued by a parish to confirm that a pauper or poor family was its financial responsibility) and removal orders (warrants for the removal of paupers back to the place which issued the certificate). Analysis of these – over 100 survive from 1698-1821 – gives a reliable picture of the geographical range of the travels of the poorer sections of society and, indirectly, a sense of the local and regional connections which Woking experienced. They show us that people frequently moved from place to place, usually over short distances – over 75 per cent of the parishes represented in the Woking documents were within a ten-mile radius – and strangers often passed by en route to who knew where. The two parishes with the closest connections to Woking, judging by the number of surviving documents, were Worplesdon and Horsell, followed by Chertsey and the town of Guildford. There are no documents relating to Byfleet (a lack of connection confirmed by the census figures of 1851, which show little movement between the two) but paupers came to Woking from much further afield: 31 other Surrey parishes, and a further 12 in Sussex, Hampshire and Middlesex, are represented, and there are also certificates issued by parishes in Gloucestershire, Buckinghamshire, Dorset and Essex. There is another side to the picture, impossible to establish in detail. Many people from the area went elsewhere looking for work or economic advancement and by the mid-18th century the huge drawing power of London was being exerted. Other indications of a shifting, mobile population of paupers emerge. Occasionally, for example, the parish registers record the baptisms of their children, as on successive days in 1706 at Woking parish church – 'William, son of a travelling woman of Knaphill' and 'James, son of a travelling woman of Sutton'. 'William, son of William Clay, a traveller born at Brookwood' was baptised in January 1714, and the previous summer 'John, an unknown child left in the parish' was christened. Such entries can hint at sad circumstances of which we can never know more: the Byfleet register for 1718 records the baptism of 'Sarah Lane, a beggar's child dropt in the Parish'. These are the unknown and forgotten people of 18th-century Woking.

22. The Basingstoke Canal

Thus, isolation could be exaggerated. Nevertheless, north-west Surrey was *relatively* undeveloped throughout the 18th century, because its agricultural potential was limited and it had no resources such as coal which could generate industrial expansion. The apparent backwardness of agriculture was a major concern to the landowners who wanted to increase rent income from the land. Enclosure and improvement of the wastes was seen as essential but this task was extremely expensive and (since lime for top-dressing had to be brought from elsewhere) the absence of modern transport was a major constraint. In the late 1770s a group of Hampshire landowners promoted a new canal scheme, to link Basingstoke with the Thames via the Wey Navigation at Byfleet. Approved by parliament in May 1778, it was intended to open up the heaths and commons and to allow agricultural produce to be sent to feed the voracious appetite of London. The Act for the Basingstoke Canal was passed during a major economic downturn, brought about by the end of the American Wars, and only in October 1788 had sufficient capital been raised for John Pinkerton, the contractor, to begin work on the canal.

The first sod was turned at Woodham, a mile from the junction with the Wey Navigation, but the first short section, from Byfleet to Horsell, was not opened for another three years. By 1792 the canal was navigable to Pirbright and at last in September 1794 it was completed through to Basingstoke. Ambitious plans to extend to Newbury or the south coast came to nothing and the Basingstoke Canal settled down to a slow and almost entirely unprofitable existence as an agricultural carrier. Even in that role it was largely a failure, for the heathlands were not reclaimed and the farming produce did not materialise. Paradoxically, the busiest period for the canal was the 1830s and 1840s, when it was used to carry construction materials for the new railway that paralleled its route, and for the development of the army town of Aldershot which swallowed up much of the heathland that had remained unimproved. The original estimates of the cost were exceeded by 60 per cent and in 1859 the arrears of interest on the original debt of £32,000 were said to be £105,000.

J. Lindley and W. Crosley published their map of Surrey in 1793, the year of the opening of the Basingstoke Canal through the Woking area. Their map emphasises the empty and unpopulated heaths and commons across which the waterway was constructed, its route using as much of such land as possible to minimise costs and disruption to agricultural estates.

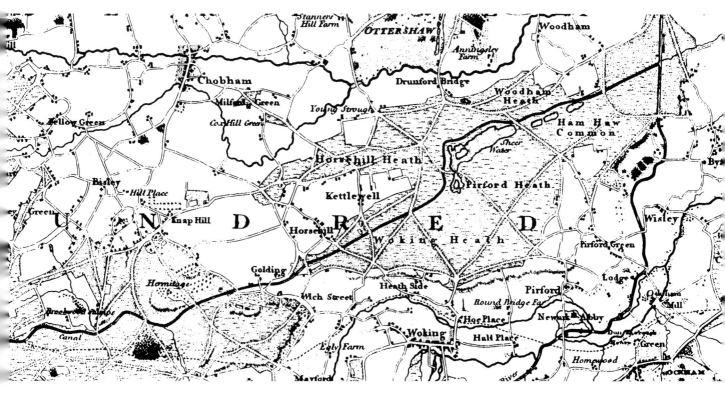

RIGHT *By the end of the 19th century the Basingstoke Canal was largely disused for commercial traffic above Woking. Beyond the town its idyllic setting, where it passed through fields and pinewoods, lent it a certain charm and there was a modest amount of pleasure boating. That, too, eventually disappeared as the canal silted up and became heavily overgrown with vegetation.*

From the Wey Navigation the canal followed the boggy valley of the Rive Ditch through Woodham and then crossed Woking Common to Arthurs Bridge, where it cut through a minor watershed into the shallow basin of Parley Brook. The natural gap between Knaphill and Hook Heath provided a convenient route into a third marshy valley, between Hermitage and Brookwood, after which it rose steadily to the great excavation which gave its name to Deepcut. The rise from New Haw to Brookwood was 90 feet, achieved by six locks at Woodham, five at Goldsworth and St Johns, and three at Brookwood. Although it passed almost entirely through heathland and empty boggy valleys, the canal stimulated some limited development. The demand for bricks to build lock chambers and bridges encouraged local production at Goldsworth, St Johns and Knaphill – it was uneconomic to bring this low value bulk commodity from further afield. The canal had country wharves at Woodham, Wheatsheaf Bridge, Arthurs Bridge and Goldsworth, where a modest amount of development followed, but at Kiln Bridge the wharf, together with brickworks and the new *Rowbarge* public house, was the origin of the new community of St Johns. In the longer term the presence of the canal helped to shape the growth of Woking, for with only eight bridges between Byfleet and Brookwood, and just two in the area of the later town centre, it constrained development, acting as a barrier and focusing traffic onto a small number of crossing places. Even today, closely followed by Victoria Way, it sharply defines the edge of central Woking.

In 1866 the Basingstoke Canal Navigation Company went bankrupt and during the next fifty years there were seven owners, each of which found the canal to be nothing but a financial liability. The Woking, Aldershot and Basingstoke Canal Company (1896) had modest success in developing a timber trade from London docks to the wharves at Spanton's and Brewster's timber yards, but even this ended in September 1899 when the bed collapsed into a tunnel being built beneath it on Horsell Moor as part of the Woking Council sewerage scheme. The canal was closed for six months and most remaining traffic ended. After 1910 the Council waged a largely fruitless battle to force the owners to repair the bridges, by then derelict and danger-ous, and in 1921 all traffic above Horsell ceased. About 14,000 tons of coal a year was still brought to Woking gasworks, which had its own wharf, but in 1936 the Woking District Gas Company stopped manufacturing its own gas. The last commercial traffic to Woking was a load of timber delivered to Spanton's Yard by Chertsey Road in 1949. After 157 years the canal had closed completely, lying weed-choked, silted and decaying, and people who knew Woking in the 1950s and 1960s will recall the sight, the remaining water scarcely visible in summer amid the riot of vegetation, the locks crumbling and the towpath overgrown.

23. Nurserying

Another important change under way when the canal was being planned was the development of nurserying and horticulture, for despite their general unsuitability for agriculture the sandy soils of the area were recognised as ideal for this specialised business. The main areas for horticulture and market gardening before the mid-18th century were east and south London, but by 1750 the outward growth of the city was swallowing up the nurseries. At the same time the beginnings of suburban development, and of commuting by the wealthier city men, generated a major new demand for ornamental garden species for 'edge of town' properties. For Woking's landowners nurserying at last offered the chance of making profits from the soil, and by the 1850s the area was one of the most important not just in Britain but also in the western world for this new consumer trade.

Goldsworth Nursery, the best-known of the early businesses, was founded in 1760 by James Turner and at the beginning of the 19th century was bought by Robert Donald, a specialist in rare and unusual trees and shrubs. He was a friend and business colleague of John Claudius Loudon, the highly influential landscape architect, writer and opinion-former whose magazine columns and books on design were instrumental in shaping the English gardens of the half century before 1850. Donald not only used this invaluable connection to build up his trade, but also eventually branched out into design work himself and in the late 1850s was responsible for the superb planting of Brookwood Cemetery, perhaps his crowning achievement. During the early 1790s the Waterer family, farmers of Lower Knaphill, switched to nurserying and began to buy up extensive tracts of land for the purpose: in 1802, for example, 'Michael Waterer of Knaphill, nurseryman, bought Ryde Heron for £132 5s'. They eventually owned almost the whole area around Barrs Lane and Whitfield. At the same time William Jackman (1763-1840) and his sons Henry and George were expanding their properties in Mayford and Goldsworth and establishing the nursery business which in the 20th century became the most famous of all. George concentrated especially on the clematis, and in 1863 produced the glorious purple *Clematis Jackmanii*, though there were many dozens of other varieties and the names of some pay tribute to the town in which they were developed: who could resist the allure of the pink and white *Belle of Woking*!

By 1840 the nurseries of Woking were nationally renowned and Brayley gives a vividly scented pen portrait: Waterers' in Knaphill, he says, 'comprises about [120] acres of ground which were enclosed from the bog and heath and progressively stocked with numerous exotics from America, which now flourish with even more than their native beauty and luxuriance … In May and June one entire mass of blossoms which perfumes the air for miles around.' In the vicinity of Horsell village, where Rosehill Avenue and Nursery Close are now, were the rose gardens managed by Henry Cobbett: 'many persons visit them in the summer season, for the purpose of seeing the flowers in a high state of perfection.' During the 1850s and 1860s there was a temporary decline in the trade, and in 1870 the formerly flourishing Goldsworth Nursery had shrunk to 24 acres, 'weedy … in bad repair [and] of little importance'; but in 1877 Walter Slocock, a friend and protégé of Anthony Waterer, bought the nursery and revived its fortunes (helped by hefty piles of London stable manure and human excrement, shipped up from the city by barge and offloaded at Goldsworth as fertiliser). When Slocock died in 1929 the business, with its 420 acres and 161 employees, was the largest in Britain.

In the years after 1890 some of the smaller and older nurseries closed because their sites had become more valuable for building. Woking had become a nurserying area partly because London nurseries had disappeared under bricks and mortar, but now Woking was itself sprawling outwards and the pattern was repeated. On the death of George Jackman in 1893, for example, the family sold his properties on either side of St Johns Hill for building development and the attractions of the site were greatly enhanced by its former use: 'situated on high ground, commanding most beautiful Scenery, and adorned with fine specimen Conifers, Deciduous and other Flowering

The staff at Jackman's Nurseries in about 1880: there are 18 gardeners and two boys. The foremen wear bowler hats to denote their superior status, and the head gardener carries a measuring rod and a bundle of papers signifying his importance. Note the saplings in the background, standing ready to be transplanted.

Trees, and Shrubs of Mature Growth.' By 1900 nurserying was one of the most important aspects of Woking's economy and extensive areas around the town were given over to plantations of shrubs and trees, rose gardens and greenhouses, and colourful beds of herbaceous plants. The nurseries of the area had played a key role in introducing and popularising beautiful plants which are now standard in English gardens – the clematis, rhododendron, azalea and magnolia, among others.

24. *Parliamentary enclosure*

The exhortations of the agricultural improvers to improve the waste and divide up the commons had the desired effect. The early 19th century saw the passing of three enclosure acts: Byfleet and Weybridge (1800), Sutton next Wokeing [*sic*] (1803) and Pyrford and Chertsey (1805). Parliamentary enclosure (as distinct from private enclosure by the agreement of landowner and tenants) required the permission of the owners of two-thirds of the enclosed land in a parish. By it, all common rights were extinguished, common systems of farming abolished, and the land was parcelled out among private owners. Commissioners were appointed to oversee the process and for the Byfleet and Weybridge Enclosure Act of 1800 their working minutes have survived. The three commissioners met on 27 June at the *Ship Inn*, Weybridge, and during the next six months heard the complaints of those who anticipated loss or damage as a result of enclosure and also received the claims of those who wanted an allocation of land. They inspected the commons of Byfleet and Weybridge (mainly on the slopes of St George's Hill, for Byfleet then extended onto the east side of the River Wey, and in the vicinity of Dartnell Park and West Byfleet) and drew up a plan showing the new boundaries of land ownership and field patterns. On 7 December 1801 they ordered that a total of 92 acres of land should be sold to defray the costs of the exercise, including the payment of their fees, and this was duly done, fetching the princely sum of £1,915 17s. St George's Hill was cheap then! From 1 June 1802 all common rights in the two parishes were extinguished, legal title was vested in the new owners, and completion of the fences and hedges was ordered. On 17 November 1802 all public footpaths and other informal routes across the former commons were stopped up and by 1 July 1803 the new boundaries had been marked out and fenced. The process was complete, and Byfleet's commons were consigned to the historical record.

The allocation of land on the former commons was determined by a rough and ready rule, whereby the lord of the manor received one-sixteenth of the land as of right, and also a substantial allocation of the remainder in proportion to his landholding. He would also normally buy some of the land offered for sale. He was thus the major beneficiary, just as he was invariably the leading petitioner in favour of enclosure. All tithes on the newly enclosed land were normally commuted, so the Church usually received an allocation of land in compensation for loss of revenues. Locally, each parish was given land for a gravel pit, to provide road-mending materials, and the poor of the parish, who had hitherto put their animals to graze on the commons, were given a modest piece of land (often in the least attractive location) to continue to graze their cows and geese and to afford the possibility, often more nominal than actual, of maintaining their fuel supply by cutting turf. Thus, in Pyrford 51 acres was allocated 'For Fuel Allotments for the Poor of Pyrford Parish' while in West Byfleet the Camphill Road recreation ground is public property to this day because it was reserved, under the Byfleet and Weybridge Act, for fuel allotments for the poor.

amount of land allotted to	Byfleet (1800)	Sutton (1803)	Pyrford (1805)
parish land and gravel pits	2	2	16
parish poor lands	49	0	70
to Church in lieu of tithes	114	51	151
sold to defray expenses	92	93	423
general distribution	494	191	803
TOTAL [acres]	**791**	**337**	**1463**
amount raised by sale	£1,196	£1,390	£2,510
average price per acre	£20 18s.	£15 0s.	£5 18s.

Note: Figures for Byfleet *exclude* Weybridge, enclosed by the same Act; but those for Pyrford *include* New Haw (256 acres), enclosed by the same Act.

The remaining land was then divided among the freeholders and leading tenants of the manor, approximately in proportion to their existing holdings, while small plots were allotted to those who held no land but exercised common rights. The wide disparity in costs in the table is explained by the method of sale: at Byfleet there was an auction, at Sutton a private treaty, and in Pyrford the land was so poor that it would not sell except at giveaway prices. Sutton was a 'closed manor', in which the lord and his estate were overwhelmingly

type of allocation	Byfleet (%)		Pyrford and Woodham (%)		Sutton (%)	
lord of the manor	23		46		63	
Church in lieu of tithes	15		6		15	
parish lands	8		5		2	
large allocations [50 acres+]	13.5	[1]	14.5	[4]		
medium allocations [10-49 acres]	26.5	[9]	24	[19]	4	[1]
small allocations [2-9 acres]	9.5	[15]	3.5	[15]	14	[7]
fragments [less than 2 acres]	4.5	[12]	1	[15]	1.5	[13]

Note: Figures in brackets refer to number of recipients of land in each category.

dominant. The lord, John Webb Weston, was the instigator of enclosure and by far its greatest beneficiary with an allocation of 63 per cent of the newly enclosed land. Most of the cottagers received no benefits from the change and, uniquely in north-west Surrey, there survives circumstantial evidence of strong but futile opposition, in the form of a poem entitled 'The Cottagers Complaint on the Inclosure of Sutton Green'. It is written in a literate style and is not the work of a cottager, but it surely reflects the opinion of those whose common rights were abruptly distinguished. Its anonymity perhaps indicates the dangers of antagonising the lord in such a small closed society.

The Cottagers Complaint on the Inclosure of Sutton Green

How sweetly did the moment glide
How happy were the days
When no sad fear my breast annoyed
Or e'er disturbed my ease
Hard fate that I should be compelled
My fond abode to lose
Where threescore years in peace I dwelt
And wish my life to close

What little of the spacious plain
Should power to me consign
For want of means I cant obtain
Would not long time be mine
The Stout may combat fortunes frown
Not dread the rich and great
The young men fly to Market Town
But where can I retreat

My eaves are few my stock is small
Yet from my little store
I find enough for natures call
Nor would I ask for more
That word Inclosure to my heart
Such evil doth bespeak
I fear I with my all must part
A fresh employment seek

What kind of feelings must that man
Within his mind possess
Who from an avaritious Plan
His neighbours would Distress
Then soon in pity the every case
To reasons ear incline
For on his heart it stamps disgrace
Who form'd the base design

Chorus: Oh the time the happy time
Which in my lot I've spent
I wish the Church-yard was his doom
Who murders my content

In contrast, Byfleet was an open village, without a resident lord and with a diversity of landowners and smallholders. The lord of the manor was the Crown, but it acquired only 23 per cent of the waste, while the king's son, Frederick, Duke of York, was granted another 13 per cent. Even so, two-thirds of the new land was shared out among other landowners large and small. In

Byfleet, too, the parish poor were granted six per cent of the area, a relatively generous award, for turf-cutting and grazing.

25. *The landscape of enclosure and its fate*

The Commissioners concentrated the small fragments and allocations to the poor in certain areas. In Pyrford the Townsley and Walsham Meads, Coldharbour Lane and Woodham Lane were used, while in Sutton little plots were carved out of Pile Hill Common and the long narrow strips of former roadside waste. This was certainly not for the convenience of the cottagers – Woodham Lane, for example, was a long way from any habitation – but it solved the problem of disposing of small or awkward corners of the waste. It placed into single ownership the large tracts of open heath where the expense of fencing, hedging, and ditching could more readily be borne by a wealthier landowner. Thus, the expanses of Pyrford Heath and Woodham Heath, between the Woking road and the Bourne, were almost entirely given to or bought by Lord King, and in Sutton the Webb Weston family took possession of almost the whole of Whitmoor and Prey Heath. These families thus acquired hundreds of acres on which the poor, as well as the wealthier tenants, had previously grazed animals and enjoyed access to the resources of the commons.

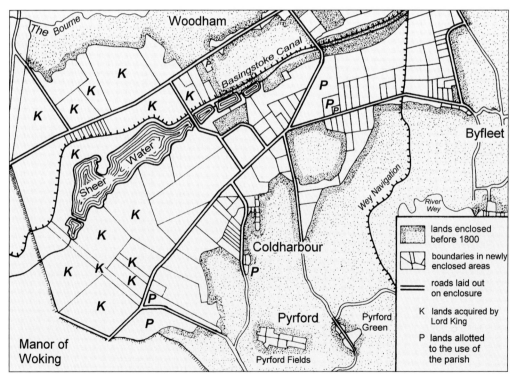

The landscape of enclosure in Byfleet and Pyrford: this map highlights the huge extent of the heathland which existed before 1805, and the strategy of laying out plots of very varied size – leading landowners were granted the large parcels of land around Sheerwater, the middle-ranking owners had the smaller plots in the vicinity of Coldharbour and West Byfleet-Parvis Bridge, while the cottagers and smallholders received tiny plots in Woodham Lane and Coldharbour.

Across the empty heaths the surveyors appointed by the enclosure commissioners plotted straight roads and geometric property boundaries which bore little relationship to the topography. Sometimes existing rough tracks and roads were adopted, straightened and widened, but others were completely new. Thus East Hill was laid out in 1804 when the Pyrford enclosure was under way, as a completely new road running along the parish boundary with

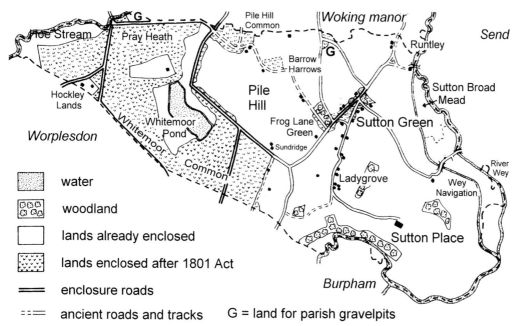

The enclosure of the manor of Sutton.

Woking, while Prey Heath Road, Woodham Lane and Old Woking Road are examples of older routes improved on enclosure. There is still, two centuries later, a striking contrast between the winding unimproved stretch of the Old Woking Road between Hoe Bridge and the Maybury Inn (in Woking parish and not enclosed) and the broad straight alignments from East Hill to West Byfleet, across what was once Pyrford Common. A new landscape was created across the whole area from the edge of Byfleet village, through what became West Byfleet, into Coldharbour and across to Sheerwater and Woodham.

Yet the effort of enclosing, draining and fencing was largely wasted. After 1815 much of the economic incentive for converting the heaths to agricultural land faded away and the cost of improvement was simply not affordable. The Webb Westons undertook extensive works in Sutton manor, emptying Whitmoor Pond and trying to drain the wetland heaths, but though large sums were spent the work was well-nigh useless. The land was so waterlogged that only plantations, rough grazing and scrub could be supported and two centuries later the site, given over to boggy plantation woodland, is still known as Whitmoor Pond. In the Rive Ditch valley the results were even less impressive. Lord King spent a vast sum of money draining the shallow 110-acre lake, Sheer Water (the largest natural lake in Surrey) and he laid out some plantations, but even in 1950 the site remained as scrub-covered bog. To the south the gentle slopes of Blackdown had more potential, and after enclosure Norfolk Farm was built here, but all around stretched great tracts of land which had been fenced, ditched and enclosed … yet remained more or less useless.

As animals no longer grazed the former heaths, and cottagers cut no more brushwood, or dug turf, or collected thatching materials, the heath vegetation was gradually superseded by birch and willow scrub and towards the end of the 19th century mature woodland, with silver birch and conifers, had developed. Thus, the tall pines and heathery glades which were regarded as so typical of Edwardian Woking were of recent creation, for in the late Georgian period this was a bare, unwooded landscape. The sons and daughters of the enclosure landowners must have rued the day that their fathers involved themselves in remodelling the landscape, spending large sums to saddle their families with expanses of useless land. The grandchildren, though, were much more charitably inclined to the memory of the enclosers, as the urban growth of Woking and Byfleet altered the financial equation. By the 1880s these agriculturally hopeless heaths became prime building land and the second generation reaped rich rewards when this became a favoured residential district. Golf courses were laid out among the heather and pines of West Byfleet and Pyrford, and around them sprawled low-density housing estates, with large and opulent residences. The heaths had come into their own and their value was infinitely greater than the farmland so eagerly and pointlessly anticipated by the enclosers. Yet the shapes of the roads, the lines of the property boundaries, and even the names of the leafy avenues, recall the

The enclosure landscape of the area which became West Byfleet dictated the shape of the residential and commercial areas which developed 75 years later. These two plans show how the post-1805 boundaries of fields guided the location of new roads and housing schemes.

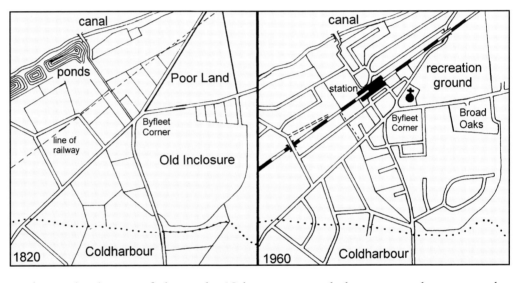

enclosure landscape of the early 19th century and the men and women who received allotments of former commons: who would now remember William Tegg and Susannah Bolton of Pyrford were it not for the roads which bear their names?

The manor of Woking, with its even greater tracts of common, was not formally enclosed until the arrival of men with very different ideas, the directors of the London Necropolis Company in the early 1850s. Horsell, though its commons were among the most extensive in the district, was one of the few Surrey parishes where no formal enclosure, by Act of Parliament or private agreement, was ever sought. This helps to explain the survival of the commons in Westfield, Mayford and Brookwood and, especially, the highly fortuitous continued existence of Horsell Common. Quite why the landowners and manorial lords in Woking and Horsell did not seek to emulate their neighbours in Pyrford and Byfleet is unclear. The survival of the open arable field in Woking into the 20th century – one of the last working instances in southern England – suggests that there was a strong 'commoner's interest' in the parish, and we know that it fought hard and with some success against the Necropolis Company in the 1850s. Perhaps, though, it was no more than a matter of chance. The Onslows, lords of Woking, were certainly not averse to enclosure, but they may merely have had the parish low on their list of priorities, because – unlike Lord King and the Webb Westons – they realised that enclosure for profit was not a realistic policy.

26. *Dealing with poverty in early 19th-century Woking*

The process of enclosure inevitably caused social and economic disruption, though historians differ in their views on the extent of its impact. It is certainly the case that in the Woking area, as in other parts of the south-east, the half century from 1790 was a time of acute distress among the poor, a problem which manifested itself not only in the higher cost of dealing with poverty but also in the growing level of rural crime and violence. The parish was the major unit of local government, its decisions being approved by a 'vestry' or meeting of ratepayers. Each parish was a miniature kingdom with powers and responsibilities over a wide and confusing variety of business ranging from the administration of the Poor Laws, via the upkeep of highways and the fabric of the parish church, to giving the payments for 'Taking Sparrows 6d pr Dozzen from Mich[aelmas] to Lady Day & 3d, [ditto] from Lady Day to Mich[aelmas]' which are recorded in the minutes of Woking vestry for January 1820. In this area

Byfleet parish workhouse, photographed in 1968: Byfleet vestry established this small poorhouse in the early 18th century to accommodate paupers and other people on temporary poor relief. The building closed in 1835 and became a cottage, which survived until the early 1970s. It was at Stream Close, Rectory Lane (formerly known as Workhouse Lane).

many minutes and other papers of the vestries have been lost through the ravages of time, but those for Woking 1818-30 and Byfleet 1795-1830 survive.

The vestry had long since dropped the close connection with the Church which gave it its name. By 1818 the Woking vestry normally met in a public house – the *Bird in Hand* at Mayford, or the *White Hart*, *White Horse* or *Crown and Anchor* in Woking village. The most important business, and the largest expense, was dealing with the poor – those paupers who legally belonged to the parish had to be helped, at the discretion of the overseer of the poor (an unpaid 'volunteer' chosen from among the ratepayers). The evidence suggests that Woking vestry was genuinely concerned to provide assistance for its paupers, and to be generous within its own limited horizons. Individuals could be privately charitable, as they had been for centuries: in September 1818, for example, 'the late Mr Brisks' willed 'a Feather Bed, Stead & Covering to the Children in the Workhouse' and in January 1830 Mr Robertson of Hoe Bridge gave '£5 for Bread for the Poor of this Parish at this Inclement Season of the Year'. The vestry, like most others up and down the country, made grants to the poor for clothing: 'Towards Shoes', 'for a shirt', 'Wm Baileys two Boys a Roundfrock each'. Each year it advertised for the supply of 'Meat, Drink,

An extract from the minutes of the Byfleet vestry, 1814, referring to the contract for the 'management' of the poor agreed with William Bicker. The arrangement, with numerous exemptions dictated by Bicker to avoid any unexpected expense on his part, was unsatisfactory and was soon terminated.

Clothing and Lodging to those poor Persons as shall be from time to time in the Workhouse' and in 1826 it asked for 'Persons willing to bake Bread of the Best Household Flour' for consumption there.

Each parish had its own small workhouse, in which the 'impotent poor' – those unable to help and provide for themselves – were housed on a more or less temporary basis. Orphaned and abandoned children, single women with young children, the disabled and chronically ill, and the old and infirm were the most important groups given such accommodation. Although in theory, as its name implies, the workhouse was intended as a place where paupers could be put to useful tasks to raise some money and thereby reduce the rates bill, in reality that aspect was never – in the Woking area at least – seriously tackled. The Woking parish workhouse was built in the late 18th century close to the *Cricketers Inn* on the edge of Westfield Common, and nearby were some small patches of arable land on which food for the inmates was grown. The Horsell workhouse was at Grove Barrs Farm, just east of the village behind St Mary's church. Pyrford's tiny workhouse was behind some cottages on the west side of the green at Pyrford Green and at Byfleet the workhouse building, which survived until the 1960s, was in Rectory Lane. It, too, had an allotment where able-bodied inmates grew food.

The workhouses were too small to accommodate all paupers and the parish authorities preferred to pay a rudimentary form of social security to the able-bodied, so that they could continue to live in their own homes. This system, known as 'out relief', was supplemented by purchasing or leasing cottages to house the poor. Thus, Horsell owned five cottages on the outermost edge of the parish at Dunford Bridge, Byfleet had three at Camp Hill, and Pyrford two on the edge of the Common. In 1818 Woking vestry seriously considered what would have been a pioneering move, when it debated the idea of 'Building Cottages for the Reception of Parishioners', but this foreshadowing of the later idea of council housing was not pursued. Medical needs were addressed. George Daborn of Woking agreed in September 1820 to attend the poor, charging the parish £2 for a birth and £1 5s. for a death. In January 1822 William Freeman undertook to be 'Doctor for the Poor within 7 miles of the Town of Woking … including Broken Bones &c (but with the Exclusion of Midwifery)' at an annual salary of £45. The danger of epidemics among the ill-housed, under-fed and overcrowded poor were considerable even in this rural district. In the summer of 1830 Woking vestry bought Thomas Sanders' house in Westfield for £65 to use as an isolation hospital, 'the Parish Officers having recently felt the dangers & inconvenience arising from the want of such a necessary asylum'.

27. Unemployment, distress and unrest

Woking vestry records show that the overseer regularly assessed the number of poor people in the parish. There were inevitably seasonal fluctuations, but from the early 1820s the overall trend was clearly upwards. This accords with what is known of patterns across south-east England as a whole and reflects developing problems in the agricultural economy of the region. In May 1819 there were 164 paupers, of whom 57 per cent lived in the notably impoverished Kingfield tithing: in total, about 10 per cent of the population was so poor as to be eligible for assistance even according to the very frugal and restrictive criteria in operation. Ten years later the proportion had risen to 13 per cent and the volume of business was such that a paid assistant overseer was appointed 'To manage the Poor of the Parish, their Labour & the Workhouse'. Increasing numbers posed other problems. Before 1820 the overseers of Woking had regularly hired out able-bodied inmates of the workhouse to local farmers, as cheap labour and to help to defray the rate burden. In October 1826 it was decided to extend this scheme to include those who received poor relief but lived in their own homes: 'Weekly Parish Meetings should regularly be held … by Tything in Rotation … or a Committee of a Given Number of Persons [should] meet on Tuesday in every week for the Purpose of furnishing Employment to the Different Labouring Poor who may Apply for it at such Meetings.' Work introduced under this scheme included 'Diggin Gravel' and 'Diggin Ditches on the Roads'. By 1830 this system was unable to provide even basic work for the poor, as unemployment grew rapidly, and the vestry frequently expressed its concern over the fast-rising cost of the system.

An increase in unemployment and rural poverty underlay the widespread unrest and sporadic violence in the country areas of southern England in the early 1830s. During the autumn of 1830 west Surrey was involved in disturbances which swept the country from east Kent to Dorset. Ricks and farm buildings were fired, machinery smashed and labourers assembled in violent and vocal demonstrations. Tithe day, when the deeply unpopular payments for the forthcoming year were set and those from the previous year were due, was 19 November. On that day in 1830 a large band of labourers and small farmers gathered in Woking village to oppose the payment of tithes to the Church. They were led by an unknown man who wore a smock-frock and shouted radical slogans, urging the crowd to march towards Dorking to free prisoners from the jail there. The meeting was addressed by Henry Drummond, the liberal local magistrate who two years later was to become MP for West Surrey, and he persuaded the men to disperse. They later blamed the unrest on agitators from Horsham (which, improbable though it may now seem, was a centre for militant radicalism) but it is clear that there was a great deal of genuine, if essentially low key and non-political, discontent in Woking and neighbouring parishes. Blaming foreigners from Horsham may, indeed, have been a clever way of exonerating the local men and enabling them to avoid the draconian punishments for riotous assembly.

As these strains developed there were moves towards reforming the local government system. In January 1822 Woking parish applied for 'select vestry' status, by which the existing procedures of ratepayers' meetings in which anyone could speak and vote was replaced by a committee structure of key ratepayers and officials. This was established in December 1822 and by 1826 the select vestry – in effect, a local council – was meeting more or less weekly to transact the increasing volume of business. Under the 1834 Poor Law Amendment Act, though, central government legislated to create an entirely new administrative structure for dealing with the pressing problems of poverty. Parish vestries lost this key role to Poor Law Unions, groups of parishes controlled by boards of guardians. In Surrey the old hundreds were used as the geographical basis of the new system, so that Woking came within the Guildford Union, which built a new central workhouse at Stoke, while Horsell, Pyrford and Byfleet were in the Chertsey Union with its workhouse at Ottershaw. The old parish workhouses were closed down and decision-making shifted from local ratepayers to centralised administrators. It was a clear harbinger for the future.

A NEW TOWN GROWS

28. The coming of the railway

Thus, changes were under way in the area by the end of the 18th century and gathered pace during the next thirty years. The open heaths were disappearing and parliamentary enclosure accelerated that process. The growth of nurserying was the first economic activity in the area which was of more than purely local importance, while the depression in farming produced unemployment and serious social unrest and distress. The canal placed Woking on a new routeway which, although it was conspicuously unsuccessful, gave rise to small-scale change in the neighbourhood. But from the mid-1830s all these changes to society, economy and landscape were eclipsed by the dramatic consequences of building the London and Southampton Railway through the heart of the district. The first serious proposals for a trunk railway from London to Southampton were announced in February 1831 and in 1834 a revised scheme was approved by parliament. Edward Ryde of Woking village recalled many years later that the original route involved a line 'parallel to the old Turnpike Road through Esher, Cobham, Ripley, Guildford, Farnham, Alton and Winchester' but that 'the landowners opposition in those places was so great that the application … was unsuccessful'. Had that route been followed the subsequent history of Woking would have been entirely different, but the 1834 Act for the London & Southampton Railway authorised a line which ran across the great open heaths of Surrey and Hampshire. It was a route chosen partly by future considerations (Basingstoke was intended to be the springboard for extensions to the West Country), partly by engineering requirements – the alignment was superb, with long straight stretches and long sweeping curves, though the civil engineering was heavy and expensive – and partly, perhaps primarily, by the fact that heathland was cheap, readily acquired and perceived as useless for other purposes.

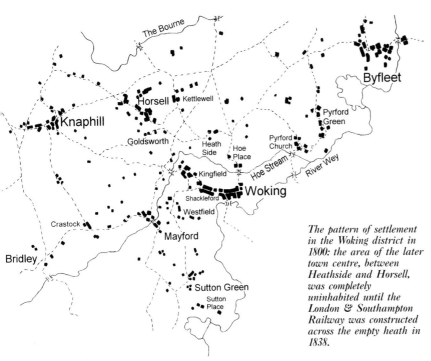

The pattern of settlement in the Woking district in 1800: the area of the later town centre, between Heathside and Horsell, was completely uninhabited until the London & Southampton Railway was constructed across the empty heath in 1838.

Work began in the autumn of 1834. John Francis, writing in 1851, noted that the eventual cost was almost twice the original estimate. The line sliced through St George's Hill by the deep cutting in which Weybridge station is situated, then crossed the Wey valley on a long high embankment. An early version of the route followed the Basingstoke Canal very closely, running for long stretches along the bank of the waterway, but the final choice was a line half a mile south, giving a more direct alignment and easing gradients. This had enormous significance for the geography of the later town, because it produced a long narrow strip of land squashed between canal and railway. As the line passed into the hillier land of the Surrey-Hampshire border there were deep cuttings at Hook Heath and beyond Pirbright, and equally immense embankments at St Johns, Hermitage and Brookwood. The effect of these prodigious works was to create a formidable barrier to communications and to focus the increasingly heavy traffic of the growing town on a small number of bridges across the line – even today the ten miles of line between Weybridge and Pirbright have only 11 road bridges.

Woking Common station and the London & Southampton Railway, looking westwards in the autumn of 1838 shortly after its opening. The artist has misrepresented the details of the topography (the line runs on a high embankment west of the station, and the road bridge at what is now Victoria Arch is not shown) but the details of the station buildings and the prevailing impression of an entirely rural and completely unpopulated landscape are convincing.

Construction was slow and the first section to be completed, the 23½ miles from Nine Elms (Lambeth) to Woking Common, was not opened until 21 May 1838. A party of dignitaries, directors and guests travelled from London by special train and enjoyed a buffet lunch in a marquee pitched beside the line on the open heath. It was the most important day in the history of Woking and within fifty years the empty heath on which they ate their salmon and cold beef would be a thriving town. The line was extended to Shapley Heath (Winchfield) on 24 September, and the final section, from Basingstoke to Winchester completing the through route from London to Southampton, on 11 May 1840. In marked contrast to the Basingstoke Canal it was an instant success: passenger traffic was four times the predicted level and the railway was profitable from the beginning. From its opening day Woking Common station assumed a major traffic importance which it never lost. As it was the railhead for much of west Surrey, including Guildford and Godalming, the stagecoach operators on the Portsmouth road diverted their services to connect with trains at Woking and the traffic through Ripley fell sharply. Previously 'Woking people would meet these [coaches] at the junction of the road from Woking at Sendhurst Grange' but after May 1838 they had a nearby station, though the Guildford road through Mayford was soon heavily congested:

> 66the roads in many places were too narrow for such traffic, it being only with the greatest difficulty that two stage coaches could pass each other in many places; and there was an entire absence of stable accommodation at Woking station. In addition to the public conveyance the whole of the

inhabitants of Guildford who possessed horses found that their best way to get to London was to arrive at Woking station.**99**

The 23-mile journey took one hour. The name of the station was Woking Common (the story that it was called 'Horsell for Woking' is entirely without foundation) but by the 1860s the simple name 'Woking' was in common use. The first station was a plain square two-storeyed building on the south (Woking village) side of the line. There were two platforms and minimalist freight facilities and that was all. The station was surrounded by open heathland, dotted with a few trees and a lot of gorse, and across the canal to the north could be seen the tower of Horsell church a mile away. That total isolation was not destined to be of long duration. Edward Woods, a local man, bought a parcel of land on the common a quarter of a mile from the station where the main road from Guildford to Chertsey crossed the old track along the side of the heath – Heathside Road in other words – and there he built the *Railway Hotel*. It opened in 1840, supplying travellers with refreshment, accommodation and stables for their horses. This was the first building in New Woking.

29. *The railway network 1840-1910*

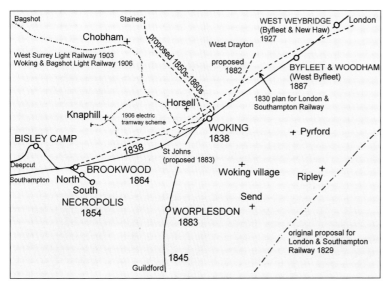

Railways (built or projected) in the Woking area 1830-1910.

From the beginning the railway company (which changed its name to the London and South Western in 1839) intended to build a branch to Guildford. In 1843 the Guildford Railway Company was authorised to build a branch and on 5 May 1845 the line was opened (the LSWR having already absorbed the local company). It was extended to Godalming in 1849 and ten years later to Havant, at which date it became the main through route from London to Portsmouth, so that Woking became a major junction on the national railway network. Further stations were opened later in the century: Brookwood (June 1864); Byfleet and Woodham, now West Byfleet, (December 1887); and Worplesdon, the most rural and the least busy (March 1883). There were frequent unsuccessful attempts to persuade the LSWR to provide a station at St Johns and Hook Heath. Other minor branch lines were added to the network. That serving Brookwood Cemetery opened in 1854, while in July 1890 Brookwood also became the junction for the short branch to Bisley Camp. Other more important lines which affected the Woking area were also constructed. The line from Pirbright Junction to Farnham was opened in 1870 and the new services from Waterloo to Alton on this route resulted in a major increase in the frequency of trains through Woking, adding to its growing attraction as a residential area for commuters. The branch from Weybridge to Chertsey opened in 1848 and was later extended to Staines, with a triangular junction allowing trains from the Woking direction to reach the line.

There were several serious attempts to construct other lines. In 1851 the Staines & Woking Railway planned a route from Victoria Arch to Egham, via Wheatsheaf Bridge, Kettlewell Hill and Horsell Common, with a separate Woking station on Commercial Road. Variants on this idea were revived several times in the next fifteen years, while in 1862 and 1882 plans for a line from Woking via Staines to West Drayton, with a train service to Paddington, were proposed but defeated by the fierce opposition of the London and South Western which rightly saw them as attempts by its bitter rival, the Great Western, to capture some of the increasingly lucrative Surrey traffic. In 1906 parliament authorised the proposals of the Woking and Bagshot Light Railway Company to build an electric tramway between the two towns, via Bullbeggars Lane, Parley Bridge, Millbrook and Chobham, with an electric street tramway network in Woking itself serving Goldsworth, Knaphill and Walton Road. Although work on the 12½-mile system was scheduled to start in October 1906 nothing was ever accomplished. Had it been built there might well have been a substantial re-orientation of Woking's growth towards Horsell Common and the Littlewick area.

30. The impact of railways

It is of course impossible to overstate the consequences of the railway on the Woking area. Had the line been built along the route of the A3, as originally suggested, Woking village would have remained more isolated and the area would have waited another twenty or thirty years before it began to expand. It is quite likely that a line from Guildford to Chertsey would have been constructed eventually, but it is doubtful if the rapid urbanisation of the Woking area would have materialised. Naturally we can

The impact of the railway around Woking station: all roads across the common were diverted to pass under the line at Victoria Arch. Station Approach and Chertsey Road mark the old alignment of the Guildford to Chertsey road while Commercial Road [Way], Guildford Road and the inner end of Goldsworth Road were diversions constructed in 1838.

never know, but the fact that all the development after 1850 in the district was, directly or indirectly, a consequence of the presence of a main-line railway speaks for itself. It did not make the development of a town inevitable (that process resulted from the decision of the cemetery company to sell its land around the station) but it created the circumstances within which urban development became feasible.

In a more detailed sense the physical form of Woking was fundamentally controlled by the geography of the railway and the road pattern which it influenced. When the Southampton line was built across the heath the existing tracks were either closed or diverted and all traffic was concentrated on one narrow railway arch under the embankment. Victoria Arch, as it was renamed when eventually rebuilt and widened, became a point of congestion and remains so to this day. Had the railway lines to Staines been built the problems of the town, chopped into four portions by embankments and cuttings, would have been even harder to solve. As it was, the hemming in of the central area between railway and canal posed serious traffic, planning and environmental difficulties for later generations. In few towns in England was the railway so important, but Woking – though for over 150 years heavily dependent upon the railway – was not a company town like Crewe or Eastleigh or Swindon. The town was, instead, the product of a circumstance which has no parallel anywhere in Europe. Woking was the child of a cemetery company. Out of death it had its birth!

31. *The London Necropolis and National Mausoleum Company*

Woking as a town owes its origins to the desperate overcrowding of the churchyards in early 19th-century London. These were the only places in which burial could legally take place and, with the massive increase in the population of the capital in the 18th century, they were bursting at the seams. Semi-decomposed bodies were hastily shifted aside to make way for new burials, dogs roamed freely, and the stench and pollution of ground water from rotting corpses were intolerable. Growing awareness of public health issues combined with revulsion against the disgusting circumstances of the churchyards to force the Board of Health (formed in 1848) to take action. In 1850 the Burials Act forbade interment in churchyards in urban areas and required the construction of new municipal or privately owned cemeteries. The Board of Health had already begun work on two huge new cemeteries for London – at Kensal Green and Erith – but it also proposed that a vast national cemetery, to be known as a *Necropolis* (City of the Dead), should be developed outside the capital but conveniently located for it. The site which it tentatively identified was Woking, which fitted the requirements in every way. It was only 25 miles from the city; had extensive unenclosed non-agricultural land (an increasingly scarce commodity in the south-east); sandy soil which was eminently suitable for burials; very cheap land prices because of the lack of farming potential; and since 1838 had enjoyed almost unequalled accessibility thanks to the London and South Western Railway line which bisected the great expanse of commons.

The Board of Health plan for a state-owned public cemetery at Woking foundered on the rock of *laissez-faire* attitudes, most interested parties being vociferously hostile to such a costly interventionist scheme, but the idea did not die. In 1851 a mixed bunch of businessmen, landowners, social reformers and philanthropists promoted a private alternative, and in October of that year the London Necropolis and National Mausoleum Company was formed. A huge national cemetery was proposed, in which the wealthy would be buried at premium rates in highly-desirable landscaped plots, while the poor (numerically, of course, vastly more significant) would be buried in 'public plots' – that is, unmarked mass graves – at the expense of parish authorities, their bodies brought to Woking by rail or water into the heart of the cemetery. It was a quite extraordinary vision: the reformers and philanthropists were persuaded of its social merits, the businessmen and landowners of its commercial charms, and the mid-Victorian love of the grandiose was fully satisfied. The first essential, however, was to acquire the land at Woking and for that purpose a special Act of Parliament had to be promoted, because the effect would be identical to that of enclosure.

32. The London Necropolis Company Act of 1852

The Necropolis Company's private bill was introduced in February 1852 and at its second reading a lengthy and highly acrimonious debate centred on the dubious character of the undertaking and the questionable wisdom of the plans. Henry Drummond, MP for West Surrey, declared roundly – taking advantage of parliamentary privilege – that the men behind the project were dishonest: 'no question of local or general interest was involved in the Bill, but the promoters, he should shew, contemplated a direct fraud on the public.' Their prospectus was misleading, he said, and he claimed – with remarkable accuracy – that 'the promoters intended to take powers to purchase 2,600 acres, while they themselves calculated that 400 would be necessary for the purposes of the cemetery, and they proposed to let on building leases the remaining 2,200 acres as a more commercial speculation'. This, he said, was not a cemetery company: 'They meant to make their money by building leases and it was in fact a Building Society under the mask of a Necropolis.' Other members, especially those with metropolitan constituencies, supported the Bill,

An imaginary aerial view of the proposed Necropolis at Brookwood, produced in 1852 when the legislation approving the project was going through Parliament. In the right foreground is Hook Heath and Wych Hill, with Hook Heath railway bridge prominently shown. To the right [north] of the railway line the cemetery is depicted occupying the land later used for Brookwood Hospital and reaching as far as Knaphill village. The large church in the bottom centre stands approximately in the middle of what is now Hook Heath golf course. Naturally, hardly any of this grand scheme was implemented.

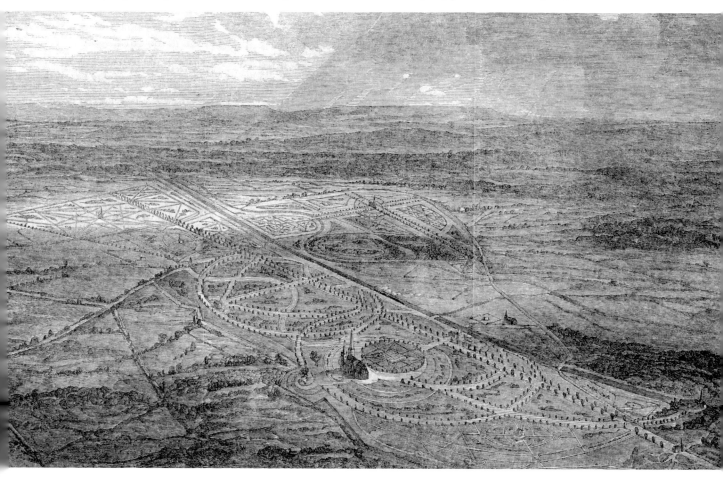

highlighting the acute nature of the burials crisis in city churchyards. James Mangles, MP for Guildford, pointed out that the commoners of Woking were mostly small farmers and manorial tenants who stood to lose heavily by this wholesale conversion from common grazing to private cemetery or building land. Victorian legislators were not at all hostile to private commercial builders as such, but the parliamentary opponents of the Bill instead objected strongly to what they saw (correctly as it turned out) as a deviousness of a project designed for public benefit being exploited for private gain. Nonetheless, the Bill was approved by the Commons with a majority of just 12, and passed easily through the Lords. It received the Royal Assent on 30 June 1852.

The new Company was authorised to purchase, by agreement with Lord Onslow, the lord of the manor, all or part of the common lands in the parish of Woking, together with 101 cottages, gardens and parcels of land which were earlier piecemeal enclosures from the waste and were required – in theory – because they would otherwise be surrounded, in an awkward and untidy fashion, by the cemetery lands. Their acquisition would allow rational planning of the new landscape to be created. The Act allowed the Company to stop up or divert any footpaths, highways and watercourses which crossed their land (though main roads such as that from Bagshot to Guildford were to remain open). Charges could be levied for burial, and for headstones, religious services and other accoutrements of interment. The railway company was permitted to enter into contracts for the carriage of bodies and other Necropolis business and railway facilities could be constructed at Nine Elms and the Cemetery. Most important, perhaps, was the clause which stated that land not required for cemetery purposes could only be sold or otherwise disposed of if parliament gave its consent and authority. This provision was inserted only after the strong expressions against land speculation which had been made during the Commons debate.

33. *Acquiring the land and the 1854 Act*

Discussions with the Onslow family had started in February 1852 and in April that year a provisional contract was agreed whereby the Company would purchase the lordship of the manor of Woking, all the common rights, and 2,326 acres of land for the sum of £38,000. The parish vestry sought compensation for those tenants and freeholders who would lose their common rights but no agreement could be reached – the amount offered was deemed inadequate – and so the matter went to arbitration. Not until October 1853 was it decided, on the judgment of a special jury sitting at Guildford, that £15,000 should be made available to the commoners as compensation. This was handed over to the Woking parish vestry and in July 1854 a private Act of Parliament gave legal force to the compensation procedure. This was required because the payment to those holding common rights was the second stage of an enclosure process. Usually known as the Woking Commons Act of 1854, it appointed commissioners to distribute the money and as a result, in October 1854, an agreement was signed between the vicar of Woking, the Onslow family and the Necropolis Company whereby the Company took full and final possession of 2,268 acres of the former common lands of Woking parish. Of this, 2,118 acres had already been discommoned – that is, they were no longer available to tenants, cottagers and freeholders and had become private property.

The remaining 150 acres, comprising Westfield Common, Prey Heath and Smarts Heath, were not discommoned because, as isolated and distant fragments, they were not appropriate for inclusion in the cemetery scheme. They remained as grazing land and the common rights continued, which is why they remain as commons to this day. In addition, the 60 acres of St Johns Lye were,

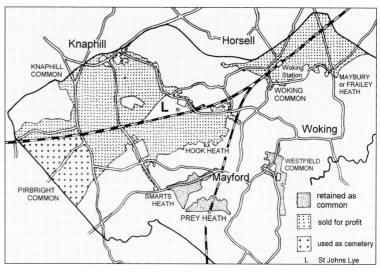

The land acquired by the London Necropolis Company in 1852-1854.

after pressure from the vicar, also excluded from the 1854 sale so that they could be used in perpetuity by the people of Woking for recreation and as common land. Dividing the compensation among the claimants took several years. It was to be available to copyholders (that is, manorial tenants) and to freeholders, and also to any others who could establish a claim based on the customary exercise of common rights. This latter category meant essentially those who had over the decades taken land illegally from the waste without challenge from the manorial courts. If they could show that they had exercised common rights without interruption for 30 years or more they were held to have permanent and *de facto* legal possession, a major benefit because this also gave them title to their land. The last claims were only settled in the autumn of 1857.

34. *Later amending Acts: 1855, 1864 and 1869*

With the exceptions noted above, the 2,268 acres acquired by the Necropolis Company should have been laid out as a cemetery and in 1852 the Company produced outline maps indicating its intention to close most of the public roads and lay out a necropolis stretching as far as the eye could see westwards from Maybury on both sides of the railway towards Brookwood and the Pirbright boundary. There is no evidence that this was anything but window dressing for public relations purposes. The first stage of the cemetery to be laid out was the 400 acres south of the railway and west of the Guildford-Bagshot road, at the westernmost extremity of the parish and in the most remote and inaccessible location. This 'first stage' of the cemetery was opened in November 1854. Not only was its area precisely that foretold by Henry Drummond during the parliamentary debate (did he have inside information?), but it was also the land with the least commercial potential. Had the Company really intended to use the whole of the Woking commons for the cemetery it would surely have started at the other end of its land, around the existing railway station, where access was easiest, but Brookwood was the least promising area for speculative land sales and the vicinity of the railway station had the most commercial potential.

The confirmation that the cemetery scheme, though in itself laudable, was merely the route to land speculation is that in the autumn of 1854, even before the first part of the project had been completed, the Company was preparing a Bill to allow the sale and disposal of 'surplus' lands. This was introduced in the Lords in May 1855 and received Royal Assent in July. Although some disquiet was expressed during the debate on its passage, the Act allowed the Company to sell (within ten years) large portions of its recent acquisitions which 'could never be properly appropriated to the purpose of the cemetery'. These included lands at St John's and Knaphill, the Hermitage estate at Brookwood, and – of vital significance – 400 acres around Woking station, Maybury and Hook Heath. The Company was to build a new 60-foot wide road (now Hook Heath Avenue) from the Wych Street corner to the Hook Heath railway bridge, opening up this land for building. Most important, perhaps, was the foreshadowing of the new town centre, for five acres were to be set aside within 600 yards of the railway station for a church, churchyard, parsonage and 'schools for the poor'. These provisions reflect what now seemed certain – that a completely new community was destined to arise, in the near future, on the empty heathland around the station.

Land sales were slow to develop and by 1864, when the ten-year time limit expired, the Company had only been able to dispose of 343 acres. Most of that was, perhaps unexpectedly, in Knaphill, where the War Department had bought land for a prison and the county justices had purchased the site of the lunatic asylum. A short private Bill, passed in 1864, granted a five-year extension to the period for land disposal. In 1869 the Company's fourth Act in 15 years freed it from all the earlier restrictions. The preamble to the 1869 Act stated categorically that the Company had 'laid out and enclosed for burial purposes a sufficient space to meet the estimated requirements of their undertaking for the next hundred years' but that the shareholders had not received an adequate financial return. The Act therefore repealed the main cemetery provisions of the 1852 Act: with the exception of the existing necropolis and a further 160 acres south of the railway and west of Blackhorse Road, any other land held by the Company could be disposed of, without time limit, for any purpose. As anticipated in the Commons debate 17 years before, the cemetery company had become a land speculation company.

35. *Brookwood Cemetery*

Woking Necropolis was the usual title of the cemetery in its early years, but by the end of the 1860s the name Brookwood Cemetery was general. Work on laying out the cemetery began in November 1852, as soon as the Necropolis Company had acquired legal title to the land. The original intention was to include the land north of the railway as far as the Basingstoke Canal, with a new station as the focal point of the design where a series of radiating avenues would meet. In the event the cemetery stopped at the railway and the land on the north side was never used. Originally, too, the company proposed a more radical redesign of the existing network of roads and tracks. Only the Bagshot-Guildford road and Blackhorse Road were to be retained. An almost straight road would follow the south side of the railway from Triggs Lane to Pirbright

Arch, with an equally direct link to Saunders Lane and Mayford, while a winding road would follow the edge of the heath from Wych Street to Blackhorse Road. The Mayford link was built (it is now Pond Road) and the heath edge road was constructed in stages and is now Hook Heath Road, but the others did not materialise, while the track from Knaphill to Pirbright which bisected the site of the cemetery was retained, widened and straightened and is now Cemetery Pales.

The Necropolis Company sought to transform the 450 acres of windswept treeless heathland into an oasis of sylvan beauty, a suitably delightful and peaceful last resting place for thousands upon thousands of inhabitants of dirty, smoky London. The architect, Henry Abraham, based his design on radial avenues linked by long curving paths and drives, with a more basic grid pattern in some areas where lower status graves were anticipated. Complementing this plan were a variety of buildings, including chapels and two railway stations designed by Sir William Tite, the prominent architect employed by the London and Southampton Railway in 1836-8 and also involved with the earlier cemetery at Norwood in south London. The landscaping work was to Abraham's design but was implemented under the auspices of Robert Donald of Goldsworth Nurseries, who exploited the opportunities presented by thin acid soils to plant many thousands of shrubs, including the rhododendrons and azaleas in which his nursery specialised, and to create extensive groves and avenues of conifers. While the Necropolis Company undoubtedly had many glaring faults and inadequacies, nobody, then or now, could question that it made a remarkably good job of laying out the cemetery itself.

The necropolis was divided into separate 'grounds', delineated by paths and avenues, which were offered to different London parishes and to various religious denominations. Between the main railway and Cemetery Pales were Catholic and Nonconformist areas, to which Muslim and Parsee 'grounds' were later added, while south of the road was the larger Anglican area. In the 1920s a large military cemetery was laid out in the northern half, later extended to accommodate Second World War graves. This section also had 'grounds' for

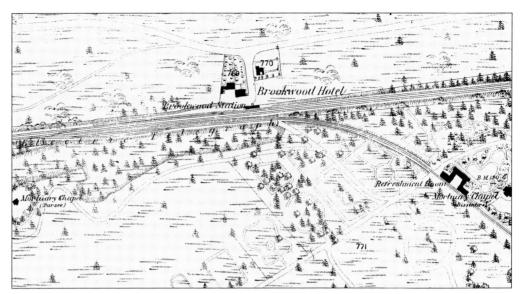

The Ordnance Survey 25-inch map of 1871 shows the cemetery railway and the North Station, with its refreshment room. Note the two mortuary chapels for the Nonconformist and Parsee faiths. Brookwood village did not then exist.

different nationalities, including American, French, Turkish and Dutch. Wealthier occupants were housed in tombs and mausolea, and an immense variety of such memorials can be seen, architecturally ambitious, embellished with sculpture and classical and religious motifs. The pauper burials, in contrast, were unmarked and uncommemorated – the company designed an 'earth to earth' coffin so that such burials would swiftly disintegrate to allow frequent re-use of the site.

The cemetery was consecrated by the Bishop of Winchester on 9 November 1854 and the first interment, four days later, was of the stillborn twins of Mrs Store of the Boro' (Southwark) – a pauper burial which set the pattern for the rest of the century. Numerically it was the poor of metropolitan Surrey, the area of London including Southwark, Lambeth, Clapham, Wandsworth and Battersea, who predominated. Their corpses arrived by rail, for perhaps the most remarkable feature of the cemetery was the mile-long private branch railway, opened at the time of consecration, which left the main line just west of Brookwood station. There were two stations within the cemetery, and at Westminster Bridge Road just outside Waterloo the company built a London terminus for cemetery trains. Every day at 11.35 a.m. or 11.45 a.m. a special left London, taking 50 minutes for the journey to Necropolis Junction. It stopped at North Station and the South Station terminus, from which it returned at 2.15 p.m. The busiest day was Saturday, when 30-35 funeral parties would be carried. By 1941 the train only ran twice a week, but in that year it – and the London station – were destroyed in an air-raid and this extraordinary rail service came to an abrupt end. After the war it was deemed uneconomic and the branch line was dismantled.

The cemetery admirably fulfilled the intentions of the reformers and philanthropists who were behind its original promotion, though whether it ever realised the slightly naïve dreams of its capitalist instigators is another matter. In 1860, only five years after opening, there were over 3,000 burials and in the peak year, 1866, 3,842 people were buried, an average of over ten per day. Every one was carefully recorded in massive leather-bound volumes, though the location of most – the pauper graves – is not indicated. After 1880 the rate slackened. Other cemeteries opened nearer London, and by 1914 cremation was becoming an acceptable alternative to burials, but by 1939 over 201,000 burials had been recorded. Today the figure is approaching 300,000. The landscaping matured superbly. The tall groves of dark conifers, the thick shrubberies, the shaded walks and glades, and the superabundance of monumental masonry all combine to give what Nairn described as 'a sombre complex landscape unlike anything elsewhere in the country', which reminded Pevsner of 'a garden suburb with all the houses become mausolea'.

But troubled times were ahead. The drastic reduction in staff (in 1980 there were five, whereas in 1880 there had been 160), the declining use of the cemetery itself, the seemingly inevitable problem of vandalism, neglect of the monuments by the descendants of the dead, and the massive task of dealing with 450 acres of mature woodland and shrubbery meant that in the late 20th century the future of the cemetery seemed very insecure indeed. Attempts by the owners to sell parts for development were both tasteless and futile, because the land is subject to strict controls as it is within the green belt. Fortunately, the efforts of the Friends of Brookwood Cemetery and high-profile campaigns to secure its long-term future were successful and today the cemetery, designated as a conservation area for its architectural and historical interest, and also protected as a local nature reserve, is gradually being restored and the damage undone. It is a magical place, as Nairn recognised forty years ago, for ever unique in its combination of an extraordinary history, a superb landscape, and a haunting atmosphere.

36. The role and importance of the Necropolis Company

Thus, the town of Woking was the product of the questionable and dubious activities of a group of businessmen who, using a praiseworthy public project as their cover, acquired large areas of real estate for the purposes of land dealing. Contemporaries were well aware of the contradictions inherent in the original scheme, and many were suspicious from the outset of the motives and strategies of the promoters, but nothing which the Company did was strictly illegal – their powers, and their policies, were authorised by parliamentary legislation – although when, in the 1880s, for example, land was being sold cheaply to the directors, or to development companies linked to the Necropolis Company, the bounds of integrity were certainly being pushed to the limit. The unpalatable aspect, for those at the time, was that much land was acquired very cheaply, ostensibly for the cemetery, when it was clear that there was never any likelihood of its being used for that purpose. Nevertheless, it must be accepted that the cemetery itself was never a lucrative business and the profits were derived almost entirely from the land deals.

The Company was not unique – there were other private cemeteries run by commercial undertakings – but unlike any other it was responsible for the creation of a town. The Victorian town of Woking certainly was unique in the means of its birth and development: there were many railway towns, steel towns, canal towns and mining towns, but nowhere else in Europe was a cemetery town. This leads, inevitably, to the character of the town which was created, and here the negligence and failings of the Necropolis Company were all too apparent. Given that land speculation was at the heart of the project the directors could have imposed a rational plan, provided public buildings, and sought to bring into being a town which was worthy and of high quality. By laying out a proper road pattern, investing in a well-designed town centre, sponsoring decent architecture, and encouraging orderly and coherent development, the company might have produced a new town of which its citizens could be proud and outside observers spoke favourably. They chose not to do so. The town which grew up was haphazard in its plan, mean in its architecture, inadequate in its facilities and inefficient in its design. For much of the next 150 years the local authorities and people of Woking struggled to remedy these glaring deficiencies. Even today the weaknesses of the original non-design are apparent and Woking's often unflattering image owes much to the self-interest and lack of public spirit of the Necropolis Company a century and a half ago.

37. *The new town centre*

The birth of the new town can be dated to the Necropolis Company's 1855 Act, which authorised land sales. The Company had a block of over 400 acres of open land, with no existing buildings apart from the *Railway Hotel* of 1840, and it had the power to remodel the road pattern in any way it chose. However, it sold the land piecemeal and made only token efforts to plan the area. The fundamental question, in retrospect, was the location of the new town centre. This lies on the north side of the tracks whereas the main station entrance is on the south side and traditionally this was blamed on the Raistrick family (who had bought the land on the south) because they refused to sell land for a town centre. In fact they were not to blame. The main entrance was on the south side when the station opened in 1838 because the main source of traffic – Guildford and Woking village – was in that direction. The real culprit was the Necropolis Company, which made the decision to sell the land on the south side of the line for high-class residences in large grounds, rather than for commercial purposes (the motive being that the slopes south of the railway enjoyed fine views across to the North Downs and so were attractive for private housing). This was not in itself a problem, because all that was required was for a suitably imposing northern entrance to the station to be provided for the town centre. That simple solution was not adopted and here, too, the Company was entirely to blame.

By 1859, as the Company's sale plans confirm, land for a church and school had been allocated on the north side and there was no doubt that this would be the centre of the infant community. But the new road plan, whereby what became High Street and Broadway lay immediately alongside the railway property, effectively denied any space for expansion of the entrance. To this day the cramped and unsatisfactory site is all too obvious: there is not a spare yard of ground between station steps, pavement and road, and there never has been. Others have compounded the problem. In the mid-1880s the railway company, when it widened the line to four tracks, wanted to rebuild the station entirely and to create a more impressive and spacious north entrance: this would have meant encroaching onto High Street and remodelling the road layout of this part of the centre, and the highway board refused permission. In 1897 the *Albion Hotel*, immediately opposite the entrance, was to be rebuilt. A number of leading citizens proposed that a town planning project should be undertaken, involving the creation of a civic square (to be called Victoria Square) at this, the highest point of the centre: it would be a focal point for the town, give a much more impressive and dignified entrance to the station, and allow the improvement of the road network. The new urban district council, parsimonious and lacking in civic ambition, refused to countenance the expenditure. It was to be 75 years before its successor, with greater ambition and enlightenment, finally created such a focus elsewhere – but the indifferent station entrance remains.

38. *The first land sales*

The earliest building in the area of the modern town centre was the *Albion Hotel*, opened in 1856 by Reuben Percy, since 1849 the landlord of the *Wheatsheaf* in Horsell. He bought a plot of land immediately opposite the northern entrance to the station and built a hotel which would rival the *Railway*. This sale was immediately after the 1855 Act which allowed the Company to dispose of surplus and unwanted land. Two years later the key site on the south side of the station was sold to John Raistrick, a wealthy retired railway contractor who purchased over 40 acres east of the station and there built his house, Woking Lodge. Later that year the Company made its

first major speculative land sale at an auction in London, offering 60 acres around the station divided into 89 lots, ranging in size from 0.15 acres to 3.6 acres. The Company architect, Henry Abraham, had designed a road network to act as the framework for the sale. North of the railway a crude and ill-formed grid pattern was laid out, based on the fixed lines of what became Chertsey Road and Commercial Road. This was far from ideal, for there were awkward junctions by the railway arch and where the two existing roads met, and the unofficial footpath which had developed from

A = Albion Hotel

Wheatsheaf canal bridge to the station over the previous twenty years was retained in the new plan, cutting at an angle across the site. In the long term, as Church Path, this early version of a pedestrian street became an attractive feature of the town centre, but its existence reflects the inept approach to urban design pursued by the Company.

South of the railway Abraham designed a rudimentary pattern of radial roads and concentric links, but he did not have the courage to redesign the existing tracks and lanes. Thus Heathside Lane (now Road) and what became Oriental Road fitted uncomfortably into the plan. Today this rather feeble venture into

The outline plan for 'New Woking', the town centre area which was delineated by the plots sold in 1859. The plan shows a rudimentary urban design south of the railway and indicates the clumsy inadequacy of the design north of the line, where no attempt was made to create a logical road network or a focus for the infant town.

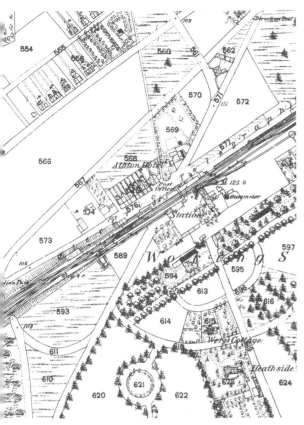

urban design is still marked by the semi-circle of Oriental Crescent and the radials of White Rose Lane and Station Approach, though here, as in the rest of central Woking, business and commercial uses – car parks, the telephone exchange, sorting office and shops – have encroached upon and partly obscured the original layout.

39. *The town centre takes shape*

Thus, the hands-off attitude of the Company determined the shape of New Woking. A substandard road pattern was to be the framework for a piecemeal development of buildings, with no coherent plan, no provision of services, and no decent architecture or design. No central square was laid out, no sites for public buildings designated, and whether shops, offices or community facilities appeared was to be entirely a matter of chance and individual preference. The diocese of Winchester chose not to take up the option of the five-acre site north of the railway and west of Stanley Road which had been allocated for a church and schools, so even that possible 'fixed point' came to nothing. As the Company offered its land for sale the speculators and builders began to move in, though

Woking Station and adjacent areas from the Ordnance Survey 25-inch map of 1871: the first buildings of the town centre were appearing in what became High Street and Church Street, while large houses stand in extensive grounds south of the station, but the 'circus' (roughly on the site of the Boys Grammar School playground) had failed to attract developers.

progress was initially rather slow. In 1863 the West Surrey Mutual Benefit Building Society opened an office at the *Albion*, and in the next few years a few new properties appeared – a row of houses in High Street, facing the railway, some cottages in Chobham Road, and some detached and semi-detached houses in Providence Street (later renamed Church Street). By 1870 some observers were sure that more substantial change was imminent: the *Surrey Advertiser* opined that 'the neighbourhood of the railway station will

A train from Waterloo arriving at Woking station in about 1900: the view shows the line of shops which had been built at the western end of Maybury Road (later renamed Broadway) in the early 1890s.

become, ere many years, covered with buildings, and … the erections now known as the town of Woking will be designated the *old*, as distinguished from the new town of Woking to spring up at the railway station'.

After 1878 a commercial centre began to evolve, more or less by accident. Shops began to appear in High Street and Chertsey Road, with offshoots in Maybury Road (the western end of which was officially renamed Broadway in 1923) and Chobham Road. In 1884-93 Christ Church was built on Providence Street (soon renamed Church Street in its honour), set down amid the straggle of houses, while in 1895-1910 a small group of public buildings was constructed – not according to any overall plan – at the western end of Commercial Road. Together the Conservative Club (1898), the Public Halls (1895), Urban District Council offices (1904) and Methodist Church (1899, with a tall and elegant spire) formed a modest civic area, facing onto Sparrow Park (laid out when the road junction was remodelled in 1903). Also in view were the public lavatories and the massive and dominating railway embankment. Utopia it clearly was not.

By 1895 most of Commercial Road, Chapel Street and Bath Road had been built up and in 1896 Duke Street was laid out across the land once reserved for a church and schools. This helped to open up more of the lower end of Chertsey Road, where building was

ABOVE *The public buildings at the western end of Commercial Road, c.1908: (left to right) Woking Public Hall (later Grand Theatre), 1895; Woking Urban District Council Offices (1904); the Constitutional Club (1898); and Commercial Road Methodist Church. Though built as individual projects they had a 'house style' characterised by the use of red brick with stone quoins, window surrounds and ornamental details. All these buildings were demolished in the late 1960s and the scene is completely unrecognisable today.*

BELOW *The growth of Woking town centre 1870-1914.*

1. *The Albion Hotel*
2. *The Red House Hotel*
3. *Christ Church*
4. *Gammon's store*
5. *Baptist chapel*
6. *Victoria Hospital*
7. *Commercial Road Methodist Church*
8. *Constitutional Club*
9. *Woking Council offices*
10. *Woking Public Hall*
11. *St Dunstan's RC Mission Church*
12. *Co-operative store*

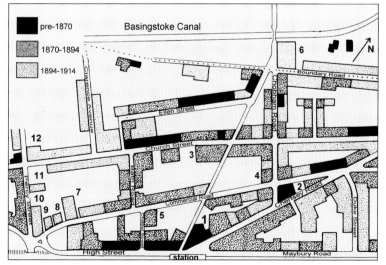

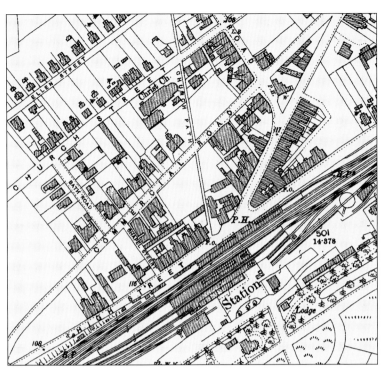

Woking town centre in 1894: the station had been rebuilt with a larger entrance, on the south side of the tracks, but the unsatisfactory northern entrance was now a fixture.

already in progress by the mid-1880s. Typically, in all these streets, shops were either built with accommodation above, or were converted from the front rooms of houses only a few years old. Even today the essentially domestic scale of the architecture of parts of Chertsey Road is very clear. Commercial Road, too, was originally residential but by 1914, as the town grew and the central area expanded, it was succumbing to commercial pressure. In the 1930s and 1950s a couple of small redevelopment schemes removed some of the erstwhile domestic properties, though others survived, still recognisable as houses, until the whole area was cleared in the late 1960s. In Clarence Avenue, which was roughly where the Peacocks centre is today, a small lower-middle-class enclave was developed with semi-detached villa housing. It was named after Prince Albert Edward, Duke of Clarence and Avondale, who died in 1892. Here a few residential properties remained until the town centre redevelopment, though most had been converted into offices, dental surgeries and other business uses.

By 1914, therefore, a town centre had been created. It had arisen piecemeal over the previous forty years, without planning or design. With the honourable exception of the small group of public buildings in Commercial Road, and the brick bulk of Christ Church, it had no architectural merit. The shops, workshops, and offices were intermingled with houses, traffic circulation was deficient, and a sense of civic dignity or identity absent. The failure of the Necropolis Company had produced what Ian Nairn, writing in the mid-1960s, called 'a period piece, though not a very creditable one … a Victorian gridiron mushroomed around [the station, with] mean and joyless public buildings, offices and chapels'.

40. Walton Road and Goldsworth

The choice of the north side of the tracks for the new centre and, conversely, the south side for high-quality residences ensured that the areas east and west of the developing commercial area would become the working-class part of the town. These districts lacked the key advantages which made the land south of the railway potentially so attractive – they were lower lying, with poor drainage in the shallow marshy valley through which the canal had been built seventy years before, and they had none of the views to distant hills and across green vales which appealed to the upper-middle-class housebuyer in the late 19th century. Proximity to the railway and the canal encouraged a variety of small industries and workshops to emerge, and the policy of the Necropolis

Company in selling the land here mainly in small plots suitable only for terraced housing or small semi-detached 'villas' reinforced the inferior social status of the district.

The Goldsworth Road area differed from much of the area on which the new town grew because there the Necropolis Company owned little land. The ancient hamlet of Goldsworth had comprised small farms and cottages straggling along the winding alignment of Goldsworth Road itself. The land around was sold off piecemeal in the years after 1860, with a large number of small developments scattered along the main road or on short streets built off it, unconnected with each other. The result was an untidy and miscellaneous new suburb: a walk along Goldsworth Road from Victoria Arch to the Triangle still demonstrates this haphazard origin. The road bends just as its predecessor, the unmade track from Knaphill to Heathside and Woking village, wound across the heath and through the fields. A variety of housing types, many of them the 'cottage' style villas of the 1890s and the Edwardian period, reflects the many local builders who had a hand in the development of the area. More recently, Goldsworth Road has experienced the advance of business and commercial use as the centre of the fast-growing town of the post-1945 period has crept out of its old confines – shops, restaurants, garages, small industrial units and (in the past twenty years) new office redevelopments have transformed the inner end, but the residential origins of many of the properties are still apparent at first-floor level.

Bird's eye view of central Woking in about 1900, taken from the roof of Commercial Road Methodist Church. Commercial Road is in the left foreground with the Baptist chapel (familiar to many in a later incarnation as Woking Library) at the junction with Chapel Street. The gasworks is in the left background and the white dome of the mosque peeps over the trees near the skyline. On the extreme right is Woking Lodge, home of the Rastrick family. Every building shown in this view had been built in the previous 40 years, and almost none of them remains today.

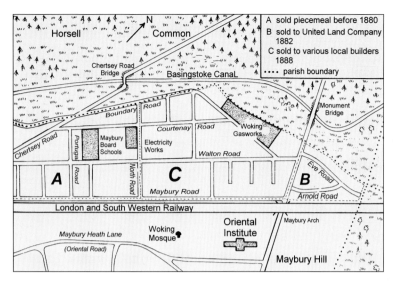

Map legend:
A sold piecemeal before 1880
B sold to United Land Company 1882
C sold to various local builders 1888
···· parish boundary

The east end of Woking 1870-1914.

East of the town centre there was only scrubby and marshy heathland until 1869, when the Necropolis Company began to construct a rough grid pattern of roads and to mark out plots of building land for sale. The old parish boundary between Horsell and Woking, which followed the line of what is now Boundary Road, marked the northern edge of the Company's property, and this dictated the shape of the new development – neither roads nor building plots could cross the boundary, hence the sharp curve in Boundary Road at its junction with Omega Road, and the tuning-fork shape of Arnold Road and Eve Road which fitted into a corner of the Necropolis Company land. Auctions of land were held in the years after 1873 and in 1879 large-scale building operations began. Substantial areas were purchased by the shadowy United Land Company, one of a number of speculative firms which had directors in common with the Necropolis Company. The intention was always that this area, north of the railway, would be for the lower orders – the manual workers, artisans and clerks.

Even so, the area was socially graded. In 1888 the last major area of the 'Woking Common Estate' was sold by the Necropolis Company, comprising 201 plots between the railway, Boundary Road and Board School Road. The frontages of the houses facing the railway, along Maybury Road, were 60-80 feet in width, but those on Walton Road were only 40-50 feet and on Boundary Road

This fine image of Courtenay Road was taken in 1904, just before the road was made up by the team of Woking Council workmen who are standing in the distance. The deplorable state of roads even in the built-up area of the town is all too obvious.

a mere 30 feet. Today it might seem surprising that the houses facing the railway were deemed to be in the most desirable location, but the Company saw a publicity value in the long row of neat and attractive (though often very small) detached and semi-detached villas easily viewed from passing trains. Today, the situation is reversed. The quieter location on Boundary Road, facing the common, is perhaps preferred to the noise and encroaching commercial development of Maybury Road.

The housing erected on these new streets was generally inferior in design and quality. Builders openly flouted many of the bye-laws introduced to try to raise standards, and even after the formation of the Woking Local Board in 1893 regulations were ignored. The Necropolis Company had laid out the lines of the roads but made no attempt to provide sewers or drains, water supplies or even to surface the roads. In 1889 the electricity power station was built in Board School Road and in 1892 the gasworks opened in Boundary

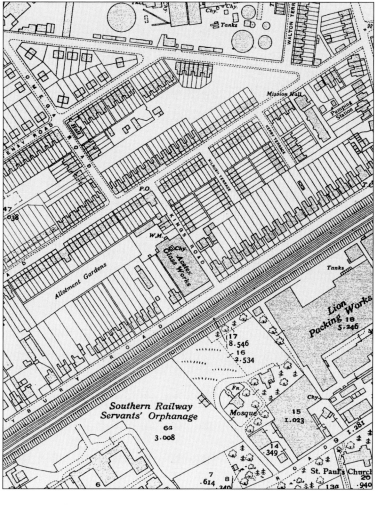

Part of the east end of Woking, 1936, showing the densely-packed terraced housing away from the railway, the small semi-detached villas which faced the tracks on Maybury Road, and the gasworks and other industrial sites cheek by jowl with housing.

Road, further emphasising that this was the working-class corner of the town, conveniently segregated by railway, canal and common from the remainder. In 1897 newly-built houses next to the gasworks, constructed by a developer named Cohen, were described as 'the worst property in Woking … built of old materials, very badly-constructed … exceedingly damp and inadequately drained'. Only eighteen months after their construction they were declared to be unfit for human habitation and closed by the order of the Medical Officer of Health. Thus, slum housing was found from the very beginning of the life of this part of the town. This did not have to be so, but the failure of the Necropolis Company and its directors to ensure proper, or even minimum, standards, and the weakness of the local government structure in dealing with these problems, stored up major difficulties for future generations.

41. The Royal Dramatic College and Oriental Institute

South of the railway line at Maybury the open heathland became the site of the strangest of Woking's several major mid-Victorian institutions, the Royal Dramatic College of 1859-77 and the Oriental Institute of 1884-99, either of which could, given slightly more favourable circumstances, have developed a national or international importance. Had this happened the history of Woking

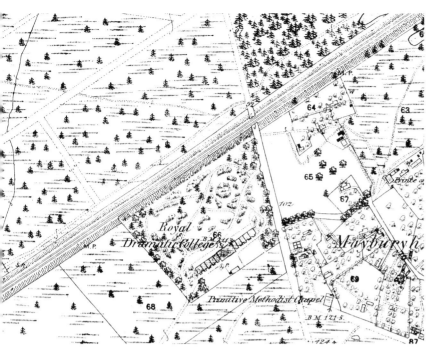

The Royal Dramatic College in 1871: its surroundings are largely undeveloped heathland (the railway bridge shown is Maybury Arch) but the first streets of the Walton Road district had been laid out north of the railway.

might well have been very different – indeed, it could have become a university town with a highly influential cultural role. The Royal Dramatic College was the brainchild of a group of leading actors, theatrical patrons and literary figures (including Dickens and Thackeray) who in 1858 held a public meeting to discuss founding a home for retired actors and actresses and a theatrical training school for the profession. The outcome was the formation of a trust, which received the patronage of Albert the Prince Consort, followed by a royal charter granted in June 1859. The site for the new college and residential home had to be out of London (because of cost considerations) but within very easy reach of the city, since that was the centre of the theatrical world. Woking, with its combination of excellent rail access and plenty of cheap land already on the market, was the perfect location. In 1860 the trustees bought 10 acres just south of Maybury Arch and on 1 June that year Prince Albert travelled on a special train, to a temporary platform adjacent to the site, and laid the foundation stone.

Residents were admitted from September 1862 though the Royal Dramatic College was not formally opened by the Prince of Wales (Albert having died in 1861) until June 1865. The chief sponsor of the project, Thomas P. Cooke, was a wealthy actor who poured a great deal of his personal fortune into creating the College because 'he had private means himself but knew that other members of his profession had not'. He died in 1867 and left a large sum to the College in his will. The buildings, in a strangely hybrid Victorian-Tudor style, were of solid red brick with terracotta reliefs. There was a large central hall, a pillared cloister or arcade along the front to provide a sheltered area where elderly residents could sit, and ten self-contained 'houses' (in reality, sets of rooms) each providing accommodation for two people. The college was run by a master and his wife, who acted as matron: the 1871 census records 16 elderly occupants (the youngest 60, the oldest 85) and no staff other than Mr and Mrs Webster, the master and matron. By this time, though, it was

The Royal Dramatic College in its heyday, c.1870. Its impressive and ambitious architecture was one reason for its failure – it had been an expensive project – but had they survived as the Oriental Institute these buildings would eventually have become the centrepiece of the University of Woking.

The medal struck to commemorate the laying of the foundation stone of the Royal Dramatic College by Prince Albert on 1 June 1860. The reverse has a bust of Shakespeare, with figures representing Youth and Old Age, and around the edge is the quotation from As You Like It, *'All the world's a stage & all the men & women merely players'.*

being reported that there were financial difficulties. Cooke's money had been almost exhausted and public and private interest had waned. In November 1877, admitting that the project was now bankrupt, the governor and trustees announced the immediate closure of the College. The Charity Commissioners ordered the sale of all assets and in June 1880 the site and buildings were bought by Alfred Chabot, a land and property speculator. What would he do with this large red white elephant?

Fifty years later there would have been no question: the buildings would have been demolished without delay and the site covered with new houses. But in Woking in 1880 developable land was not yet a precious commodity, and when in 1883 Dr Gottlieb Wilhelm Leitner came looking for somewhere to realise *his* private dream the College buildings still lay vacant and available. Dr Leitner was surely the most extraordinary man in Woking's history. Born in Budapest in 1840, he was soon discovered to have an exceptional talent for languages: at the age of ten he was fluent in most European tongues, together with Turkish and Arabic. When he was 15 he became an interpreter with the British Army in the Crimea, and at 19 was lecturer in Arabic, Turkish and Modern Greek in the University of London. At 23 he was professor of Arabic and Mohammedan Law. By the time he was 30 he had founded the University of Lahore in what is now Pakistan and this experience, together with his passion for Middle Eastern, Arabic and Oriental culture, inspired him to imagine a European centre for the study of the languages, culture and history of the East. Looking round for a possible site, he came upon the Royal Dramatic College, bought it, and set about realising his ambition.

The complex was renamed the Oriental Institute, and part was made into what was said to be the finest private museum of Oriental artefacts in England – all the priceless objects which Leitner had acquired on his travels were housed there. The Institute trained Asians in Europe who wanted to enter the professions, undertook and promoted the study of linguistics and history, and taught Eastern languages to Europeans who wished to travel there. Woking was somewhat bemused by this oddity in its midst, and Leitner remarked that 'There is no place in the world where the Institute and its publications are less known than in Surrey'. But his ambition did not stop there, for he aspired to even greater achievement. By 1896 the Oriental Institute was awarding degrees, validated by the University of Lahore (a curious reversal of the usual position – colonial universities normally had their degrees validated by English establishments) and Leitner planned that in due course it would be upgraded to become the Oriental University of Woking.

Woking Mosque: an engraving published soon after it was opened in 1889. The first purpose-built mosque in western Europe in modern times, it is perhaps the most historically significant of the town's buildings, as well as one of the most beautiful.

Would that it had, but here, too, over-reliance on the energies and financial support of an individual proved to be disastrous. In 1899, having been ill for some months, Leitner travelled to Germany to take cures at the Rhineland spas. He contracted pneumonia and at the end of March died in Bonn. His body was returned to England and he is buried, appropriately, in Brookwood Cemetery. His death meant the death of his Institute. It closed in the summer of 1899, its priceless library and museum were sold off, and the buildings again stood vacant. Think what might have been – a university of worldwide reputation next to Maybury Arch … Woking as a cultural centre of global significance … but of this wonderful dream there are just two tangible reminders. One is the name Oriental Road, so incongruous unless the history of the area is appreciated, and the other is Woking Mosque, the town's most delightful and historically most important building.

42. South of the railway

Confirmed in 1859 as the higher-class residential area of New Woking, the land south of the railway acquired a completely different character from that to the north. It was also the only part of the growing town where the Necropolis Company made any serious effort to plan development, though even here the attempt was limited in extent and half-hearted in execution. The sale of former common land in the Station Estate, south from the railway to Heathside Road, began in 1859, but the Necropolis Company found that take up was comparatively slow. South of Heathside Road was meadow and pasture, and it was another twenty years before the owners of this farmland began to appreciate its development potential. Between 1859 and 1875 a few large houses, such as Heathside House and Wergs Cottage, were built in the White Rose Lane district, but most of the rest of the heath stayed as open land. The building of the Royal Dramatic College close to Maybury Arch in the early 1860s encouraged development at that end of the common, and houses were built on large plots on what had been known as Maybury Rough but which became, far more decorously, Shaftesbury Road. The *Surrey Advertiser* noted in 1869 that 'The disposition to erect Dwellings in this neighbourhood is becoming more manifest' and after 1870 most of the

The 1894 25-inch Ordnance Survey map shows, south of the station, very large houses in extensive wooded grounds – note that Beechcroft has drives, shrubberies and lawns which extend from Heathside Road to Hillview Road. These properties are typical of the high-class and expensive character which was deliberately promoted for this attractive part of the growing town.

Maybury Heath Lane, c.1900: this rutted, muddy and tree-hung country lane is now Oriental Road. Originally it was a track crossing the open heathland near Heathside Farm, but woodland had grown up on the heath-land in the previous fifty years and after 1900 this was seen as an asset giving a delightful setting for new housing.

Guildford Road in 1905, with the Railway Hotel, *the first building of New Woking, on the right. Even in the 1960s this scene was comparatively unaltered but in the past forty years the combination of redevelopment and road-widening has transformed the view.*

land between the *Maybury Inn*, the railway and Heathside Farm was developed for expensive low density housing, high in quality and in an exceptionally attractive setting – the emptiness of the open heath gave way to architect-designed residences set amid shrubberies, pines and leafy avenues.

In 1882 the owners of Heathside Farm sold 16 acres of land between Park Road West and Heathside Road, marking the beginning of a westward extension of development. In the following year the Fladgate family of Cross Lanes Farm sold their entire property, 136 acres extending from Elm Bridge to the *Railway Hotel* along the Guildford road and east to White Rose Lane. The farm was sold not as a going concern but for speculative building, the prospectus enticingly suggesting that 'from its being so admirably situate between Main Roads, and from its beauty and healthfulness, [it] offers an Opportunity for Investment seldom met with'. The sale catalogue summed up the new and exciting commercial potential of what was now being identified as a perfect area for wealthier people to settle and – crucially – to commute, for the ever-improving rail service from a main-line station within easy walking distance made this an ideal location:

> 66 It is in the heart of one of the loveliest parts of the country, and from its commanding position all the beauties of the neighbourhood are open to it … its surroundings of large heath covered Commons constitute it one of the healthiest spots in the Country, a fact well known to the leading physicians who strongly recommend it to their patients … railway communication, which is exceptionally good [is] another feature in its desirability to city men and gentlemen whose daily occupations require

their presence in the metropolis ... the Estate is [so] admirably situated ... that it lends itself most readily to many excellent schemes for subdivisions ... it offers an altogether exceptional opportunity to Capitalists and others of making a most genuine and profitable investment. **"**

The development of the Cross Lanes estate determined the form and character of a large swathe of south Woking. From 1885 expensive houses in large and carefully landscaped plots began to appear on and behind the main Guildford road, covenants in the sale contracts preventing undesirable uses and the asking prices precluding anything but housing of the 'most superior character'. The Mount Hermon estate, with its sequence of long gently curving roads making attractive use of the hillslope, was developed from 1885 onwards. The York estate, laid out in 1893 (the year of the marriage of the Duke and Duchess of York, later King George V and Queen Mary) was slightly less ambitious and, being close to the railway, a little lower down the social scale, though the sale catalogue omitted to mention the railway and referred only to the proximity to 'the favoured Mount Hermon area ... in a most advantageous position surrounded by superior residences'. In both these areas, despite the impact of infilling and redevelopment in the later 20th century, many fine examples of late Victorian and Edwardian suburban residences survive, with their white-painted balconies, bargeboards and balustrades, laurel shrubberies and conifers.

On the east side of Guildford Road the Suburban Land Company bought the whole tract between Hoe Stream and Heathside Road, marketing most of it as the Hillview Estate (the name being fully justified – the distant views of Merrow Downs are still obvious from Constitution Hill). In 1904 part of the land was acquired by the urban district council for a public park and, preserved from further building, it enhanced the quality of the landscape in the area. In all these schemes the land was resold in large plots to owners who usually employed an architect to design the house, or who bought architect-designed plans for their contracting builder to carry out. Only at the southern end of the Cross Lanes Estate was the land sold in smaller parcels, to speculative builders. There was thus a greater diversity of house types, and most of the houses were rather smaller than in the majority of the Cross Lanes land. A new road was built from the foot of Guildford Hill to Elm Bridge, to open up this land and to provide a shorter route from Woking village. Completed in 1887, it was christened Claremont Avenue after the home of the Duchess of Albany, who in that year laid the foundation stone of Christ Church.

Building in the area continued until the First World War. Typically, the houses constructed on the Cross Lanes land were large, expensive and often very beautifully designed. Many were intended to be staffed by two or

Mount Hermon 1880-1914, showing the main sub-divisions of land sold for development in this period.

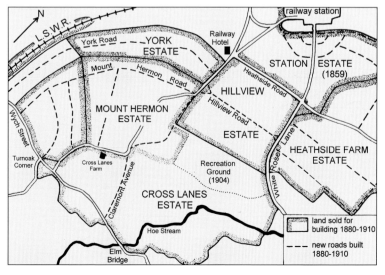

three live-in servants, as well as 'dailies'. Their owners walked up to the railway station each day, and at the weekend or on days of leisure played at one of the golf clubs which were appearing in the neighbourhood. Meanwhile the gardener and his boy tended and nurtured the expensive and fashionable plants bought in from the nursery gardens nearby at Goldsworth and Knaphill. But despite superficial appearances this was not the most exclusive part of late Victorian Woking. The 1885 sale catalogue, in its subtle reference to 'city men and gentlemen', drew a social distinction which any contemporary would recognise. City men may have had plenty of money, but they were socially not of the very top drawer. The gentlemen (who were) did not live in areas such as Cross Lanes. Instead, they were just up the hill in Hook Heath.

43. Hook Heath

Hook Heath in 1914: a scruffy area of squatters and hovels in the early 19th century, by the time of the First World War this was one of the most exclusive residential areas in England. The great houses set in acres of well-wooded grounds and enjoying fine views across the Wey Valley were a result of Woking's growing appeal for the wealthy.

The highest part of the borough of Woking, Hook Heath was originally one of the most disreputable. It was remote from centres of population and, since the land was poor and the soils sandy and infertile, had never been much use for agriculture. In the 17th and 18th centuries it was known as the haunt of squatters, tinkers, and vagabonds. Around College Lane and Wych Hill was an untidy collection of hovels, sandpits and smallholdings, scattered amid the open heath. When the railway line to Basingstoke was built in the late 1830s and the Guildford branch in 1844-5 the area became further isolated from the rest of the parish by deep cuttings. In 1854 it was, like the other heathlands of Woking, acquired by the Necropolis Company and after 1855 the wide road which is now Hook Heath Avenue was built across the northern edge. However, the company made no attempt to market or sell its land here, presumably considering that it was not worth the effort.

In the late 1880s, though, circumstances changed. The conspicuous success of the Cross Lanes and Heathside sales, and the general feeling that the Surrey heathlands were eminently desirable for residential development, meant that this once-worthless tract of sandy waste had acquired prime building potential. From 1889 onwards, using experience learned from the sale of land elsewhere in the neighbourhood, the Necropolis Company began to concentrate on selling Hook Heath. Its persuasive marketing emphasised the seclusion – remoteness, no longer a disadvantage, had become a prized asset – and the splendour of the position, with wide uninterrupted views south to the Downs and the Hogs Back. It opened

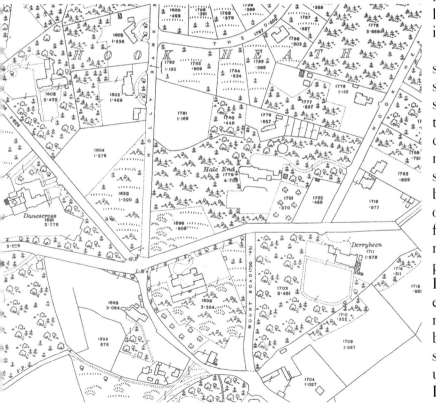

an estate office at Hook Heath itself, providing a personal service to wealthy prospective purchasers, and it enticed them by the offer of membership of the new exclusive Hook Heath Golf Club.

Two more wide, tree-lined and generously landscaped roads, Holly Bank Road and Golf Club Road, were cut across the heath, and Hook Heath Road wound along the edge of the hilltop. All the plots were large – most of them at least an acre – and the houses correspondingly impressive, many-roomed and many-servanted, hiding behind high hedges of holly and yew and surrounded by pines, firs and laurels. The main period of building, 1895-1914, produced an aura of Edwardian luxury, as befitted one of the most exclusive and expensive residential developments in south-east England. Some of the houses were designed by architects of international reputation, most notably Fishers Hill and Fishers Hill Cottage, by Sir Edwin Lutyens with gardens by his celebrated colleague and enthusiast for all things West Surrey, Gertrude Jekyll. It was a mile and half and another world away from the jerry-building of Courtenay Road and the terraces by the gasworks.

44. The institutions

During the mid-19th century the Woking area was seen as a particularly appropriate location for a series of public and private institutions, all of considerable historical importance, which had a major long-term effect upon its development. Today, when this is one of the most expensive places in Britain, with some of the highest land values anywhere in Europe, it seems perhaps strange that these institutions came here because of the cheapness of the land. But not until the 1880s and 1890s, when commuting began to play a role in the town's development, did the residential market begin to inflate prices. In the 1860s and 1870s Woking had shown signs of becoming a working-class, institutional and industrial community. Land was cheap not only because private housing demand was in its infancy, but also because – another factor conspicuously absent today – so much land was available. The sale of the commons by the Necropolis Company meant that the government and the county justices were able to acquire large tracts of former heathland at bargain prices. Accessibility was excellent but the western half of the parish, in particular, was sufficiently remote from major settlements to make it acceptable as a location for a prison and an asylum, which people did not want on their doorstep. The institutions were important players in the development of the town, bringing not only great complexes of buildings set in carefully segregated estates, but also generating a major demand for labour. At their peak, in the late 1890s, they occupied almost ten per cent of the land area of Woking parish and employed several hundred people, many of them attracted from outside by the prospect of work. A significant part of the population increase in 1861-81 was the result of their expansion.

45. The convict prison and barracks

In the late 1840s it was widely recognised that the national prison system was in chaos. Prisoners were still being housed in rotting hulks moored in the

Thames at Woolwich and elsewhere (the last being finally emptied of its human cargo in 1853) and no provision was made for sick, chronically ill and invalid prisoners. The Home Office therefore planned a prison designed specifically for those inmates who needed medical care. A wide range of possible sites was considered before the government chose, in 1858, to purchase almost 65 acres of Knaphill Common, between Robin Hood Road and the track to Crastock and Bridley. This land had recently been offered for sale by the Necropolis Company, which was very happy to make a quick profit even though the presence of the prison would inevitably damage potential land values in the vicinity. The new prison, designed by Sir Joshua Jebb and the nationally known architect Arthur Blomfield, was built very rapidly: the first section was opened, for the reception of prisoners transferred from Lewes, Carisbrooke and Dartmoor, less than a year after the site was purchased. The official opening was on 22 March 1860, and by that time it housed over 300 inmates. Those prisoners who were able to work were drafted to labouring gangs which constructed the next stages and landscaped the grounds:

> **"** … the prisoners have been most industrious and their conducts generally very good … [many] have been employed in digging foundations for the prison walls, gas works, gas and water mains and drains, also in the formation of exercising grounds, paths and roads. Latterly a gang has been placed at the disposal of the farm bailiff for the purpose of clearing the brushwood and raising a mud wall to enclose the property. **"**

The austere and functional building, dominated by a 190-foot clock tower, had a west wing designed specifically for the chronically sick and insane. Its hilltop site made it a conspicuous new feature in the Woking landscape, the tower being visible for miles. In 1867 work began on a second prison, this time designed with another new prison reform in mind – the strict segregation of male and female prisoners was a recent element in government penal policies. The Woking female prison was opened in 1869, and by the end of that year accommodated 70 women, giving a total of 1,400 inmates. The men were employed on the home farm and in many of the labouring and outdoor tasks, while the women were put to cooking, cleaning, gardening, or sewing mailbags, prison clothes and uniforms for the boys of Greenwich Hospital. Others were employed in craft workshops, making mosaic tiles and panels for churches, museums and St Paul's Cathedral. Most of the people housed in the two prisons were not in what would later be called 'high risk categories', though during the Fenian emergency of 1868-9 several

Woking convict prisons, 1871: the large-scale OS map shows the internal layout of the twin jails, with their exercise yards and cell blocks, and the rows of terraced cottages for prison officers and their families sheltering under the perimeter walls.

Inkerman Barracks in about 1900: the tall square tower, a landmark for miles around, was designed by Arthur Blomfield and closely resembles that of one of his more famous works, St Barnabas' Church in Jericho, Oxford. The parade ground is the former prison exercise yard.

Irish prisoners were accommodated and special detachments of troops from Aldershot guarded the prisons.

In 1886, though, it was decided that the two prisons should be closed. This is very surprising, given that the female prison was only 18 years old, but the reasons are simple. The criminally insane, a significant proportion of the inmate population, were now being accommodated in separate special institutions such as Broadmoor, while the changing (and more lenient) sentencing policy in the courts meant that prison numbers were falling sharply. More important, though, is that the army was in urgent need of more accommodation in the district – in 1888-1902 it acquired most of the commons in Pirbright, Bisley, Frimley and Chobham parishes, and military activity expanded rapidly. This, in itself one of the most important decisions in the history of north-west Surrey, meant that a viable alternative use was readily available. The War Department took over the ownership of the entire prison estate between 1889 and 1895 and converted both prisons into what was renamed Inkerman Barracks. They remained in use as barracks, extended by the construction of married quarters in the grounds, for over half a century. From 1955, though, as Britain's global military role dwindled and national service was phased out, they too became redundant. In 1965 the Inkerman Barracks was closed and the site was acquired by Woking Urban District Council. Since then it has been used for housing, public open space and the St Johns bypass, and today there is little obvious evidence of the great institution which dominated the area for over a century.

46. Brookwood Hospital

In 1841 the Surrey county justices opened the Wandsworth County Asylum, a model institution where advanced methods of treatment for what was then universally known as 'lunacy' or 'imbecility' replaced the abuses and harsh cruelties of the 18th century. By the late 1850s the huge population increase in metropolitan Surrey meant that Wandsworth was stretched to capacity and the justices searched for a site on which to build a second asylum to serve the western half of the county. They were looking for an open and healthy environment, away from towns and large villages (strict geographical segregation was seen as essential) and not using agricultural land because that meant higher prices and higher rates. They did not have far to look, for the Necropolis Company was, as usual in this period, offering large tracts of land for sale at very favourable prices – the convict prison was already under construction so land values were even lower than they might have been. In 1860 the justices bought 150 acres between Knaphill village (sufficiently lower class for the proximity not to matter) and the canal for a mere £10,500. Work on building an asylum began in 1863 and the first patients were admitted in June 1867.

The asylum, later known more sympathetically as Brookwood Hospital, was designed as a self-contained community in accordance with the contemporary principles of segregation and useful employment. There were no public services available, so the institution had its own gasworks, water supply and sewage farm. Patients who were sufficiently able were employed in the various departments of the asylum, cooking, cleaning, washing, carrying out repairs, growing vegetables, cereals and potatoes on the Home Farm which was established in 1886, making baskets and rugs, and weaving. All this was therapeutic, but it also played an important part in keeping the costs, and the rate burden, under control. By the standards of the time the regime was relaxed, calming, sympathetic and humane: patients could attend concerts and dances, play cards, dominoes and draughts, read books, illustrated papers and newspapers in the library, and either listen to or play in the brass band.

Unfortunately many of the potential benefits of this genuinely progressive institution could not be realised because local poor law unions, which could send patients here instead of to their own establishments such as the Guildford Union Workhouse at Stoke, showed a persistent tendency to regard the Brookwood asylum as

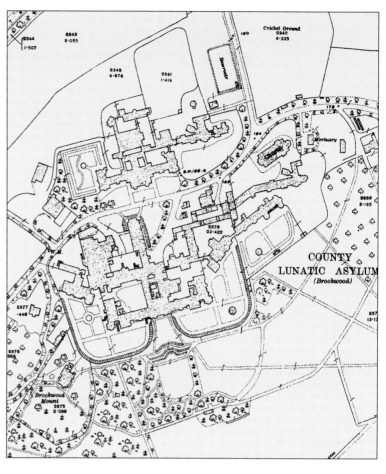

Brookwood Hospital or Surrey County Lunatic Asylum, 1916: with its monumental architecture and layout which comprised a series of self-contained and segregated units within one great complex, Brookwood Asylum typified later Victorian philosophies for institutional design and dealing with mental illness – it was at once relatively humane yet emphasised exclusion and isolation.

somewhere to offload their incurable, chronically sick or violent patients. The hospital visitors rightly deplored this, noting that the main purpose of Brookwood Asylum should have been to assist with the convalescence and recovery of curable patients and to assess and help those newly admitted. Instead, they declared angrily in 1868, 'some [patients] arrived in such a hopeless condition that they appeared as if they were sent here only to die'. Eventually, as the national policy on treating the mentally ill and mentally disturbed changed, these problems were eliminated, though as late as 1884 only about 40 per cent of admissions were deemed 'curable'. By then, though, the death rate in the hospital was significantly below the national average, a tribute to the humane and caring environment which had been created and maintained.

The patient numbers grew rapidly. In 1875 there were 672 residents, but by 1931 this had grown to 1,477, so that Brookwood was one of the largest mental hospitals in England. With such large numbers on a permanent basis the impact on the local community was very considerable. The hospital was the largest employer in west Woking, many of the residents of Knaphill and St Johns being hospital staff and, although visually the hospital was screened by woodland and well-hidden because of its location away from the road network, it was an essential element in the local economy. During the first half of the 20th century tradesmen in the two villages relied heavily on supplying the hospital with goods and services.

By the 1980s, though, those involved in the treatment of mental health problems had formulated new principles, often summed up as 'care in the community'. The large Victorian institutions, segregated from surrounding areas and hidden behind high walls and dark shrubberies, were generally regarded as inappropriate. Furthermore, many such buildings were physically obsolete or required massive expenditure to bring them up to modern standards. The preferred policy was to close them and gradually introduce the patients to other forms of care. In 1981 the closure of Brookwood Hospital was announced – with the obvious financial advantage that, given the extremely high price of land in the Woking area (how the times had changed), the extensive and very attractive site was clearly ripe for commercial and housing development. Today, with the Sainsbury's store as its retailing showpiece and a network of small residential roads and closes spreading across much of the former asylum land, the landscape of the hospital site is transformed. This, perhaps, is the last major development area within the borough unless green belt land is released for building in the future.

47. Knaphill and St Johns

The selection of the heathland south of the old village of Knaphill as the location of the convict prisons and lunatic asylum reinforced the historic tendency for this area to be regarded as lower-class and inferior. After 1860 the district, too distant from the railway station to develop as a commuter area, and too unappealing to would-be superior residents because of the great public institutions on its doorstep, grew in a piecemeal and unplanned fashion, adding to its already incoherent and straggling layout. The patches of common and smallholdings of the old village were infilled and built over with short rows of cottages and single dwellings, to which were added, by the end of the 19th century, a multiplicity of workshops, small local shops, brickpits and market gardens. Even today Knaphill, though now an important local centre, has an irregular and unplanned character as a result of three centuries of haphazard growth. During the 1870s and '80s the Necropolis Company sold the

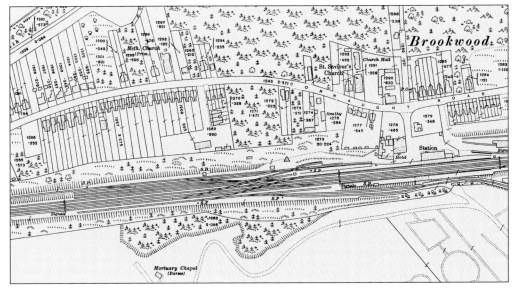

Brookwood in 1934: the village had grown up along both sides of Connaught Road, hemmed in by the railway to the south and the canal and wet heathland to the north, to give a distinctive linear form. When the station opened in 1864 there was not a single building in the area of the later village.

remaining areas of Knaphill Common, south and west of the village, for housing development. These lots were mostly purchased by local builders who erected a variety of terraced cottages and semi-detached villas. The quality of the building was often poor and there was a good deal of slum clearance in Knaphill after 1950. Many of the people who lived in this housing worked in the asylum and the prisons, but there were also labourers and artisans, so that the social tone was definitely working-class. Because the village lay so close to the parish boundary the Necropolis Company owned no land to the north or east, and until the mid-20th century these areas remained in agricultural use, the built-up area stopping abruptly at the border.

Beyond Knaphill there was very little building until the late 19th century even though the railway station at Brookwood was opened in 1864. Its services were not yet attractive to potential commuters, and the proximity to the cemetery meant that land in this area was retained by the company for much longer than its properties in the eastern part of the parish. Much of the land was so wet and inaccessible, cut off by the railway and canal and subject to waterlogging, that it could never seriously be considered for development. The first houses in what became Brookwood village were built in the early 1880s, close to the railway station, and by 1930 a long narrow community had grown up, scarcely more than one house deep on either side of the road all the way from the Guildford Road crossroads to the Pirbright border.

St Johns, at the southern edge of Knaphill Common, was also the location of smallholdings and squatter cottages in the late 18th century, but the

Conaught Road, Brookwood, c.1905: the arrival of a photographer was evidently a novelty in this out-of-the-way place. Brookwood village was still developing, and although new villas can be seen at the junction with Station Approach, the road from Knaphill still passed stretches of scrub and woodland.

construction of the canal and the opening of modest wharfage facilities at Kiln Bridge encouraged the development of a settlement whose inhabitants were mainly labourers and their families. The canal itself, the brickfields and the nursery gardens all provided employment and by the late 1830s the village – generally known as Kiln Bridge – was large enough to be given a chapel of ease dedicated to St John the Baptist. This provided, in turn, a 'proper' name for the growing community. The opening of the prison and the asylum offered further employment in the neighbourhood and in the 1870s and 1880s terraced housing was built on both sides of the canal, while small cheap villas appeared in Barrack Path and Copse Road. The village expanded outwards along the main road towards The Hermitage and Goldsworth, but the steep slope of St Johns Hill marked more than just a physical transition. It became a favoured area for upper-middle-class housing, and on the higher slopes large properties were built, with fine views across the valley of the Bourne towards the heathery expanses of Chobham Common. Here, as in Hook Heath across the railway, the large houses were soon vanishing behind thick plantations of trees and shrubs, a process encouraged by the Jackman family who not only provided many of the plants from their nurseries, but in 1893 sold for house-building 40 acres of nursery on the hill itself.

48. The crematorium

As well as Britain's largest cemetery, Woking also has the country's oldest crematorium. This method of 'disposal' was illegal in England in the mid-19th century, though there was growing pressure for it to be permitted on grounds of hygiene, lack of burial space in some areas (though not of course Woking itself) and a developing secularism. In the 1870s a Cremation Society was established and in 1878 it bought a small plot of land at Hermitage on which to build an experimental crematorium, where animal corpses could be used to test different methods, observe any problems with smoke or odours (this being regarded as a likely offensive nuisance), and so convince sceptics and critics that all could be done decently, efficiently and respectably. In January 1879 the *Sanitary Record*, commenting on the project, noted that the site was 'in a secluded part of Woking parish, admirably suited for the purpose, and sufficiently remote from habitations … no better site could have been obtained, nor will many of the large towns which are eager to avail themselves of the coming reform be able to suit themselves as well'. It cannot have been mere coincidence that only two miles away was the largest cemetery in the country – the contrast between the two methods was certainly in the minds of the Cremation Society members.

Local opposition was nonetheless strong, the vicar of Woking vehemently denouncing the plan as an anathema. His lawyer prepared a paper on the subject which referred to the feelings of 'the greatest abhorrence' felt by the inhabitants of the district and claimed that house and land prices would fall, that 'one schoolmaster has lost a Pupil through the Parents reading of the Crematory in the papers, and the wife of a Warder at the Gaol refuses to live in a nearby house'. After two test cases – a private cremation in Dorset in 1882 and the famous Price case in Wales in 1884 – the courts ruled that cremation was legal provided that no nuisance was caused. The vicars of Woking and St Johns and the lord of the manor, the Earl of Onslow, desperately tried to prevent the Society from using its St Johns Crematorium, but to no avail. On 26 March 1885 the body of Mrs Pickersgill, a member of the Society, was conveyed from Woking station to St Johns to be 'disposed of' by officers of the Society, the first definitely legal cremation in modern Britain. The method was slow to attain popularity – in the first 15 years only 1,340 cremations were carried out at Woking and the local press continued to report them as special events – but after 1918 attitudes began to change and in 1968 the number of cremations for the first time exceeded burials. The extremely plain and utilitarian Woking Crematorium was rebuilt in 1889 in a more elaborate style, red brick with stone dressings and 'in the style of the early 13th century' – a medieval crematorium is a curious notion indeed.

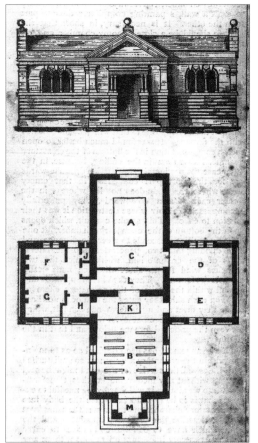

The modest unassuming design for Woking Crematorium, the first in Britain, which was built at St John's in 1879 but not used for human cremation until legal test cases approved this method of disposal in 1885. This drawing and plan appeared in The Sanitary Record *in 1879 when the process of cremation was still barely understood and a careful explanation of its technical details was needed.*

49. Horsell

Horsell village remained a backwater until the 1880s, its ancient street almost untouched by new development, surrounded by farmland and nurseries and entirely rural in character. However, as Woking town expanded on the south side of the canal the village gradually succumbed to development pressures. By the 1890s Woking was large enough to be spawning its own new suburbs, and as the rail service improved and commuting became more important it was inevitable that Horsell, only a 15-minute walk from the train to Waterloo, would be eyed by speculators and land developers. The area around Wheatsheaf Common was the first to be built over, followed by the southern end of Horsell High Street. The Necropolis Company had no land or influence in the parish, but there were other small landowners who were very happy to sell smallholdings and little farms for building. The fragmented nature of land ownership had a clear influence upon the way Horsell developed. Individual owners sold separately, often to small local builders, and so each housing scheme was unconnected with any other. Each had its own access road, hence the series of cul-de-sac estates on either side of the High Street. Abbey Farm was sold in 1890 and Abbey Road built in two phases in 1892 and 1896; Horsell Nurseries went on the market in 1899; and Waldens Farm in 1900, when it was described as 'most eligible and ripe for development as a Small

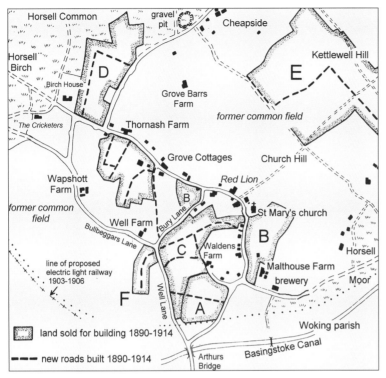

Horsell Common

gravel pit

Cheapside

Kettlewell Hill

E

Horsell Birch

D

Birch House

The Cricketers

Grove Barrs Farm

Thornash Farm

former common field

Grove Cottages

Church Hill

Red Lion

B

Wapshott Farm

B

St Mary's church

former common field

Well Farm

Bury Lane

Bullbeggars Lane

C

Waldens Farm

Horsell

line of proposed electric light railway 1903-1906

Malthouse Farm

brewery

Moor

F

Well Lane

A

land sold for building 1890-1914

Woking parish

new roads built 1890-1914

Arthurs Bridge

Basingstoke Canal

ABOVE *Growth and change in Horsell village 1890-1914, showing the main land sales which took place in the period*
A *Abbey Farm*
B *Horsell Nurseries*
C *Waldens Park estate*
D *Horsell Common estate*
E *Horsell Rise and Kettlewell Hill*
F *Woking Co-operative Society Garden Suburb*

BELOW *Horsell High Street and St Mary's church in about 1897, a view which captures the rural atmosphere of the village in the late 19th century. Children played in the road and a heavy farm cart laden with timber stands outside the church. Within a decade Horsell would be mushrooming into a suburb of New Woking, and would be administratively absorbed by its larger neighbour.*

Building Estate. Woking Station is a very rapidly growing Town, and this Estate must greatly increase in value'.

The types of houses being built in Horsell varied from very small semi-detached properties in low-lying Arthurs Bridge Road, to middle-class detached homes on the Waldens Park estate. North of the village Russell Road was built in two phases in 1902-04, with 125 plots of 20-foot frontage, designed for 'small Villa residences … or Cottages, which are urgently needed in the neighbourhood'. The promoters claimed, stretching the truth considerably, that it was within 20 minutes' walk of Woking station – but it is very significant that this was regarded as a main selling point, for it indicates the powerful influence which commuting was now playing in the development of the Woking area. East of the village the slopes of Kettlewell Hill were bought by the National Land Company, another of the ephemeral and shadowy firms which flourished in the Woking area in the years after 1890. Between 1900 and 1914 a series of superior estates of large houses was developed by the company, which laid out roads and plots, and then sold on to

individual purchasers. Among the farms purchased were Potters Corner on Woodham Road, Castle Farm, and parts of the Horsell Grange estate. The Kettlewell area thus differed sharply in tone from the village proper.

Perhaps the most unusual of the housing schemes in Horsell in this period was the Woking Co-operative Society Garden Suburb, which originated in the purchase by the Society of land off Well Lane in 1908. In 1912 work began on a project for 30 dwellings and a small co-operative store, as the first stage of a more ambitious plan intended to accommodate lower-income families who could not afford the increasingly high rents demanded by property owners in the district. The first phase was the only one completed but, as Holyoake Crescent, it remains almost unaltered from its origins in the idealistic social planning of a century ago. Overall, though, there was little that was utopian about the way Horsell developed. Much of its charm and all its rural character were lost, and in 1963 the architectural writer Ian Nairn

Kettlewell House, an attractive 18th-century building with large grounds, was demolished in the early 1930s and its land used for superior housing.

was moved to pass a harsh judgement: 'swamped by Woking. A few battered cottages remain from the old village'. Today, when it is a conservation area, the remaining historical interest of Horsell is more carefully protected and valued than it was in the heyday of its expansion, but it is sad to reflect on how many of the old farmhouses and cottages were lost – but intriguing, perhaps, to realise that the brash new houses of the years around 1900 are now themselves the subject of protection, conservation measures and historical appreciation.

50. Byfleet

The old village of Byfleet survived unscathed by modern development longer than Horsell, but its subsequent fall from tranquillity was even more complete. Its relative inaccessibility had protected it until the beginning of the 20th century – the railway stations were too far away, road access was poor, and the landowners were not anxious to sell to the speculative builder. After 1860 a few large houses were built north of High Road: all have now gone, but their names are recalled in later developments, such as Weymede, Shrapnells and Grasmere. These properties were built by wealthy Londoners who could, like their colleagues just over the Wey in St George's Hill, afford to spend most of the week in their country residences. A few terraces and small villas had appeared by 1900 but the local authorities were very concerned at the inferior quality of these, and Chertsey Rural District Council sought unsuccessfully to prevent 'the building of dwellinghouses upon sites so lowlying and waterlogged as to be absolutely unsuitable for the purpose and a constant danger to the health of the district'.

But in 1905 this peace and calm was shattered for ever. The Honourable Henry Locke King, the best known local resident, largest landowner in the

The old Blue Anchor *Inn in Byfleet village, 1898, with Byfleet Lodge in the background. The attractive 17th-century inn was demolished soon after this photograph was taken and replaced by the building later notorious for its role in the 'Bluebeard' murder case.*

The eastern end of Byfleet village in 1871, showing the winding alignment of what became High Road and the farms and large houses on either side of the Blue Anchor *(centre of map).*

parish, and prominent benefactor of village causes, began work on the construction of the race track at Brooklands, which was then largely within the parish of Byfleet. Local opinion was almost unanimously hostile. The parish and district councils protested in vain, but work went ahead. Two ancient farms, Brooklands and Wintersells, were demolished, the Wey was diverted, access roads built, and the high embankments of the track were raised across the valley. The problem of noise during building work was exacerbated by the damage to the roads caused by heavy traction engines, and once the track was finished the motor racing brought frequent intrusion – and, since Locke King was a pioneer aviator, and turned Brooklands into one of the first airfields in England, the parish council found other reasons to protest: in 1913 it asked him 'to stop the practice of Aviators practising with their Machines over the Village on account of the danger to life & property'. The calm of the Weyside village was gone for ever.

51. West Byfleet

Until the middle years of the 19th century the area which became West Byfleet was largely undeveloped. At Byfleet Corner, where the roads to Woking village, Pyrford, Byfleet and New Haw met, there were a few cottages, but the rest was agricultural land with some areas of heath. In the late 1870s, though, the break-up of some of the larger farms began as owners observed the high prices which real estate now fetched in this part of Surrey. Sheerwater Court was auctioned in 1881 and the land between the railway and the canal, from Old Avenue to Camphill Road, was acquired by building developers. In 1883 almost 11 acres between Byfleet Corner and Camphill Road, described with immense artistic licence as being 'very agreeably situated … on high ground, with fine views, and therefore admirably suited for the Erection of small Residences', was sold for building. The sale catalogue for this property notes that a new station had been proposed, and that promise helps to explain the sudden rush of interest in this previously overlooked district. The London & South Western Railway had indicated that it wanted a station in the Byfleet area, to break the long gap between Woking and Weybridge, and in 1887 it duly opened what was then called Byfleet & Woodham and is now West Byfleet station. By this time such a move, on the main line out of Waterloo, was guaranteed to produce not only increased land values but also a fever of sales and building activity. By 1900 West Byfleet had become a sizeable village and all the land around was being parcelled out and developed.

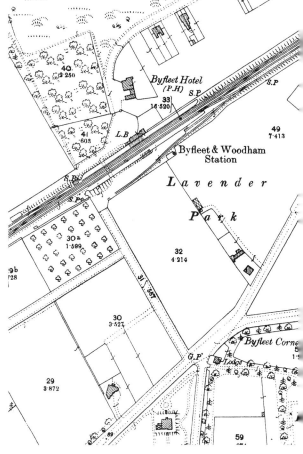

West Byfleet in 1894: although the railway station had opened in 1887 little development had yet taken place apart from a few large houses on the Old Woking Road. At the bottom centre is Rosemount, destined to be demolished less than twenty years later and to give its name to the shopping parade built on the site.

Oyster Lane, Byfleet, in about 1905, with the lodge of Petersham Place on the left. This quiet country road was destined to become a major inter-urban highway, its tranquillity destroyed by the building of Brooklands racetrack from 1906 onwards and then by the commercial development of this part of the lower Wey valley.

The village centre grew haphazardly (the lessons of Woking were not learned) but at least the road junction at Byfleet Corner provided a focus of sorts. Some higher density housing, of the 'small villa' variety, was built north of the railway in Station Road and Claremont Road, and in Camphill Road and Lavender

Newly-built shops at Byfleet Corner, c.1900, looking west along a still undeveloped Old Woking road. The sign outside the shop on the left advertises a house and estate agency, a sign of the times in a fast-growing community such as this. Rosemount Parade was soon to be built where the trees can be seen behind the group of youths. Today standing in the middle of this road would not be advisable.

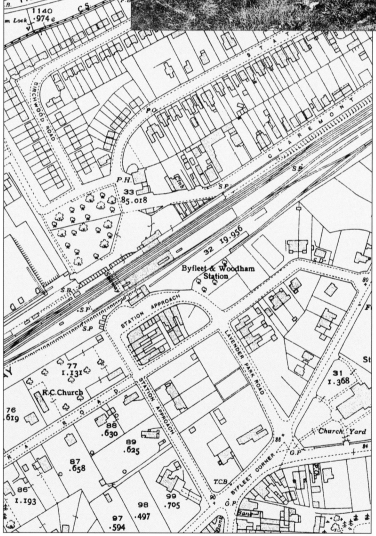

West Byfleet in 1934: a substantial community had appeared in the previous forty years, centred on the station with its fast commuter services to London. There was no overall design and streets and housing developments were constructed haphazardly. Note the large houses south-west of the station, an area of increasingly high land values where large-scale redevelopment in the 1960s and 1970s capitalised on the commercial potential of the site.

Road to the south (the name refers to the growing of lavender in the vicinity, to supply the essential oils distillery in Pyrford). Elsewhere, though, the building was generally at low densities with large detached houses in tree-lined streets and with a good deal of the existing woodland retained for landscaping. As the village grew, and shops and other amenities were required, redevelopment took place with large houses making way for commercial and business uses. In 1906, for example, the grounds of 'Rosemount', only 30 years old, were used for road-widening and for the shopping parade which bears its name.

Dartnell Park, east of the new village and south of the canal, became one of the most exclusive of the low-density estates in the Woking area. The land was enclosed from the wet heath in 1806 but was never used for agriculture because the ground was so poor. By 1870 Dartnell's Wood, named for its previous owner, was thickly grown with conifers. It was parcelled out into building plots in 1884-98 in several phases, with individual properties in the earlier period of building being notably large – some were over three acres in extent. The sales publicity focused on the 'country residence near town' theme: 'The estate is adorned with Majestic Timber ... giving richness and beauty to home new ... possessing so many advantages that it is probably without equal in the country ... the dry healthy soil [not strictly true!] and air, varied drives and walks amidst some of the most beautiful Pine and Sylvan Scenery [fulfil all] the requirements of a country gentleman, or those whose vocations call them to town.' In its combination of flattery and euphemism this description sums up the sales technique which was so widely employed in the Woking area in the decades around 1900, cleverly exploiting the ambitions of the newly moneyed classes. These were manifestly not the country estates of real gentlemen, but living in Dartnell Park or in Hook Heath or Kettlewell realised the social aspirations of people whose immediate forebears (say it not) were much lower down the scale. Later sales were accompanied by enticing references to the boat club and the tennis club, one brochure announced that the plots offered 'excellent sites for full-sized tennis lawns at no great expense', and the vendors chartered special trains from Waterloo and provided would-be purchasers with free lunch in a marquee beside the romantically decaying Basingstoke Canal.

52. The southern borders: Pyrford to Mayford

Of all the communities in the Woking area, Pyrford was least touched by change. In the Old Woking Road and Coldharbour area the growth of West Byfleet meant that some new housing spilled over the parish boundary by 1914, and a few very large properties were built elsewhere, but in the days before widespread car ownership the greater distance from a convenient railway station (and the absence of any main road) militated against

A row of 16th-century cottages in High Street, Woking village, at the junction with Church Street: this view was taken in April 1907 just before the demolition of the whole row and the redevelopment of the site. The picture gives an excellent impression of the traditional architecture of the village, but also demonstrates what has been lost over the last century as a result of renewal and clearance. Today these cottages would be considered to have major architectural and historical value.

Kingfield Green in 1905: the splendid elm tree at the junction with Stockers Lane has long since gone and the poplars which fringe Kingfield Pond have grown to an immense height. The green itself has been altered by road widening and the planting of plane trees in the 1930s, but its northern part, next to the pond and Loop Road, still retains something of its historic character, edged with cottages and damp and rushy in the centre.

Gongers Lane in 1905: this scene is now completely unrecognisable and even the name of the road is forgotten. The picture shows what is now Westfield Road, looking from the junction with Granville Avenue eastwards towards Vicarage Road and Loop Road. In the 1920s the road was widened and council housing and private housing were built on either side, so that the hedges and trees disappeared and a country lane became an urban highway.

development. The entire area between Pyrford Church and Old Woking Road was either common land or part of the Pyrford Court and other large estates, whose owners did not intend to sell for building, and the agricultural landscapes of this part of the middle Wey valley thus remained unscathed.

The little old town of Woking was also relatively untouched, gradually becoming a backwater as, like a cuckoo in the nest, its vigorous child by the railway station grew and flourished. Woking village, Kingfield and Westfield were too far from the station to be, as yet, the subject of pressure from developers building commuter housing, and their economic activity stagnated. The growth of population in this part of the parish was very slow and, although a few new houses and cottages were built in the years after 1880, their impact was but small. In 1914 the distinctive linear form of the old village and its extension through Shackleford to Kingfield Green was almost unaltered, a ribbon of housing stretching (usually only one property deep) for nearly a mile and a half. Mayford, too, remained small, while at Sutton Green the fact that the majority of the land was part of the Sutton Place estate further protected it from speculative building. Most of the farming estates in this part of the parish of Woking continued intact until the 1920s. The single important exception was 122-acre Frog Lane Farm, between Mayford and Sutton Green, which was offered for sale in 1894. Forty acres remained in farming use but the rest was sold off in large plots (one was 7½ acres) and huge private residences were built along what was christened Pyle Hill, the line of an enclosure track laid out in 1811. The use of 'y' in the name was an indicator of Good Taste, as befitted the most secluded and superior of all the housing developments in 19th-century Woking.

53. *Images and reflections*

The wealthier residents came to Woking to enjoy peace, space and beauty, in contrast with the noise and congestion of the metropolis. In their writings and in the literature of the time we may see something of their perceptions of the area. The combination of natural beauty, cheap land and easy access to London was rare, and inevitably the first two factors dwindled and disappeared as Woking grew, but for the first generation of affluent residents the landscape was delightful – groves of tall scented pines, glades of heather and gorse, and views across green valleys to distant hills and ridges. An eccentric enthusiasm was expressed by the overbearing and disagreeable Mrs Cosham in Virginia Woolf's 1919 novel *Night and Day*, set in the years before the First World War: 'I come from Woking, Mr Popham. You may well ask me, why Woking? and to that I answer, for perhaps the hundredth time, because of the sunsets. We went for the sunsets, but that was five-and-twenty years ago. Where are the sunsets now? Alas! There is no sunset now nearer than the South Coast.' More conventionally, but reliably, Arthur Munby, the Victorian diarist, who lived at Wheelers Farm from 1878 to 1910, was enchanted by the soft and gentle landscape of the Wey:

> **"**There was a melting yellow sunshine over all the valley … diffused through a warm and melting haze, and the abbey, grey beyond a yellow belt of corn, and the elms and firs of Warren Wood, and the long waving lines of willows by the water, and under their green & their silver grey stood groups of red and white cattle … the freshness and quiet, & the sense of infinitude … that the remote heaths and meadows of the Wey can bring.**"**

The combination of rural peace and easy access brought some famous residents. Sir Charles Dilke, the Liberal cabinet minister whose career was ruined by a notorious divorce case, bought land at Pyrford Rough from Lord

Onslow in 1894 and built himself a bungalow. This was intended as the most exclusive of all Woking's residential areas, a series of great houses in extensive grounds at the top of the slope above the Wey, but the estate was sold to the Guinness family, the earls of Iveagh, in 1892 and they instead built one of the last English country houses, Pyrford Court, in 1908-10. In 1898, however, Dilke wrote to Onslow recounting a clash of cultures: on the one hand, the new wealthy residents and their staff, on the other the traditional poachers of west Surrey:

> 66 A fire broke out when a poaching party was collecting from three pheasant nests in the young self-sown pines to the west of us [Pyrford Rough] … [the keepers] got it out by hard work, though the spot is an especially dangerous one. The ex-policeman did not appear and the cottagers looked on and jeered. Sunday is the … only poaching day, so I doubt if the ex-policeman does his duty … pheasant egg shells everywhere shew what an extraordinary natural game country it is. 99

The Honourable Gerald Balfour, brother of the prime minister Arthur Balfour, built himself a house at Fishers Hill, Hook Heath, designed by Edwin Lutyens. He was active in local community life and his wife, Lady Betty, helped in relief organisation and charity work during the First Word War. In 1919 she was elected as Conservative councillor for the St Johns ward and was important in advancing housing and public health policies. Balfour Avenue in Westfield is named after her. One of her closest friends was the formidable and eccentric Dame Ethel Smyth, composer and suffragette. She lived at 'Coigne', Hook Heath, from 1908 until her death in 1944, with a housekeeper and a succession of Old English sheepdogs all named 'Pan'. Dame Ethel was president of the Woking branch of the National Union of Women's Suffrage Societies and, at the height of suffragette agitation in 1912-13, she gave lessons in guerrilla warfare to the equally remarkable Emmeline Pankhurst, whom she once 'took at nightfall to a deserted spot on Hook Heath to throw Stones at a Tree'. Vera Brittain recalled how Dame Ethel, a familiar Woking figure for many years as she strode vigorously about the streets, once told a meeting that if she was given a title she would choose to be known as 'Ethel, Duchess of Woking'. Sir Arthur Conan Doyle used Woking as the setting for a Sherlock Holmes short story. In *The Naval Treaty* the Mount Hermon district is described by Doctor Watson:

> 66 We were fortunate enough to catch an early train at Waterloo, and in a little under an hour we found ourselves among the fir-woods and the heather of Woking. Briarbrae proved to be a large detached house standing in extensive grounds within a few minutes' walk of the station … through the open window … came the rich scent of the garden and the balmy summer air. 99

But the town's greatest and most enduring literary fame is that between the summer of 1895 and autumn 1898 H.G. Wells lived at 'Lynton', a small detached villa in Maybury Road. The house was cramped and too noisy for Wells's liking, but in that period he produced a number of short stories and three of his best-known novels, *Wheels of Chance*, *The Invisible Man* and one of the most famous of all science fiction works, *The War of the Worlds* (published in 1898). It is set in Woking and the author's detailed knowledge of the town is revealed, while his incidental descriptions give us vivid glimpses of the landscape of the area over a century ago. Some aspects of the area have changed relatively little – 'the undulating common seemed now dark almost to blackness, except where its roadways lay grey and pale under the deep-blue sky of the early night' (no orange streetlights pierced the night then) – but no longer might we see 'over the Maybury Arch a train, a billowing tumult of white, firelit smoke, and a longer caterpillar of lighted windows' because soulless electric trains have replaced the drama of steam. He notes small details: 'there was a noise of business from the gasworks, and the electric lamps were all alight' – Woking in 1898 was one of the few provincial towns with electric streetlights – and a survival from the rural past was 'the little one-roomed squatters' hut of wood, surrounded by a patch of potato-garden' at Bunkers Hill near College Road. Roads busy with traffic were then country lanes: 'We were spanking down the opposite slope of Maybury Hill towards Old Woking. In front was a quiet sunny landscape, a wheatfield ahead on either side of the road, and the Maybury Inn with its swinging sign … The scent of hay was in the air through the lush meadows beyond Pyrford, and the hedges in either side were sweet and gay with multitudes of dog roses.' Wells did not much care for Woking, and in the book he killed off his neighbours in painful and eccentric ways. The invading Martians land in the old sandpits on Horsell Common and destroy much of the town, an event which he describes with obvious pleasure:

The Mayford village blacksmith, 1937: this small village or hamlet had two smithies in the later 19th century, one on the green at the junction of Guildford Road and Smarts Heath Road, south of the Bird in Hand, *and the other over the bridge at the Westfield Road junction. A few smithies in the district survived to the Second World War, and one or two even into the 1950s (for example, Burdon & Bates at Kingfield forge) but the advent of the motor vehicle and farm mechanisation eventually spelled the end for all of them.*

      ❝ The town had become a heap of fiery ruins … the valley had become a valley of ashes … Where flames had been there were now streamers of smoke; but the countless ruins of shattered and gutted houses and blasted and blackened trees that the night had hidden stood out now gaunt and terrible in the pitiless light of dawn. ❞

    New Woking was considered by contemporaries to have very many faults and very few virtues, but the southern parts of the district remained, until the advent of the motor age, relatively quiet and unaltered. The old ways of West

Surrey life were drawing to a close, but even just before the First World War there was a sense of timelessness about the landscape and the traditional farming practices. One of the observers of this dying world was Eric Parker who, in *Highways and Byways in Surrey* (1908), described a visit to Woking in which he walked down White Rose Lane and over the fields to the village. His lyrical prose, over the top by today's standards, might serve as a memorial for the old and a judgement on the new:

> **"** In whatever way you may choose to travel through Surrey, it is difficult to avoid making Woking a centre and a rendezvous. All the trains stop there; at least, I cannot remember ever passing through the station without stopping, either to change trains … or to wait in the station until it is time to go on again … I never found anything else to do at Woking, unless it were at night, when the railway lights up wonderful vistas and avenues of coloured lamps. Then the platform can be tolerable. It was that Woking, the Woking of the station, which for many years I imagined to be the only Woking in Surrey. One did not wish for another.
>
> But there is another Woking, and it is as pretty and quiet as the railway Woking is noisy and tiresome. It stands with its old church on the banks of the Wey two miles away, a huddle of tiled roofs and old shops and poky little corners, as out-of-the-way and sleepy and ill-served by rail as anyone could wish. I found it first one day in October, and walked out from the grinding machinery of the station by a field-path running through broad acres of purple-brown loam, over which plough-horses tramped and turned. It was a strange and arresting sight, for over the dark rich mould there was drawn a veil of shimmering grey light wider and less earthly than any mist or dew. The whole plough land was alive with gossamer and Old Woking lay beyond the gossamer as if that magic veil were meant to shield it from the engines and the smoke. **"**

PEOPLE AND GOVERNMENT

54. The population in the 19th century

While maps and the landscape itself help us to trace the physical growth of a new town, the censuses taken every year from 1801 onwards give us the statistical evidence for that extraordinary expansion. The table below shows the population of the four parishes of Woking (and thus of the present borough) between 1801 and 1911. They reveal that growth was not evenly spread geographically and neither was it steady over time. There were pauses and slackenings, interspersed with phases of extremely rapid population increase but, over that period of rather more than a century, the growth was indeed exceptional.

decade	Byfleet	Horsell	Pyrford	Woking	whole area
Percentage population increase of the Woking parishes 1801-1911					
1801-1811	8.3	14.4	14.8	17.8	15.4
1811-1821	8.9	9.4	11.4	14.7	12.5
1821-1831	19.4	9.1	4.4	9.1	10.1
1831-1841	31.8	13.8	8.5	25.7	22.8
1841-1851	2.2	-0.5	9.6	14.3	9.3
1851-1861	12.1	3.4	4.4	34.6	23.8
1861-1871	18.8	13.8	-6.3	72.5	52.1
1871-1881	37.8	0.3	-3.9	29.9	26.3
1881-1891	9.8	13.4	25.7	14.3	14.1
1891-1901	22.0	108.4	22.5	65.9	63.1
1901-1911	75.4	42.3	85.4	34.3	39.8
1801-1911	**717.6**	**513.8**	**325.6**	**1525.9**	**1085.4**

During the early years of the 19th century, in common with much of rural southern England, there was a substantial population increase, but this slackened in the 1820s as agricultural depression encouraged a drift from the land. In Byfleet and Woking the 1830s saw a substantial amount of in-migration, as the building of the railway, the expansion of nurserying, and the opening of some industries attracted labour. Writing of Woking in 1840 Brayley commented that 'since the introduction of the Printing establishment and Paper Mills here and of the fixing of a Railway Station at Woking Heath, the population has of late years increased considerably'. After the 1840s, though, the agricultural slump returned with a vengeance and there was a serious decline, exacerbated by the beginning of mechanisation in farm work, a factor not present in the 1820s. Horsell parish lost population in the 1840s, while Pyrford and Byfleet experienced little growth. By the 1860s Pyrford, as the smallest and most agricultural of the parishes, was experiencing major haemorrhage of population, losing over 10 per cent of its people in just 20 years.

The contrast between Woking and the other three parishes is thus dramatic, for there the construction of the prison and the asylum in the 1860s, bringing as it did not only inmates but also warders, labourers, clerks and their families, was primarily responsible for a large population increase – indeed, the 1860s were, in percentage terms, the fastest period of growth in the history of the parish. Without the institutions the growth rate would have been less impressive: of the 1871 population about 3,000 were inmates of the prison and the asylum, or warders and other staff and their families. Even so, the start of full-scale urban development in the same decade meant that the rate of increase was sustained. By the 1880s not only had a town developed, but it had started to expand into the neighbouring parish of Horsell and suburbs were growing at Knaphill, Hook Heath, St Johns, Maybury and Mount Hermon. Between 1891 and 1911 Woking grew at an astonishing rate, doubling its population in 20 years, while Horsell outpaced even its larger twin. The development of West Byfleet was responsible for a rapid acceleration of population growth in that parish, and even Pyrford saw its decline suddenly reversed. During the 1890s the town of Woking grew so fast that by 1901, with about 14,000 people, it had eclipsed Chertsey and Egham to become the largest town in north-west Surrey. At the 1911 census, when its population had increased to over 20,000, Woking had overtaken Guildford to become the most populous town in Surrey outside the metropolitan area. It has retained that position ever since.

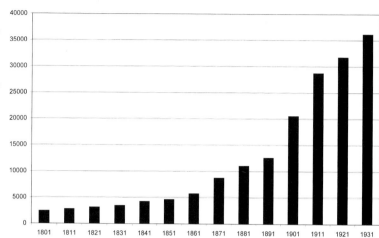

ABOVE *The population of the present borough of Woking 1801-1931: the relatively slow growth rate until the 1860s, and the exceptionally rapid increase in the twenty years before the First World War, are notable features.*

LEFT *The growth of the built-up area 1850-1914.*

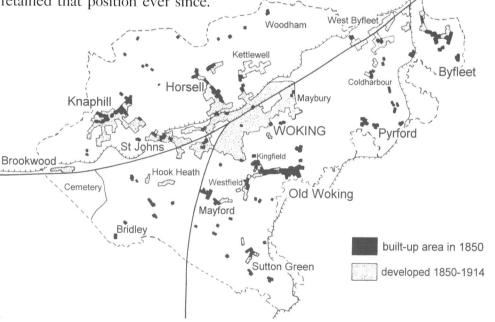

built-up area in 1850

developed 1850-1914

55. Where they came from

Most of the dramatic increase in the population of the Woking area can be accounted for by in-migration, rather than natural increase. The evidence of the census returns from 1851 onwards, which record birthplaces, establishes the origins of the newcomers and so identifies Woking's developing 'catchment area'. A revealing statistic, looking at the four parishes as a whole, is that in 1851 almost precisely two-thirds of the population was born in the area of the present borough – local people, born to local families, many of them of many generations standing. But only twenty years later that proportion had fallen very sharply – in 1871 just over half the people of the Woking area came from *outside*. Furthermore, the percentage who came from the immediately adjacent parishes, such as Wisley and Pirbright, also fell significantly over the same period. So we can be certain that Woking's attractions were not only drawing more people to live here, but that they were coming from a good deal further afield.

One obvious factor helping to account for this is the development of the railway network. The number of Woking residents who were born in the five south-western counties rose more than fivefold between 1851 and 1871, and those from the outer parts of south-east England (that is, beyond west Surrey) increased from 276 to 655. The town's position as a major railway junction, and especially its role as one of the key places on the expanding London and South Western Railway network which was extending its tentacles towards the Atlantic coasts of Devon and Cornwall, is clearly important. Indeed, in a few cases we can identify the details of the process – for example, the family whose children were born in Exeter, Yeovil, Salisbury, and Woking, as they gradually moved up the line towards London. In the growing town there was plenty of industrial, transport and service employment, an attractive prospect for displaced farm workers from the country areas of Sussex, Hampshire and Berkshire. Thus, simultaneously with its early growth of commuting and the arrival of the first wealthy citizens came much larger numbers of poor country people, hoping to make good in the boom town.

Birthplace of inhabitants, 1851 and 1871 (percentage of total)		
place of birth	*1851 census*	*1871 census*
four parishes of Woking	62.8	49.8
adjacent parishes	12.4	10.3
rest of West Surrey	7.1	6.6
south-eastern counties	6.9	10.3
Greater London	5.7	9.1
East Anglia	1.6	2.9
South Midlands	1.2	2.2
south-western counties	0.9	3.4
rest of England	1.2	2.2
Scotland, Wales and Ireland	0.5	1.9
other (not known or overseas)	0.7	1.2

Note: excluding inmates of prisons and asylum; 'adjacent parishes' are Chobham, Chertsey, Weybridge, Wisley, Ockham, Ripley, Send, Stoke next Guildford, Worplesdon, Pirbright and Bisley.

Occasionally, too, we can see very specific flows of people. In 1871, 54 residents of the Woking area had been born in Suffolk, but of these 21 came from Cockfield, Bradfield and Stanningfield, adjacent small villages near Bury St Edmunds. The reason is that the Hilder family, owners of the Hoe Bridge estate, were from Cockfield and when they moved to Woking they brought many of their farm servants with them. Similarly, 36 of the 136 Sussex-born residents came from Kirdford, Wisborough Green and Billingshurst, where the Locke King family, lords of the manor of Byfleet, had important properties.

But many of the moves were over much shorter distances, as they always had been: 106 of the inhabitants of Woking parish were born in Horsell, and 103 Horsellians were from Woking, proportions which were probably little different from those of three hundred years before.

56. Governing the growing town

The problems of the new town of Woking were primarily the fault of the Necropolis Company, but weaknesses in the local government system were a significant contributory factor. As the town grew the existing parish administration was ever less able to cope with the demands placed upon it, while the other administrative bodies in the area, geared towards rural problems and needs, were unsympathetic to urban aspirations. The first major reform of the mid-19th century in Surrey was the division of the county into highway districts in 1864. These were managed by boards, elected by the parish vestries, and took over the highway powers and functions which since the 16th century had been the responsibility of individual parishes. As the districts were based on the petty sessional divisions, themselves derived from the medieval hundreds, Woking came within the Guildford district (on which by 1880 it had four of the 17 board members) and the other three parishes under Chertsey. Whereas the 1862 Highways Act, under which the districts were set up, was aimed at improving an existing system, the 1872 Public Health Act was designed to fill a gap in local government coverage – until that date there was no provision for public health or sanitation measures in rural areas.

The Empire Day celebrations in Woking town centre, 1908: the procession is passing the public buildings at the Victoria Arch end of Commercial Road, headed by children of the Goldsworth Road Council School. The banner hanging from the window of the Public Hall announces an exhibition of flower-making by 'crippled girls'. By the Edwardian period the town was half a century old and was developing a sense of civic conscious-ness and community identity despite the manifold problems caused by its haphazard growth.

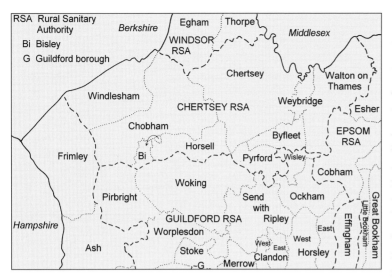

RSA Rural Sanitary Authority
Bi Bisley
G Guildford borough

Local government in north-west Surrey 1872-1893.

The Act established rural sanitary authorities, empowered to administer health, drainage and sewerage, lighting, building regulations and nuisance control. They were closely related to the existing Poor Law boards of guardians – the guardians themselves automatically formed the boards of the new authorities – and inevitably therefore Woking parish became part of the Guildford RSA and the others were brought within the Chertsey RSA (though the areas covered were not the same as the highway districts of the same name). Woking was much the largest constituent of the Guildford RSA, with twice the population of the next largest parish in 1872 and contributing almost 30 per cent of the rateable value in 1892. It was, in effect, a substantial and fast-growing urban area which was for local government purposes treated as if it was a thinly populated rural community, and that naturally produced discontent and tension. The Guildford RSA demonstrated a strong pro-rural bias, as indeed did the Guildford Highway District, and both bodies served Woking badly, neglecting its ever greater and more pressing problems and refusing to spend the substantial sums of money on infrastructural improvements which the developing town urgently needed.

57. The introduction of urban government

Woking parish vestry, increasingly under the influence and control of ratepayers in 'new' Woking, campaigned long and hard for a reform of this inequitable position. It sought to obtain powers for the separation of Woking parish as an urban sanitary authority, but the Local Government Board, the 'ministry' which oversaw these matters, refused sanction. It allowed the Guildford RSA to levy additional rates within Woking, in order to provide extra services in that area only, but the procedure was lengthy and cumbersome and each service had to be treated separately. Thus, a special rate could be levied for lighting, or fire services, or sewerage provision, but each had to be individually approved and separately administered. In 1890 the Guildford RSA attempted to delegate its powers to a 'Woking Committee' (thus freeing itself of the torrent of complaints but retaining control of the rateable value of Woking town) but the government rejected the application.

In 1890 the vestry yet again applied for a grant of urban status but Guildford RSA promised to build a long-delayed sewerage scheme and the application was turned down. Eighteen months later nothing had happened, the vestry tried once more, and a public enquiry in June 1892 gave overwhelming local support for the establishment of a Woking Urban Sanitary District. At last the Local Government Board conceded the force of the argument, the application was accepted, and on 1 October 1893 the Woking Local Board (or Council) and Urban Sanitary District came into being. The parish was divided into five wards which between them elected 18 councillors (six of them for the Woking Station & Maybury Ward). Parliament was already debating the first stages of a comprehensive reform of local government and only 15 months after it came into being the Woking Local Board and Urban Sanitary Authority was abolished, to be replaced by a new body, the urban district council which formally took office on 1 January 1895. The change was one of name only, since the officials and almost all the councillors remained the same.

In the Chertsey area matters were more complicated. On the insistence of the county council, Walton on Thames, Weybridge and Chertsey, each of which had been a parish in the rural sanitary authority, became (as had recently happened with Woking) separate urban districts. The remainder of the Chertsey RSA then became the Chertsey Rural District, an inconvenient and administratively incomprehensible authority which comprised seven parishes divided into three quite unconnected parts and administered from Chertsey, which was not even within its area. In the new Chertsey Rural District, Byfleet acquired a greater importance, with the largest population (except for Windlesham) and 23 per cent of the rateable value in 1895 – but with only two of the 12 councillors. Here, as was often the case, the small and most rural parishes were heavily over represented. The 1894 Local Government Act abolished the old system of vestries and replaced them with democratically elected parish councils to provide for purely local needs and in some cases to act as agents for the rural district councils. At New Year 1895, therefore, the parish councils of Byfleet, Pyrford and Horsell met for the first time.

58. Further changes 1900-1933

As early as the spring of 1894 there had been talk of Horsell amalgamating with Woking to form a single urban district. Although that did not happen immediately it was clear that the parish, as it grew rapidly with new housing, was becoming more closely linked with its larger neighbour. By 1900 they were beginning to coalesce physically into one built-up area – the ancient parish boundary ran along the Rive Ditch but in 1900 its line was altered, on the suggestion of Woking UDC, to follow the canal east of Wheatsheaf Bridge.

Local government in north-west Surrey 1895-1907.

Under this tidier arrangement Horsell lost 58 acres and 23 people. Horsell's problem was that as it became urbanised it needed the higher quality services expected in a town, such as sewerage, street-lighting, and refuse collection. Chertsey Rural District Council conspicuously failed to provide these and, inspired by the example of Windlesham (which included Bagshot, and in 1902 applied successfully to become an urban district in its own right), Horsell Parish Council voted to break away from Chertsey RDC and similarly become an urban

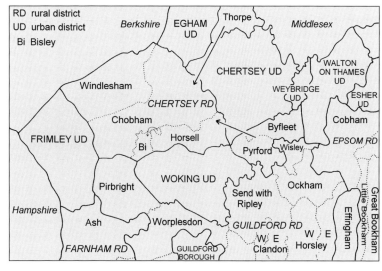

authority. The county council rejected the proposal after a public enquiry but Horsell still desperately required a sewerage and drainage system, so in January 1906 it formally asked Woking UDC if it would be willing to annex Horsell and build the long-overdue sewers. Woking naturally agreed, as did the ratepayers of Horsell by 195 to 118 votes. With the blessing of Surrey County Council and the approval of the government the amalgamation of Horsell with Woking took place on 1 October 1907. Chertsey Rural District, without Windlesham and Horsell, was now even more of an absurdity. It had five parishes in three portions and was an administrative nonsense. Many Byfleet residents favoured the creation of an urban district council for their parish, while the parish council itself supported union with Pyrford as a tiny rural district. In the event Chertsey RDC, which had actually voted for its own abolition, was reprieved and struggled on. In 1929 the council's administration was moved from Chertsey to West Byfleet (since by then Byfleet parish had almost 60 per cent of the population and rateable value) but only four years later in 1933 the Chertsey RDC was abolished under further reforms and Byfleet and Pyrford were amalgamated with Woking, an idea which in 1902-08 appears to have occurred to nobody at all.

59. Water supplies

The essential role of the new local government structures after 1893 was the provision of high quality public services, since private enterprise had achieved relatively little. The absence of piped water supplies until the mid-1880s gave the new town of Woking an especially primitive character. In other parts of the country since the 1840s there had been successful attempts to bring clean drinking water to towns, and municipal authorities had invested heavily in such projects. However, because the 'godmother' of Woking, the Necropolis Company, had no interest at all in making such provision, and because local government was still in a confused and weak state, nobody was able to tackle this most essential requirement of civilised urban living. For its first two decades the fast-growing new town was dependent on wells which (in the absence of sewerage systems) were often seriously polluted and insanitary. In 1881 the Woking Gas and Water Company was formed, to supply water to the new town, the rest of Woking parish, and the rural areas around – Chobham, Send, Ripley, Pyrford, Ockham, Bisley, Horsell, East and West Clandon and Merrow. The reason for the large area of supply south of the Wey was that the water came from a borehole in the deep chalk aquifer above Clandon Crossroads on the slopes of Newlands Corner, so intermediate parishes could easily be served. At the end of 1883 the mains were laid through Woking village and by 1895 had extended as far as Horsell and Pyrford. Another firm, the South West Suburban Water Company, was authorised to supply a wide area of the Thames Valley, including the parishes of Byfleet and Chertsey, and by 1900 these areas also had pure piped water. Today the North Surrey Water Company supplies over 40 million gallons per day, mainly treated water abstracted from the Thames at Chertsey, to a population of more than half a million.

60. Roads, bridges and their repair

The failure of the Guildford Highway District to meet the needs of the growing town meant that the Local Board which took office in 1893 had to tackle a large backlog of essential repairs as well as to contemplate more substantial projects for road improvement. The minutes of the Highway Board demonstrate that almost nothing was being done to provide proper surfaced town streets, let alone to upgrade the main roads outside the urban area. In 1871 a resident described White Rose Lane as 'in so rough a state as to be impassable', in 1890 drainage and gutters were so inadequate in Church Street and Percy Street, in the heart of the town, that one observer suggested that they were 'a natural course of water', and in the same year the Board had to purchase chemicals to spray the unmade surfaces of Brooklyn Road and Mount Hermon Road which were 'overgrown with weeds and grass'. Residents tended to make matters worse. Thus, in 1871 James Woods, wanting some building materials, simply dug a large hole in Wych Hill Lane and took away a cartload of sand and gravel, while in the summer of 1886 there were so many fishmongers' and butchers' stalls outside the railway station in High Street that the road was blocked.

Part of the problem was that the equipment available for road-mending suited a small rural parish, not a large town. In 1869 the Board allocated to the 45 miles of public road in Woking merely '3 Wheelbarrows, 3 Rakes, 4 Scrapers and 1 Pump' and, given its reluctance to spend a penny more than necessary, it also refused to adopt and make up streets in the newly developing residential areas. Although a steamroller for Woking parish was bought in 1887 and a second in 1890, the real need was for a concerted long-term programme of improvement, not *ad hoc* patching. The new Local Board

LEFT *The decrepit and inadequate railway bridge at Victoria Arch before its reconstruction in 1907: through this 20-foot wide arch passed all traffic between the two halves of the new town as well as that between Guildford and Chertsey.*

ABOVE *Wheatsheaf canal bridge, Chobham Road, in 1910: the narrow brick bridge, built in 1792, was replaced with a timber decking and parapets by Woking Urban District Council in 1911, and fully rebuilt in 1921, but attempts to recover the costs from the Canal Company failed since it was bankrupt.*

This frail timber structure is the temporary bridge (built by Woking Council in 1910 on the brick abutments of its predecessor) carrying Chertsey Road over the canal. In 1922 the Council constructed the impressive bridge which carries the road to this day, at the same time eliminating the dangerous double bend by returning the road to the direct alignment followed prior to the building of the canal in 1792.

and its successor, the urban district council, regarded road improvement as a priority. In the summer of 1894, for example, Walton Road, Maybury Road, Church Street and Bath Road were at last made up and adopted. Nevertheless, ruts, mud and, in summer, clouds of dust were characteristic of roads in almost all of the area until the early 1920s.

Bridges, too, were a serious headache. The railway company was very reluctant to incur the high cost of widening the bridges under the massive embankments. They resembled short tunnels (the best surviving example is the Blackhorse Road bridge) and as road traffic grew they became major bottlenecks. The railway arch in the town centre, to which the name 'Victoria' was added in 1898, was only 20 feet wide, unlit, without a footway and it leaked alarmingly. Only in 1906 was the LSWR persuaded to rebuild to give the present 40-foot carriageway with pavements and lighting. River bridges were similarly unsatisfactory. The increased traffic generated by the growth of the town placed ever greater pressure on their frail structures. Elm Bridge was described in 1883 as 'in an unprotected state' because its parapets had fallen down. The name was originally *Ellbridge*, meaning 'plank bridge', and in the 1880s it was still an ancient wooden structure only 12 feet wide. The present 30-foot double brick arch was built in 1891-92. Chertsey RDC rebuilt Plough Bridge at Byfleet in 1906-07 after damage by floods, traction engines and general decay, and it also reconstructed Mimbridge and Dunford Bridge over the Bourne and renewed and raised the causeway between Pyrford and Newark Mill.

The most intractable problems were those associated with the canal bridges, because responsibility for ownership and upkeep was uncertain and the canal company was so financially precarious that it had no money for maintenance. The bridges, built to a standard narrow hump-backed design in the mid-1790s, were unsafe even before the motor age. Chertsey Road and

Wheatsheaf Bridges, carrying increasing volumes of town traffic, were the most unsatisfactory – they were too narrow for two lanes of traffic, the brickwork was crumbling and in both cases the arch had started to sink. In 1906 the situation was so bad that Arthurs Bridge and Chertsey Road Bridge had to be closed completely, while all others were closed at night and severe weight restrictions were enforced. Woking UDC and Chertsey RDC carried out temporary repairs in 1907 and in 1911 Woking Council successfully promoted a private Act of Parliament to recover the costs from the canal company, confirming that the company was legally liable for the upkeep of the bridges. The money was never recovered and in 1922-4 the Council gave up the fight. While not admitting legal responsibility, it completely rebuilt the bridges at Brookwood, Hermitage, St Johns, Chobham Road and Chertsey Road in a distinctive and rather grand style.

61. Sewers and drains

We forget how life used to be. This seemingly prosaic subject (actually it is endlessly fascinating) was central to life in Woking 120 years ago. It still is, of course, but no longer is it a matter for debate and the existence of drains and sewers is unremarkable and unremarked. But in the late 19th century this was the most controversial issue affecting the growing town, and the provision of a sewerage and drainage network was by far the largest and most expensive task facing the new local authorities created in 1893-5. Until the beginning of the 20th century no part of the present borough had any mains drainage or sewerage system. The new town was a sanitation-free zone. This, even more than the lack of planning, was the result of the culpable negligence of the Necropolis Company. While town authorities across industrial England were passing byelaws and obtaining powers to build sewers and drains, in increasingly affluent Surrey, only 25 miles from London, a new town was created without such facilities. Household waste and industrial effluent were disposed of directly into streams and ditches, or were dumped in brickpits, back lanes and middens. The result was a deteriorating public health record, with outbreaks of epidemic disease.

In the late 1870s, for example, typhoid and cholera (both the result of the pollution of drinking water) began to occur more frequently in the district, just as the rest of England was beginning to bring these diseases under control. Wells were sunk adjacent to cesspools and soakaways – in 1874 a newly-built row of cottages near the station was supplied with water from a well polluted by leaks of sewage. From the 1880s, as piped water was introduced, that danger diminished but the town of almost 15,000 people still had no sewers or drains. The 1875 Public Health Act permitted rural sanitary authorities to build sewerage and drainage systems, and to levy special rates to pay for them, but though the Guildford RSA repeatedly discussed the idea of implementing the Act in Woking parish it took no action. Progress was minimal – a few building byelaws were passed, but all they did was to control the location and design of cesspools. As the town centre grew, even the shopping streets were still unsewered. In 1883 domestic sewage was 'discharging into Chertsey Road' and in 1890-2 the owner of the *Red House Hotel* was prosecuted for 'allowing waste and filth to flow onto the road from his premises'. Two years later the railway company was fined because its employees had emptied the contents of several cesspools into the open gutters of Goldsworth Road. When new housing was being planned at Arthurs Bridge in 1895 the submitted designs for sanitation involved merely 'buckets for sink waste'. In the villages conditions were no better. At Byfleet the sewage of the village emptied into ditches, which in hot weather became stagnant and stinking. The watercourse which ran close to the centre of the village was described in 1890 as full of 'offensive matter … sink and urinal waste from the Plough Inn … slops and privy drains', while the Rive Ditch, between Woking and Horsell, was said to be 'a common sewer'.

In the autumn of 1890, after a mere fifteen years' discussion, the Guildford RSA put forward a plan for sewering the new town, with a sewage works on the Hoe Stream just north of Elm Bridge (close to the present swimming pool). This was turned down after a public inquiry on the grounds of cost – the princely sum of £12,000. Another scheme, proposed by the new Woking Local Board in 1894, was likewise rejected. Finally, in July 1895 the Urban District Council approved a scheme for a new sewage works at Woking Park Farm, Old Woking, at the lowest point of the district (thereby permitting gravity flow from the entire system). Lord Onslow, who owned the 42 acres required for the works, objected vociferously, not because of the loss of farmland but because he had plans to develop the Hoe Bridge estate, on the hill to the north, for exclusive housing and feared that the excellent close-up view of a sewage farm might detract from the saleability of the land. The sewerage scheme went ahead, however, as the Council purchased the land compulsorily. Perhaps indirectly it saved from development the fine sweep of open hillside at the Sheepwalks which is some of the best countryside in the Woking area.

In December 1896 the works was opened and the sewers gradually extended along the roads of the urban district, covering the entire area of the new town between 1897 and 1899, then on to St Johns (1900), Maybury Hill (1903), Knaphill, Kingfield and Old Woking (1905) and Hook Heath (1906). From 1907 onwards the Woking system was extended to Horsell, its construction being the guarantee which had persuaded Horsell Parish Council to accept amalgamation with its larger neighbour. Sewering Horsell served twice as many streets than under the previous proposals by Chertsey Rural District Council, at half the cost – a bargain indeed. When this work was completed, in 1910, it could at last be claimed that one of the most important features of modern urban living had been provided, and one of the most glaring inadequacies of 'railway Woking' had been eliminated.

Byfleet and Pyrford, too, were provided with a modern sewerage system just before the First World War. Work on a new sewage farm at Wisley, south of the river, began in September 1910 and in September 1912 the whole of Byfleet and West Byfleet villages, and the more built-up part of Pyrford, were connected. By this time a total of about £150,000 had been spent on the provision of sewers and efficient drainage throughout the developed parts of the present borough – a cost which in today's terms amounts to well over £50 million. Thus, this was not a cheap or straightforward task. Although some of the cost was met out of the rates, much of the money came from loans and borrowing. Here, as elsewhere, the upgrading of infrastructure and the financial complexities which it involved marked a 'coming of age' of local government. In 1890 the local authorities in the Woking area could still debate for hours about trivial expenditure, such as whether to buy a new shovel for road-mending; a quarter century later they were big business, and their role in people's lives could no longer be overlooked or dismissed as irrelevant. The building of sewerage systems, by a very long way the largest and most expensive work undertaken during this period, was in large measure responsible for that change.

In most English towns, refuse collection and disposal were contracted out to private enterprise in this period, and Woking was no exception. In December 1893 the newly formed Local Board gave a contract for scavenging domestic waste and emptying cesspools to John Brown, who lost it six months later because of his unsociable habit of dumping the contents of the cesspools on a waste plot next to new houses in Maybury Hill. A succession of contractors continued to work the system, using vehicles leased to them by the Urban District Council (which bought its first motor dustcart, secondhand, in 1908). The rural parishes also benefited from refuse collection services. Chertsey Rural District Council used direct labour, operating 'night carts' in Byfleet from 1894 and West Byfleet from 1897, while in Horsell a service was provided from 1901 using a cart, a horse, a pump, a shovel and a hose, bought for the grand total of £50. Chertsey continued to operate its own refuse services by direct labour throughout the 1920s until its dissolution in 1933, managing an efficient service which contrasted with the somewhat makeshift and unsatisfactory policy of Woking Council.

An aerial view of Wisley sewage works, following its enlargement in 1963: local history books rarely include pictures of sewage works, but these prosaic sites have been central to the development of communities in the past century – perhaps more so than the churches and public buildings more commonly depicted. Wisley sewage works was opened in 1912 and took the effluent from Byfleet and Pyrford parishes.

What to do with the waste – household refuse, cesspool contents and what was delicately referred to as 'night soil' – was always a problem. From about 1905 in Woking the contractors were permitted to dump everything on the low-lying fields adjacent to the Hoe Stream south of the Constitution Hill recreation ground, but by the mid-1920s the dumps were growing too large and the efficiency of the operation was manifestly inadequate. The Council took over direct control in 1929 and in 1932 bought 11 acres south of Elmbridge, beside the river, for a new tip. The old dumps were closed and levelled and in 1935 the swimming pool was built on the site. Searching ever more widely for sites for new refuse dumps, the Council was frustrated each time by local opposition and the refusal of landowners to sell, and eventually abandoned the idea altogether, in the late 1940s joining with Guildford Borough Council to build the large refuse incinerator and destructor at Slyfield.

62. Gas and electricity

Although the convict prison (1859) and the lunatic asylum (1867) had small private gasworks, there was no public supply of gas in the district until the early 1890s. Woking was one of the last towns in the country without such a facility. Although the building of a gasworks was discussed at public meetings in 1869-70, and the Woking Gas and Water Company obtained powers in 1881 to build a gasworks at what is now Elmbridge Lane, Kingfield, nothing materialised until the formation in 1891 of a new Woking District Gas Company. This was promoted jointly by George Smallpeice of Kingfield House, the instigator of the 1881 scheme, and the Holroyd family of Byfleet who had a variety of local business interests including flourmills. The new company obtained a parliamentary order to supply gas to the parishes of Woking, Horsell, Pyrford, Byfleet, and Send and Ripley. As the site for the gasworks it bought a small plot of former common in Boundary Road, Maybury, close to the canal. The land had been intended for housing and the residents of the area protested vehemently against the scheme, rightly fearing not only pollution and disturbance but also a rapid fall in property values, but their objections carried no weight. The special advantage of the site – apart from its being almost in the town centre and thus at the heart of the potential market – was the ease of transport for the huge quantities of coal and coke required. A new wharf was built on the canal and remained in use until 1936 when road transport took over. The gasworks opened in June 1892 and the company was an immediate success, paying a dividend of 3½ per cent in its first year. A profitable sideline in the sale of ammonia, ashes and tar to local authorities, for sanitary and highway use, soon developed. Supplies were extended to Horsell in 1897, West Byfleet in 1899, and Mayford and Hook Heath in 1902

In contrast, Woking was among the first English towns with a public electricity supply. Indeed, it is probably unique in having had electricity before gas. The Woking Electricity Supply Company was formed in 1889 and in the following year received authority to supply power to domestic premises and for street-lighting. Since other undertakings authorised by the same order included those in Oxford, Derby and Portsmouth there was at least one respect in which Woking could consider itself progressive. Messrs New & Maynes built their new power station (opened in November 1890) in Board School Road, laying mains as far as the *Goldsworth Arms* and the top of Constitution Hill. Unfortunately almost all the electricity was used for lighting, in buildings and streets, so the company only generated power at night, a major disincentive to extending the use of the new power. After six years' operation only 179 customers had signed up and even in 1910, twenty years on, there were only 1,500 customers. In 1898 the company almost went into liquidation, and two years later the Urban District Council threatened to make a compulsory purchase order for the undertaking because of the constant problems experienced with the electric street lamps. This fate was just avoided and the firm then began to promote electricity more vigorously, made the supply more reliable, and extended the area served, reaching Woking village in 1907, Knaphill in 1908, and Pirbright, Ripley and Bisley by 1914.

63. *Street-lighting*

The streets of Woking were a battleground between the rival power companies. The Woking Local Board, established in 1893, gave high priority to the provision of street lighting. Not least, illumination at night would help the residents to skirt the potholes and deep ruts, pools of mud, and streams of sewage which characterised the streets of the town centre. As both forms of power were available the Board invited competitive tenders for the erection and maintenance of 100 street lamps. It asked for technical details of illuminative power and as a result the electricity company was awarded the contract because its lamps were brighter and its prices somewhat lower. The first electric streetlights were switched on at the end of January 1895. Woking was one of the first towns in England to have electric street lighting. Progress again ... but not for long. The electricity supply was very unreliable, interruptions were frequent and the company neglected maintenance to save money. In October 1895, 21 of the 111 lamps failed to work when the lights were switched on after the summer break, so the Council awarded a contract for lighting St Johns and Woking village to a firm which proposed to use oil lamps, although the electricity company had offered to extend its mains to serve those areas.

In December 1895 the entire system failed just before a council meeting at which discussion of the lighting problems was scheduled. The lighting contract expired in 1900 and the Council immediately approved the rival tender of the gas company, despite threats of legal action from the electricity undertaking. Gas-lighting began in August 1902, using secondhand equipment purchased from Battersea Borough Council which was converting its system from gas to electricity. Woking appeared to be turning the clock back. The gas company extended street-lighting to areas outside the town centre. Thus, Oriental Road, still slightly rural in character, was lit in 1910 after complaints that it was 'unsafe for women after dark and ... frequented by tramps and loafers of the worst sort'. In the villages even the most basic street-lighting did not appear until the 1920s: Byfleet Parish Council, for example, rejected an 1895 plan for the magnificent total of three oil lamps on the grounds that it would cost too much, and turned down more ambitious schemes in 1896, 1901, 1911 and 1913.

During the First World War there had been no street-lighting because of the blackout, exacerbated by the acute economic problems faced by the Gas Company as its coal supplies were disrupted and employees conscripted. In 1919 the Company found it difficult to return to normal working and the Council complained officially, only to be told that over 200 gas lamps had been destroyed by vandalism and accidental damage during the war years, coal supplies were irregular, there was scarcely any labour, and 'only one lame horse'. Eventually matters settled down but when the lighting contract came up for renewal in 1931 the Electricity Supply Company won the tender, having demonstrated once again the superior brightness and regularity of its lamps. Electric light returned to the streets of Woking in October 1931 after a thirty-year break. In 1925 Byfleet was for the first time given a proper street-lighting system, with the electricity company serving the village and the gas company the outlying parts of the parish and also the northern end of Pyrford. These last were converted to electricity in 1936.

64. Fire services and wartime emergencies

If, as happened not infrequently, buildings in Woking caught fire, little could be done. Chains of buckets from a pond or stream were the only means of fighting the blaze, unless the distant and ineffective town brigades at Guildford or Chertsey could be summoned in time. As the rateable value of the parish increased there was pressure for a local brigade but, even though by 1890 the town had 8,000 people and numerous commercial and industrial properties, there was still no cover. The Local Board appointed a committee to consider the question but in August 1894 rejected the recommendation that equipment should be bought and a volunteer brigade formed. In May 1895 the new urban district council reversed that decision and accepted the tender of Merryweather for an engine and accessories. This produced the first really political issue which the new authority faced – its members divided between those who favoured spending public money on such services and those who wanted to keep the rates to a minimum by continuing to rely entirely on private provision. In October 1895, as a result of lobbying by the latter group, the decision was again reversed and only a rudimentary collection of equipment was purchased – at each of four iron sheds, located at St Johns, Old Woking, Knaphill and Chertsey Road, '1 Jumping Sheet, 1 35-foot ladder and 2 short ladders' was provided. A 20-man volunteer brigade was formed with Charles Sherlock, a strong supporter of the pro-fire engine group, as its captain.

There was intense personal antagonism between Sherlock and Councillor Kittredge, a St Johns shopkeeper who was chairman of the Fire Brigade Committee and leader of the anti-spending faction, and unseemly squabbling ensued. Sherlock, in each of his regular reports to the Committee, lamented the absence of a steam-powered fire engine, while Kittredge with equal determination rejected the notion. In 1897, after the Council dismissed a petition from the entire brigade asking for a steam engine, Sherlock and his men resigned en masse, leaving the town without a fire service. It is important to remember that all these men were volunteers, giving up their own time and energies to serve the public. They were persuaded to return by Robert

Mossop, the town clerk, but the Fire Brigade Committee, with remarkable folly, issued a public reprimand: a large section immediately resigned once more. At the 1898 council elections several anti-engine candidates lost their seats, Kittredge lost the vital committee chairmanship, and the new council at once voted to buy a steam fire engine. One was eventually delivered in August 1899, to be housed in a new fire station which had been built in Church Street. While it was not always triumphantly successful in its fire-fighting techniques – in 1900 the cart carrying the brigade's equipment caught light during a fire at Woking Laundry, and in dragging it away the firemen ran it over the hoses and severed them – the Woking brigade performed valuable service in the town. The disputes of the mid-1890s were soon forgotten and as the town grew this essential service expanded and developed further.

Byfleet had a volunteer brigade for some years before its larger neighbour. From the mid-1880s Sir James Whitaker Ellis, a local resident, organised one using his private manual fire engine. It was taken over by the parish from 1894 and the fire station in High Road was opened in 1896, being rented by the parish council until in 1902 it was bought outright. A steam engine for the village brigade was acquired in 1906, paid for entirely by the voluntary subscriptions and fund-raising of local people. With 11 men, an engine, uniforms and decent equipment Byfleet had for some years a fire service considerably superior to that of Woking. The parish of Horsell was covered by the Woking brigade under an agreement signed in 1902, at a fee of £25 per year, while in 1906 Pyrford Parish Council made a similar arrangement for the use of the Byfleet brigade in the north of its area. This was extended in 1910 so that the whole of the two parishes was covered.

On 13 October 1915 a German zeppelin passed over Weybridge and Guildford, dropping bombs on both towns but fortunately avoiding Woking. Charles Sherlock recorded the events in his diary, noting that he had hear the sound of explosions and he and his men had got the engine in steam ready for the anticipated air-raid. But what if it had happened – how could a volunteer force with one horse-drawn steam engine tackle such a potential calamity? Captain Wright, Sherlock's successor who took over in the summer of 1917, used the incident to urge modernisation and his words were heeded. In September 1919 Woking UDC took delivery of a motor engine with telescopic ladder, and thereafter expansion and upgrading of the brigade and its equipment took place regularly: a second engine was bought in 1925, and a Renault car was given by Councillor Illingworth for conversion to a fast auxiliary tender. Byfleet brigade acquired its first motor engine in 1923. A new fire station was built in Church Street in 1928 and during these years the brigade extended its area of operation as the parish councils of Chobham, Pirbright and Bisley agreed to pay a retainer to Woking Council in return for fire cover. In 1933 Woking Council took over responsibility for the fire service in Byfleet but continued to run it separately. In October 1936 there was a serious fire at Brooklands Aerodrome, during which the Byfleet engine broke down and failed. The subsequent enquiry revealed many shortcomings in the organisation of this little local brigade and Woking Council then undertook reforms – not least, because the growing threat of war meant that maximum efficiency was essential. From 1938 the chief officer of the Woking Brigade was

Inaugurating the Byfleet motor fire engine, June 1923. Giving the address is Ebenezer Mears, the well-known local building contractor. Behind him, from the left, are Mr Lock, headmaster of Byfleet village school; the rector, the Reverend H.V. Johnson; Leonard Stevens; Mrs Anne Stevens (first woman chairman of Byfleet Parish Council); and Mrs and Mrs Frederick Stoop of West Hall, prominent local benefactors.

a full-time salaried appointment, for a town of 40,000 people could no longer rely on an entirely unpaid amateur force.

The imminence of war saw much activity in the late 1930s, as fire and air-raid precautions were installed and tested, air-raid shelters were constructed, and new administrative arrangements put in place. In September 1939 the government legislated to amalgamate all brigades into county units which formed part of a National Fire Service. The Woking brigade was, like all others in the region, heavily involved in tackling the huge fires which raged in London and the suburbs during the massive air raids of 1940-44, as well as more local crises such as the major raid on Brooklands in 1940. By the end of 1944 Woking itself had experienced a total of 58 air raids, in which 434 high-explosive bombs as well as many incendiaries had been dropped on the town. About two dozen houses had been totally destroyed and another 2,820 damaged. Fortunately, casualties were light – only seven fatalities and about 60 seriously injured, though 13 Woking people were killed in the 1940 Brooklands raid. As in any town, the war years saw the people of Woking make concerted efforts to 'do their bit on the Home Front' collecting scrap iron, bones, tins, bottles and timber; taking in children as evacuees from even more dangerous area (such as the South Coast towns during July 1940); digging for victory; and attending to the minutiae of administration – in September 1940, for example, the Council requested Messrs. Spanton, timber merchants, to remove the word 'Woking' from the sides of their vans because it might give a clue to the enemy. But, all things considered, Woking was very lucky to escape so lightly. With its vital importance as a railway junction, the existence of several major industrial concerns, and the excellence of the railway line as a navigation path towards south-west London, it could easily have suffered more.

65. *Employment in the 19th century*

Between 1850 and 1914 the Woking district was transformed from a dependence on agriculture into a thriving town in which service trades, retailing and transport were dominant in the local economy. The table below summarises the extent of this change for the combined parishes of Woking and Horsell (comparable 1911 data for Byfleet and Pyrford is as yet unavailable):

type of employment	1851		1871		1911	
	no.	%	no.	%	no.	%
agriculture	858	57	847	41	962	9
crafts and trades	129	9	232	11	1658	16
retailing	87	6	145	7	874	8
services	242	16	400	19	3296	31
public employees	11	1	296	11	1258	12
industry	120	8	82	4	599	6
professions	33	2	68	3	580	5
transport	26	2	72	4	847	8
miscellaneous					638	6

The most remarkable change is seen in agriculture, which in 1851 provided 57 per cent of all employment in Woking and Horsell yet sixty years later accounted for only nine per cent, even though the actual numbers employed had increased slightly. But the figures are deceptive, for this category including nurserying, which had experienced major expansion during the 1860s and 1870s. If that trade were to be excluded a dramatic fall in employment would be apparent. Those simple statistics tell the end of the old and time-honoured ways of rural west Surrey. Other figures can deceive. The retailing sector had grown from 87 employees in 1851 to 874 in 1911, which seems impressive, but its share of the total employment had only crept up slightly – in other words, the expansion of shopping failed to keep pace with the growth of the town. Had it grown at a comparable rate the employment figure would have been almost twice its 1911 level. That highlights the weakness of Woking as a commercial centre and the inadequacies of the shopping area of the new town.

The *really* significant growth came, instead, in the sector labelled in 1911 as 'services'. That means, to a very considerable extent, such work as domestic service, for Woking, with its multitude of large new houses designed for polishing, dusting, and firelighting by skivvies, its fine drawing rooms and dining rooms where superior servants did their duties, its coach-houses and (by 1911) garages, its gardens and lawns and paths and shrubberies, was the sort of place where domestic and outdoor servants were in high demand. Servants of a different kind were also increasing in numbers. In 1851 there was no public sector worth speaking of but, by 1911, there were council clerks and council workmen, engaged in maintaining, despite the many problems they encountered, the infrastructure and administration of the town, while others, employed by the county council, looked after the patients in the county asylum.

66. The pattern of agricultural change

In 1864 the diarist Arthur Munby, celebrated today for his fascination with working women (the more muscular the better), watched women labouring in the fields between Woking and Pyrford, on the slope where Pyrford Court stands today. He records in beautiful and moving detail a vanishing world – not the romantic, timber-hung, cottage-garden west Surrey world which Gertrude Jekyll so observantly captured for posterity thirty years later, but the daily grind of field work in an isolated farming community where the pattern of life was governed by the repeated annual cycle of ploughing and sowing, weeding and hoeing, reaping and gathering. As Munby writes you hear the woman talking in her soft rounded Surrey accent, a form of speech as yet untouched by the strident tones of London, and you realise the poignancy of what she says, an epitaph for a dying world. Her children knew a very different Woking, of motor cars and electric light, commuters and council housing:

> 66 At the other end of the field, two women, clad in what seemed white garments, were moving as if from work, each with a hoe upon her shoulder. One of them turned, and came towards me … She looked hard & wide-eyed at me, as one who sees not strangers often. But she stopped readily to talk … Her fellow, she said, had gone to pick up faggots among the felled timber under the wood; and she had brought her hoe as well as her own. They had been hoeing carrots, since eight this morning … There's many women, she said, and girls too, married and unmarried, that work afield about here hoeing, and couching, and reaping with the sickle … a woman's work is tenpence a day: a man's twelve shillings a week. Men and women don't work much together: the female labourers will hoe on one side of a field, the male on the other … Hoeing is not hard work at all, says she, and its healthy is field work … Lots of the girls that works in the fields come from Maybury, & from Bunker's Hill. 99

Other evidence of women and children working in the fields of Woking is found in the census returns, though because these people often worked casually or intermittently, doing tasks such as reaping, fruit-picking, bird-scaring and tending the cattle, the numbers are certainly underestimated. In the 1840s and 1850s boys began farm work at 12 or 13, but in places such as Bridley, where there was no school, nine or ten was more usual. In the 1851 census the youngest 'official' farmworker was a nine-year-old boy at Westfield. Women labourers are also found – there were three female farmworkers at Bunker's Hill, aged 25, 24 and 19, and at Kingfield a widow of 56 and her daughters of 22 and 16. Itinerant labour was employed for seasonal or casual work, part of a tradition of vagrants, squatters and travelling people testified by the entries in the parish registers of the 17th century and continuing into the years before the First World War. Munby's woman labourer said, 'We've no Irish about here, oh no!', but the 1851 census records an itinerant agricultural labourer of 43, living in a tent on the common at Hook Heath with his wife and six children, and at Wych Street a vagrant labourer was 'sleeping in the Barn'. As late as 1911 Woking and Horsell had 76 people living in tents, sheds and barns.

In 1851 agriculture still dominated the economy. Almost two-thirds of the working population (1,294 people) were employed on the land, of whom only 53 were in the nursery business and eight in forestry. In Pyrford, the most rural parish, 91.5 per cent of the workforce was in agriculture. Between then and 1871, employment in agriculture fell by 22 per cent over the borough as a whole, but in Pyrford the decline was dramatic – 60 per cent. The result was a classic 'drift from the land' as mechanisation and the disappearance of smallholdings reduced the need for labour. In Woking and Horsell the rapid growth of nurserying, paradoxically a direct result of urbanisation and residential expansion, soaked up some of the loss – in 1921 the two parishes between them had 890 nursery workers – but Byfleet and Pyrford had no such alternative and considerable rural poverty and economic hardship was the consequence.

67. *Brick-making in the 19th and 20th centuries*

The building of the asylum and the convict prisons, followed by rapid growth in house-building in the district, led to a substantial expansion of output in the Knaphill brickfields after 1858. There were 21 brickworkers in the 1851 census, 17 in 1871 and 25 in 1911, but these were the skilled workforce – many others were employed who are listed simply as 'labourer' in the census returns and cannot be separately identified. The brickyards were on the slopes of Goldsworth Hill, Hermitage and Knaphill, though those near to Kiln Bridge had closed by 1890 after a century of operation. A description of Brickfield Cottage,

St Johns, demolished in 1907, indicates something of the primitive conditions in which the brickyard workers lived: 'an old mud cottage with a straw roof. The walls were crumbling down.' After 1894 the Kiln Bridge pits were used as a convenient site for the disposal of domestic refuse, the rubbish coming not only from the Woking area but also by barge along the Thames and the canal from Kingston and Richmond.

The brickfields in Goldsworth were opened at the same time as the

ABOVE *A section of the 1934 OS 25-inch map of Knaphill, showing the extensive brickfields north of Victoria Road. The last of these brickfields closed during the Second World War, bringing to an end over 250 years of brick-making in Knaphill and St Johns.*

LEFT *Anchor Hill, Knaphill, in about 1919, looking westwards (uphill) from the junction with Barley Mow Lane. On the left are the brickfields (with large stacks of fired bricks) and claypits. This brickworks closed in 1924 and the site has since been covered in housing, but the slope down from Anchor Hill into Hillside Close marks the edge of the former claypit.*

Basingstoke Canal. In the 1870s the Jackman family bought them and tried to operate them as a sideline of their nursery business, serving a purely local market with deliveries by horse and cart to places such as Woodham, Woking village and Pirbright. Goldsworth Brickworks, near the *Rowbarge* public house, worked from 1877 to 1889, using coal brought by canal from Radstock in Somerset and Warwickshire. It produced the bright red bricks for the Westfield Board Schools and for many houses in New Woking and Knaphill, but profits were never large and output was limited by the thinness of the clay beds. Competition from the massive brickworks of the south Midlands eventually made the whole venture uneconomic. In contrast, the brickworks in the area between Robin Hood Road, Anchor Hill and Victoria Road, with a complex of kilns close to the *Queen's Head* public house, were more extensive and longer-lived. By the 1920s almost 20 acres of claypits were being worked, and the 1921 census showed 21 brickworkers in the area. Although the Anchor Hill pits closed during a temporary building depression in 1925, those at Robin Hood Road survived until the suspension of all building work during the Second World War forced their closure in 1942. This ended brick-making in the Woking area after more than two centuries and today, since the claypits have been infilled and used for residential development, hardly any trace remains. Yet many buildings in Woking, especially those dating from 1850-1890, are constructed of locally produced bricks, and the impact of this trade on the town's development should not be underestimated.

68. *Paper and printing*

Woking cornmills closed in 1835 after a continuous history spanning eight centuries, but three years later Alderman Venables of Guildford bought the buildings and converted them to the production of paper, 'the meandering stream of the Wey affording great opportunities for such a purpose'. Venables died in 1840 but the business was acquired by Henry Virtue Bayley & Co. and under the auspices of its new owners it expanded rapidly. Paper was made from rags, which were sorted and bundled by women workers, and then bleached and boiled before pulping and processing. A steam engine provided the power, though in later years the firm had its own small gasworks. There were 55 paperworkers living in Woking parish in 1871, but a larger number across the river in Send, where a population increase after 1861 was attributed to 'the erection of houses for the workmen of a large papermill situate in the parish of Woking'. Arthur Munby recorded in his diary in 1868 that, walking from Woking station to Pyrford in the late afternoon, he 'passed the paper-mill girls on their way home from work' to their poor cottages at Bunker's Hill, Maybury. The industry suffered badly from trade cycles – economic depression always reduced the demand for paper – and in 1870 the mill almost closed: 'Messrs Bayley the well known paper manufacturers of Woking have given a fortnight's warning to the whole of the hands employed in their mills, numbering 136. If the mills are closed it must have a most disastrous effect on the trade of the town of Woking.' Although the threat was averted the mill was not well placed to meet the challenge of larger, more intensively mechanised mills elsewhere in the country and in 1894 it closed for good.

The present Unwins Printing Works in Old Woking was built in the late 1890s, but it is on the site of the watermill which dated from Saxon times and is recorded in Domesday Book. For over eight hundred years the mill, one of the largest on the River Wey, ground the corn from much of the parish of Woking and was a central element in the life of the whole community.

By this time, though, a related industry had developed in Old Woking. In 1837 John Bensley of Andover started a small printing works in Church Street. He sold it to Joseph Billing of London, who expanded the firm. By 1851 it employed 35 Woking residents and others from Send and Ripley, but in March 1856, having been sufficiently successful to outgrow its constricted site, the works closed and the business shifted to new premises in Guildford. But for an accident this would have been the end of printing in Woking. However, in November 1895 Unwin Brothers' printing works at Chilworth was destroyed in a spectacular fire and an urgent search for new premises produced only the disused papermill at Old Woking. It was certainly not an ideal site: the mills had 'a sufficient volume of water to drive two turbines and raise a total of 100 h.p. [but] all the surrounding land was low lying and perilously liable to flooding after snow or in prolonged wet weather … Housing accommodation in the nearby village was not plentiful, and the railway station was a full two miles away'. Nevertheless, the works was refurbished and partly rebuilt with a 'handsome, somewhat Flemish style … façade in warm red brick'. Willows were planted along the causeway from Hipley Bridge on the insistence of George Unwin, to maintain the beauty of the river, and in May 1896 production began. By 1906 the works employed over 200 people and was by far the largest industrial concern in Woking. Workers came from as far afield as Guildford and even Wonersh: 'one stalwart walked twelve miles there and back from Guildford six days a week, and was never late or absent … life was more leisurely and an apprentice could slip off occasionally in the summer during working hours for a swim in the river'.

Today, over a century after the firm came unexpectedly to Woking and more than 170 years after its foundation, Unwin Brothers is still flourishing. The firm is part of the MPG Martins Printing Group and with its sister firm MPG Dataworld it specialises in high quality printing on lightweight papers, including directories, yearbooks, trade price guides, academic and learned journals and magazines. George Unwin would be more than a little bemused by the equipment and its breathtaking speed of production – 'two KBA colour presses offer 4 colour perfecting or sheet work at speeds of up to 15,000 sheets per hour' – but surely pleased that his company is still in such good health.

69. Railways

As well as allowing the development of a completely new town at Woking Common, the railways also provided a substantial amount of employment. A considerable number of temporary labourers came to the area while

Woking railway station, c.1900: the station was rebuilt in the 1880s when the line from Waterloo was widened to four tracks. In this view, looking towards London, the line of shops in High Street can be seen on the left, and the overall roof which covered three of the four main platforms is prominent. The station was totally rebuilt in 1935-7 when the lines to Portsmouth and Alton were electrified.

construction was under way – works such as the deep cuttings at Weybridge and St Johns on the Southampton line and Hook Heath on the Guildford branch required armies of workers. Some undoubtedly stayed though most, as was typical of the railway age, moved on to new contracts. In the 1840s there were few workers employed permanently on the railway, for the first Woking station was small and, although its significance increased once it became a junction in 1845, it had only a limited staff. In 1851 there were just 24 railway workers resident in the four parishes. The real expansion came partly with the growth of the town itself (which generated a lot of extra business) but more especially after the opening in 1859 of the line from Godalming to Havant, which made Woking into a key junction served by two busy trunk routes. The widening of the main line to four tracks in the 1880s was accompanied by a major remodelling of the station area, with greatly extended freight facilities and the transfer (in January 1889) of the locomotive depot from Guildford. This employed over 60 men and came as more intensive use was being made of Woking freight yards. Whereas in 1871 there were 71 railway workers in the area, by 1911 there were 361 in Woking and Horsell alone and over 400 in the future borough.

70. Rural industries in the 19th century

There were several other minor industries during the 19th century, economically of little importance but nonetheless interesting. Most made use of agricultural products. Thus, the Pyrford essential oils distillery, opened in the early 1850s next to the *Sun Inn* on the road from Byfleet Corner, used locally grown flowers and herbs to produce rosewater, lavender water, essences and fragrant oils. It was operated first by the Collins family and from 1872 until its closure in about 1905 by John Newland. During the 1880s Messrs. Woodward & Co. grew and manufactured liquorice in Westfield, while the local brewing trade was supplied with hops grown in several places in the Woking area. Woking village brewery, founded in 1715, was taken over from the Strong family by Henry Charrington in 1870. The brewery was rebuilt but sold in 1887 to John Lovibond & Co., who closed it in 1890. John Stedman, maltster and brewer, carried on his trade in Horsell village from the late 1860s until just before the First World War. The brewery was at the foot of Church Hill, and today the name Brewery Road is a reminder of a trade which, it was proudly claimed in local newspaper advertisements, used only hops and barley grown by the owner and produced beer of the highest quality. Byfleet Brewery was the largest in the area. Under the ownership of Henry Dennett and then the Holroyd Brothers it flourished in the second half of the 19th century. In the mid-1890s Holroyds Brewery amalgamated with Friary Ales of Guildford and Healey's of Kingston and, almost inevitably, this larger concern closed it down in 1905 as it switched to larger and more modern premises in Guildford.

71. Religion in the growing town

The four ancient parish churches were sufficient to cater for the needs of an essentially rural population, but as the town began to develop and new communities arose additional churches were opened. The old parish churches survive today, though in each case there was extensive 'restoration' during the 19th century – the typically heavy-handed Victorian approach to improving the fabric of ancient churches is exemplified at Horsell and Byfleet, where much that would now be regarded as of special interest, or beauty, was removed during the 'renewal'. The architectural writer Ian Nairn wrote of Horsell St Mary that it is 'a sorry mess of restoration and enlargement … all new or renewed to extinction'. The least altered, as we have seen, was Pyrford, where the restoration was relatively sensitive and restrained.

The first new church was a small chapel of ease, dedicated to St John the Baptist, which was built close to the canal at Kiln Bridge in 1840. Nairn did not like this one either, despite the later fame of its architect: 'Not in [Sir George Gilbert] Scott's own list of his early "ignoble" churches. It ought to be.' St John's Church gave its name to the community which was developing around the canal bridge and in 1883 it became a separate parish in its own right, detached from Woking St Peter. In the new town the Necropolis Company was supposed to provide a site for a church and schools, and eventually a plot on the south side of what became Church Street was chosen by the diocese of Winchester in 1861 and formally conveyed to the ecclesiastical authorities in 1870. In the meantime services were held in the back room of a shop in Chertsey Road. A temporary iron chapel was provided in 1877, but by 1885 it was so rusty and leaking that the building of a proper church could no longer be deferred. In 1887 the Duchess of Albany laid the foundation stone of Christ Church, and the building was

The small chapel of ease dedicated to St John the Baptist which was opened at Kiln Bridge in 1842. The new chapel became a parish church in 1883. It gave its name to the district which by 1880 was generally known as St Johns. Architectural historians have been scathing about the building, but it is not unattractive and now, over 150 years old and with its peaceful wooded setting, it is hard to see why it provoked such hostile comment.

consecrated for public worship in 1889. William Unsworth's original design included a tall brick tower, but there was not enough money and the present flèche was substituted. In 1893 a separate parish was created. Nairn liked this church: 'big in scale, honest ... as with so many late Victorian architects, the cheaper the building, the better the design.' Christ Church survived the wholesale clearance of the centre in the late 1960s, for several years standing high above a creeping tide of wasteland and rubble, before becoming a focal point in the redevelopment scheme.

Church Street and Christ Church, c.1905: the Anglican church serving the new town of Woking was completed in 1883, apart from a tall solid tower which was part of the original design but never built. The slender and elegant copper-sheathed flèche (or spire) which substitutes for the tower is much more effective visually, for the tower would have given a top-heavy and ungainly appearance. In 1905 Church Street was almost entirely residential, a leafy suburban road though only yards from the bustle of Woking station.

As the town began to acquire suburbs, further churches were provided. St Paul's, Maybury Hill (1895) was followed by Holy Trinity, Knaphill and St Mary of Bethany, York Road (both 1907), and St Saviour, Brookwood (1909). All Saints, Woodham Lane (1893) was designed by the ubiquitous William Unsworth, whose house, Woodhambury, was nearby: it was in an 'Old Surrey' style which the opinionated Nairn described as 'frigid and expensive ... joyless and stone dead', but whether or not it satisfies the architectural purists it makes an attractive scene in its conifer-surrounded setting. West Byfleet St John, also in the 'Surrey traditional' mould, was completed in 1912 to replace a 40-year-old iron

Some of the plans for redeveloping the town centre, drawn up in the late 1950s and early 1960s, involved the demolition of Christ Church. Fortunately those eventually adopted allowed it to remain as a centrepiece of the new design. In this view, taken in 1972, its comfortable red-brick solidity represents the only element of continuity as the tide of demolition and reconstruction spreads across the (less than a hundred years old) town centre.

church: 'a complete specimen of the fussily-detailed genteelly-roofed type of design which has been the bane of English church architecture for nearly fifty years.' Nairn's many comments were written in the early 1960s, when vernacular styles were seriously out of favour and concrete was all the rage. Nearly fifty years on we have, perhaps, a different perspective. These churches, consciously designed to blend in with firs and pines, rhododendrons and birches, also fit extremely well into the overall architectural 'feel' of the Woking area. A century and more after they were built the Edwardian principles of architecture and aesthetics are much in favour, and the merits of the unambitious but pleasant churches of the period are more evident.

Roman Catholics in the Woking area – of whom there were few – had to make do with private rooms for worship, or used the family chapel at Sutton Place (since the Reformation a celebrated Catholic house) until 1876, when St Edward's, Sutton Green, was opened. In the late 1800s an iron mission church was built in Percy Street, in the town centre, and in 1925 this was replaced by the architecturally dreary St Dunstan's in White Rose Lane (about to be demolished, at the time of writing). Nonconformist worship in the area dates back to the mid-17th century and the district was an important early centre for Quaker activity. In 1668, only 15 years after the Society of Friends was formally established by George Fox in Lancashire, the Guildford Monthly Meeting attracted adherents from 'Pirbright, Warplesden and Oakinge' among other places, and in 1681 and 1682 Quakers from Woking were imprisoned at Guildford for their steadfast refusal to pay tithes. An independent Baptist chapel was established at Kingfield by the early 1770s (and rebuilt in 1782) and meetings were also being held in Horsell and probably in Knaphill by this date. In 1810 an old cottage on the edge of Horsell Common was adapted as a Particular Baptist chapel and in 1816 a purpose-built chapel was built there: its worshippers came from as far afield as Horsley and Albury. Another Baptist chapel was opened in Horsell village in 1848 and in 1879 one in the town centre, under the auspices of Henry Gloster, a leading figure in Woking's public and civic life for over 30 years.

[at the quarter sessions held at Guildford, Michaelmas 1777]

...William Huntinton having Exercised the Function of Teacher and preacher of the Holy Gospel, at an Independent Meeting House Licensed by Law at Woking in the County of Surrey: We whose names are Underwritten being Members of the said Meeting, do approve, and judge of the said William Huntinton; to be a proper person to Exercise the said Function, both with regard to his Abilities as a Preacher, and one whose life and conversation is consistent therewith ...

James Hodd
Jno. Flackman
Benjamin Reading Sen.
John Lee
Nicholas Smith
John Symmonds

Benjamin Reading
Richard Simmonds
William Lad
John Baily
James South
John Russell

William Hampshire
William Allfield
Henry Allfeld
John James
James Harding

In the 17th and 18th centuries Woking and Horsell were important centres for nonconformity in a county where dissenters were relatively few on the ground. The nonconformist chapel referred to in this document was at Shackleford, and drew its congregations from poor labouring families across the district, well beyond the boundaries of Woking. In 1788 the curate of Worplesdon and Pirbright reported to the bishop of Winchester that 'we still have near 20 persons among us, illiterate, who absent themselves from their parish church [and go] at a distance every Sunday ... and they generally find their favourite at a meeting-house in Woking'. The chapel had a good reputation for its early attempts to develop an educational role, with Sunday teaching as well as preaching.

72. *Religious faith in the mid-19th century*

Back in 1676 the church authorities had undertaken a survey of 'conformists' – adherents of the Church of England – and instructed local clergy to report on the presence of Catholics and nonconformist Protestants. Though it is highly suspect in detail the picture given is significant, for it suggests that nonconformity was already quite strong in the district. Almost two centuries later this characteristic had not altered. In 1851 a census of religious worship was taken, giving a rare statistical picture of the strength of different denominations and the level of church-going as a whole. For the Woking area striking contrasts are revealed. The percentage of nonconformists in the Woking area was well above the county average, and that of Horsell was one of the highest in Surrey. But at the same time the percentage of people who went to a religious service of any sort was lower than almost anywhere else in the county. Thus, the Woking area did not conform to the patterns evident in the rest of Surrey, a fact perhaps attributable in part to the relative remoteness which had encouraged breakaway groups and new sects in the 17th and 18th centuries and which – because of the distances involved – reduced the attraction of the Anglican parish church for regular worship. We perhaps see something of the same in the comment of the Rev. E.W. Tarbox, minister at the tiny Baptist mission chapel at Anthony's on Horsell Common, who in 1885 noted that 'it was like working in a heathen land, for many of the little folks had never even heard of the name of Jesus'.

The 1851 religious census: attendance in Woking area parishes		
parish/rural deanery and denomination	*total attendance at services 31 March 1851*	*% of total population who attended a service*
BYFLEET [C of E]	235	34.2
HORSELL [C of E]	327	42.9
HORSELL [nonconformist]	388	50.9
Horsell [total]		**93.8**
PYRFORD [C of E]	86	23.6
WOKING [C of E]	735	25.9
WOKING [nonconformist]	468	16.5
Woking [total]		**42.4**
Chertsey Rural Deanery [C of E]		43.9
Chertsey Rural Deanery[nonconformist]		12.4
Chertsey Rural Deanery [total]		**58.3**
Guildford Rural Deanery [C of E]		43.2
Guildford Rural Deanery[nonconformist]		13.2
Guildford Rural Deanery [total]		**56.4**

Note: the exceptionally high figure for Horsell reflects the fact that many worshippers came from outside Horsell parish.

73. Education

Not unexpectedly, these thinly populated parishes had little educational provision until the 19th century. The vicar of Byfleet reported in a diocesan visitation, or survey, in 1725 that in his parish there was 'Only one private school, a mistress teaching children to read', while the incumbents of Horsell and Pyrford reported that there were no schools of any sort. The vicar of Woking stated that, although there were no endowed schools (those with a charter or formal foundation deed), 'we have one poore writing master, and some dames that teach the smaller children', but he claimed that 'the better sort send their children to Guildford and other places for instruction'. A similar survey in 1788 found no schools of any sort in Pyrford or Byfleet, but in Horsell 'one unendowed school, Mrs Walker the mistress, with [number] of scholars uncertain'. This school was loosely associated with the Church of England (though formal church schools did not yet exist) but in the 1790s another school was opened in the village, linked with the nonconformists.

The Church of England school grew steadily and in 1818 had a total of 165 pupils, of whom 87 came from Woking parish (that is, Knaphill and Goldsworth, where there was no educational provision at all). In the same year Byfleet was said to have a small voluntarily maintained school, taking 24 pupils, but in Pyrford there was no school and 'the poorer classes are entirely destitute of means of education, though desirous of obtaining them'. By the 1830s national standards of education were so poor that the government was finally forced to intervene and give grants for school provision. A survey in 1833, conducted as part of this new policy, recorded that Horsell school (which also included a Sunday school) had 209 pupils, of whom 91 were from Woking parish and 38 travelled daily (presumably on foot) from Pyrford parish. Byfleet had three day schools, supported by donations from parents, but they together provided only 49 places – though a new voluntary village school was opened in 1840. In Woking village the vicar, the Rev. Charles Bowles, opened a small voluntary church school in the same year.

Woking parish was seriously deficient in school provision, a problem only remedied from the 1840s by the National Society for the Promotion of the Education of the Poor in the Principles of the Established Church (founded 1811). The National Society, with the help of government funding, opened a 32-place village school at Pyrford in 1847, followed in 1848 by the Church Street school in Woking village and in 1849 by the Westfield National Schoolroom. Church Street was enlarged in 1899-1901 and finally closed in 1981, while the Westfield schoolroom, on the very edge of Westfield Common, was superseded eventually by Westfield Infant and Junior Schools (both also now closed). Other church schools were opened, or adopted by the National Society and restructured, in the ensuing decades: St Johns and Sutton Green in the late 1850s, Knaphill in the early 1860s, Horsell in 1851 and Byfleet in 1856. Private education took root in this period and has remained a major feature in the district. Many private schools have been short-lived, not surviving the death or retirement of the founding teacher or, in more recent years, closed because more profit could be made from selling the buildings and land for redevelopment. But by 1870 the most glaring deficiency in this field was the total absence of any educational provision in 'new' Woking. Children could either walk from there to Horsell or do without schooling altogether, a state of affairs which was manifestly unsatisfactory and which provoked the greatest local political controversy of the 1870s.

Westfield in 1934: the map shows the Mission Hall, at the Bonsey Lane junction, which was built as a National Schoolroom in 1849 on a small plot of land taken from Westfield Common. It became a mission hall in 1897 when the Woking School Board built the new Infant School; the Junior School opened soon afterwards. By the 1930s council housing and small private estates had grown up all around. Both schools (which had the honour of educating me!) are now closed.

74. The school boards

The Education Act of 1870 made elementary schooling compulsory, although not free of charge, and also gave powers to local authorities to use rate money for education and schools. School boards could be established, elected by the ratepayers but directly responsible to the Department of Education, to provide schools in areas where existing facilities were particularly inadequate. A public meeting in Woking in December 1870 heard that over 200 children in the parish were still receiving no education at all, because of a desperate shortage of school places, and in June 1872 the parish vestry, unable to take action itself, recommended that a school board be set up. The proposal split the parish. Most ratepayers in Woking village, St Johns and Westfield, which already had adequate schools, strongly opposed their rates being spent in such a way. 'New' Woking and Knaphill, where provision was quite inadequate, were equally strongly in favour. In February 1873 a ratepayer poll narrowly defeated the plan (Woking village was 90 per cent opposed and St Johns 94 per cent, while the Station area was 84 per cent in favour and Knaphill 65 per cent). A year later the vote was reversed – the new town was voting more solidly – and the first elections to the Woking School Board were held in April 1874.

The rift between the two halves of the parish lasted for twenty years, the representatives of the 'rural' areas consistently voting against expenditure and equally regularly being outvoted by their opponents. The School Board set about its task with energy and determination. Within a month of taking office it had purchased land from the Necropolis Company in east Woking and in September 1875 the Maybury Board School was opened, with places for 70 infants and 180 older children – the importance attached to this project can be seen from the naming of Board School Road in its honour. Between 1874 and 1877 the National Schools at Westfield, Church Street, St Johns and Knaphill were transferred to the control of the Woking School Board, which immediately began to plan replacements for their cramped and outdated buildings. New elementary schools were provided at Knaphill in 1881, Westfield in 1897, Goldsworth in 1898, and Church Street and Brookwood in 1901. The School Board also used its powers under education legislation to regulate and inspect private schools – in 1884, for example, it ordered the closure of the village school at Sutton Green on the grounds that it was 'inefficient' (the usual euphemism for grossly unsatisfactory) and in 1881 had taken steps to exclude children from Mrs Lilley's private school in Woking village for the same reason.

In Byfleet and Horsell the existing National Schools were enlarged and partly rebuilt in the later 19th century and, although the situation there was not ideal, no pressure for school boards developed. In Pyrford, by contrast, the small village school was seriously overcrowded and substandard by the late 1880s, as population grew in the

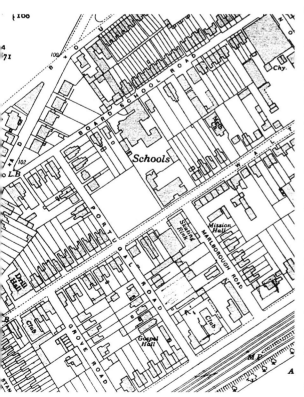

The Maybury Board Schools, opened in 1875 by the newly-established Woking School Board. This was the first school in the fast-growing town and local people were proud of the achievement – hence the naming of the road in its honour. An earlier proposal to build a church school in what became Duke Street had come to nothing and until the Maybury school was opened children in 'New' Woking had no educational opportunities at all.

northern part of the parish. The 1888 Local Government Act allowed the new county council to make compulsory declarations of school boards in areas where ratepayers refused to cooperate, and Surrey County Council used this power to establish a Pyrford School Board in December 1891. A new school was built at the junction of Coldharbour Road and Engliff Lane in the spring of 1893. But in 1902 a further Act sought to rationalise what had become a confusing and increasingly inefficient system (there were 29 school boards in Surrey alone) by making county councils responsible for the provision of free elementary education for all children in the public sector. In 1903, therefore, the Woking and Pyrford School Boards were dissolved and their assets and responsibilities were, with those of the National Society in Byfleet and Horsell, transferred to Surrey County Council. The work which the School Boards had undertaken was, in contrast to that of most other local government bodies in the area during the second half of the 19th century, efficient, prompt and decisive and they laid a good and solid foundation for the further expansion of educational opportunities during the 20th century.

75. Secondary education

Although, as the vicar of Woking had noted back in the 1780s, wealthier local people could send their children to places such as Guildford to be educated, there was no secondary education of any sort in the present borough until 1914, a deplorable state of affairs. By that date Woking was one of the largest towns in Britain without a secondary school. The Woking Mutual Improvement Society, founded by the vicar in 1867, gave instruction to adults in a wide range of subjects such as foreign languages, and also ran a small lending library, while in 1893 the Woking School Board, although it did not have formal powers over secondary education, adopted a scheme for evening classes to be provided in board schools. The Woking Local Board, established in 1894, and its successor, the urban district council, both campaigned for the provision of a secondary school but it was not until the county council acquired its comprehensive set of powers and responsibilities in 1903 that the possibility moved closer. In 1909 Surrey County Council bought a large site on Station Approach and in 1914 the Woking County School for Boys was opened, with its large and imposing buildings of red brick and white limestone. Eight years later the County School for Girls, to which rather less attention and expense was devoted, opened in a converted house in Park Road and there it stayed until in 1959 it moved to a new and spacious site in Old Woking Road. The two grammar schools were soon supplemented by other secondary schools, especially with the major expansion in secondary education after 1945.

76. Public health and medical care

The public health problems of the area in the second half of the 19th century were nothing like as bad as in large cities, but Woking had its share of epidemic diseases, which were regularly reported by the medical officer of health. Thus in the autumn of 1901 diphtheria closed all the schools in Knaphill and Brookwood for eight weeks, and in November 1905 an epidemic of the same disease in the Woking station area killed 22 children aged seven or under. Every year brought several deaths from scarlet fever and measles, and dysentery was rife in the summer months. In November 1898 a mystery illness in the Goldsworth area, unhelpfully described as 'sore throat', turned out to be cattle fever spread by milk from an infected dairy herd at Goldsworth Farm. Although such events were hardly unique to Woking, they highlighted the acute problems presented by the lack of medical facilities. Though there were private doctors in the growing town, there was no hospital – the nearest was the Royal Surrey at Guildford, itself under considerable strain from population growth in the county town. From 1882 there was an isolation hospital at Wood Street, Worplesdon, provided by the Guildford Rural Sanitary Authority for patients with infectious diseases, and ten years later a comparable hospital was opened for the Chertsey area at Ottershaw, but these were too small to cater for a serious epidemic and they served a very large area. In 1893 a temporary 'cottage hospital' was opened in a converted house in Bath Road, in the centre of the town, and in 1899 this was replaced by Woking Victoria Hospital, a small purpose-built establishment on a cramped site next to the Wheatsheaf canal bridge. It was named in honour of the Diamond Jubilee of the queen, which fell in 1897, the year the foundation stone was laid, and in 1903 was extended using public subscriptions given by the people and council of Woking as a memorial to Queen Victoria.

The local authorities were the main agents for the provision of medical facilities and in 1933, following local government reform, Woking Council, together with the councils of Walton and Weybridge, Chertsey, Frimley & Camberley and Bagshot, formed a joint hospital board which began to create a comprehensive health and hospital service for the area. The strategy, which was very far-sighted for the period, was to develop a major new centrally located hospital with resources for the full range of healthcare provision. This was the genesis of what became St Peter's, where building work began in October 1933. Complementing the new central hospital were to be several new local hospitals which would offer the typical range of outpatient, clinic, minor surgical and other small-scale facilities. When the war broke out in September 1939 work was about to begin on a new district hospital for the Woking area at Kettlewell Hill, Horsell. In 1948 the new NHS abandoned that scheme, focusing its attention on St Peter's and preferring to leave the Victoria Hospital to serve the town's more immediate needs. From the 1960s onwards threats of closure were regularly raised, and met with vociferous opposition – not least because access to St Peter's was ever more difficult as traffic congestion grew. The Victoria survived the immediate threat of town-centre redevelopment, but its position – isolated by the canal and the new relief road and in a prime development area – sealed its fate. However, continuous public pressure paid off, and in 1990 it was decided to replace it with a new Woking Community Hospital on the site of the existing small maternity unit at Beechcroft in Heathside Road. The new hospital opened in 1993, the Victoria was closed, and another Woking landmark quickly disappeared.

BETWEEN THE WARS

77. Overview

The outbreak of the First World War checked the growth of the town and the neighbouring parishes. In 1911-21 the overall rate of growth was 10.5 per cent, compared with 39.8 per cent in the previous decade. The main exception was Byfleet, where the construction of the Vickers aircraft works at Brooklands attracted substantial amounts of labour from other areas. To cope with the influx of workers the company, in conjunction with Chertsey RDC and Byfleet Parish Council, built a model housing estate on Brooklands Road. The population of Byfleet grew by 41 per cent during the war decade, much the fastest in the area. During the early 1920s the large institutions, which had reached their peak size in the years before 1914, began to contract slowly. Railway services were of relatively poor quality, and had suffered from wartime neglect and over-use, and apart from the aircraft works Woking had no significant industries to bring in workers from elsewhere. In the early 1920s growth remained slack.

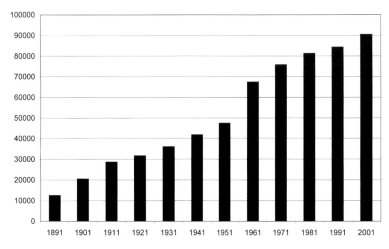

The population of the borough of Woking, 1891-2002: the rate of growth rose sharply in the 1950s and 1960s as major new housing schemes came to fruition, and then slackened in the 1980s and 1990s as the supply of easily-developed spare land dried up because of Green Belt restrictions.

However, in the late 1920s circumstances altered and Woking became a magnet for people coming to the south-east from other parts of the country, as well as for Londoners moving out of the city. New sales of building land allowed extensive house-building, while major improvements in rail transport (notably the electrification of the lines to Portsmouth and Alton in 1936-7) gave a much better service of faster, cleaner and more reliable trains, which were often non-stop to Waterloo. The result was a huge increase in commuting during the late 1930s and – after wartime interruptions – the 1950s. Woking was becoming known as a 'dormitory town'. After the mid-1920s, too, new industries were developed, including James Walker Limited and the Sorbo Rubber Company, the two largest industries by 1950. During the 1930s the population increase across the urban district as a whole was 27 per cent, but Horsell, in particular, showed much higher rates and almost doubled in size between 1931 and 1939. By that date Woking, with 45,000 inhabitants, was by a considerable distance the largest town in non-metropolitan Surrey.

78. Town planning questions

Neither the development of the town in the mid-19th century, nor its suburban expansion between 1880 and 1914, was accompanied by any framework of planning, urban design or coherent provision of services and amenities. Only in the late 1920s did local authorities in the area begin to consider shaping the patterns of development, though it should be noted that the first planning legislation (which was voluntary) only dated from 1909. In 1928 seven councils in the area, including Woking UDC and Chertsey RDC, formed a joint committee to draw up an overall planning policy for north-west Surrey. It proposed that there should be three separate urban areas in the Woking district: Knaphill-Brookwood; Woking town; and Byfleet-Woodham-Addlestone. These would be separated by rural zones, but a large new industrial area would be built on the north side of the railway between Woking and West Byfleet, at Sheerwater Farm. Woking Council was unhappy about some aspects of the policy but was inspired to appoint its first planning officer in 1931, and, although the detailed impact of this 'broad brush' scheme was very limited, it did help to establish some key principles and to guide development in a general sense.

Foremost among those outline policies were that new development should be at low densities; that some of the more attractive rural areas within the urban district should be protected from building; that existing built-up areas might expand at higher densities, but only to a limited extent; that land should be reserved for major highway projects (the first talk of a London orbital road was heard in the 1920s); and that Woking town centre should be expanded, improved and redeveloped. The assumption that most of the open and undeveloped land in the district would be available for house-building at low densities (as few as four houses per acre for large swathes of countryside) had crucial implications for the future. Had the war not intervened, and a new planning system not been imposed in 1947, Woking would have continued to sprawl across the pleasant rural land of Mayford and Bridley, Pyrford and Horsell. If we project the growth patterns of the 1930s forward to the 1970s (that is, if there had never been a green belt) the town would have coalesced physically with Guildford, Chertsey and Bagshot (as it does now with Weybridge and Addlestone) and the population would have reached almost 150,000 by 1975 (in 2003 it is 90,000). It is quite clear, therefore, that the planning policies of the post-1947 era, which were directed towards preventing such an eventuality, were instrumental in shaping the town of today by protecting the visually important countryside of west Surrey from uncontrolled building.

79. The geography of growth 1918–1939

Woking grew between the wars with three main types of development. First, there was council housing, a new feature of the period and one which became increasingly important as house and land prices rose, though its main impact came in the 1950s and 1960s. This type of housing was concentrated in four areas – Knaphill, Westfield and Old Woking, Byfleet, and Horsell – where land was cheaper and smaller properties were being sold off piecemeal. These districts were less attractive to speculative private builders than the breezy heights of Hook Heath or the pinewoods of Pyrford, so there was less competition. There was also some higher density private building, mainly on the fringes of the existing built-up area where land ownership was more fragmented and infill schemes and small estates could be developed by local builders. These sites, like those used for council housing, had a further important advantage. They were close to main roads and existing development, so were conveniently provided with services such as gas, electricity, and

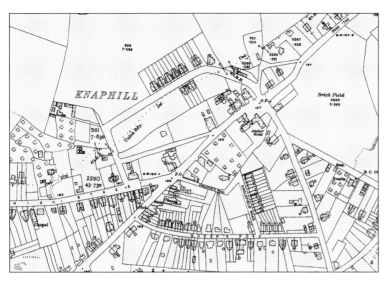

Knaphill in 1934: the Ordnance Survey map reveals that the irregular layout of the village, a consequence of its origins as a squatter settlement on the edge of the common, had been embedded in the pattern of streets and houses developed in the later 19th and early 20th centuries. There was no overall design and shops, houses and roads appeared when and where landowners or developers chose. In 1934 there was no village centre apart from a cluster of shops and the Anchor Hotel at the road junction, and when a centre did develop in the 1950s and 1960s it, too, was unplanned and piecemeal.

The growth of the built-up area between the Wars.

water. This meant that the builders did not have to spend large sums on ensuring the provision of those essentials: costs were kept down and the profits stayed up. Finally, there were exclusive and expensive low density schemes, where large detached houses stood in extensive grounds and often with the added seclusion of private roads entered through gates and set in thick woodland. These developments, characteristic of areas such as Pyrford, Hook Heath and the area of Maybury north of White Rose Lane, carried on a tradition of exclusiveness established in the Edwardian period. Because of very high architectural and design quality of some of these areas, and their distinctive social origins and character, the best examples have now been designated as conservation areas.

In 1914 the built-up area was still a series of unconnected portions. Thus, Knaphill was separate from St Johns, St Johns from Goldsworth, Pyrford from West Byfleet. The interwar years saw a very rapid expansion of the built-up area as it spread out from these older centres and in due course they coalesced. By 1939 Horsell, Woking, Old Woking and Kingfield, Kettlewell, Knaphill and St Johns formed one large urban area. Likewise, Byfleet, Pyrford and Woodham had been joined together, though they were not yet physically linked with Woking to the west. This massive expansion of the built-up area was reflected in the administrative changes of the early 1930s, which saw the four old parishes finally united into one urban district. But as well as growing,

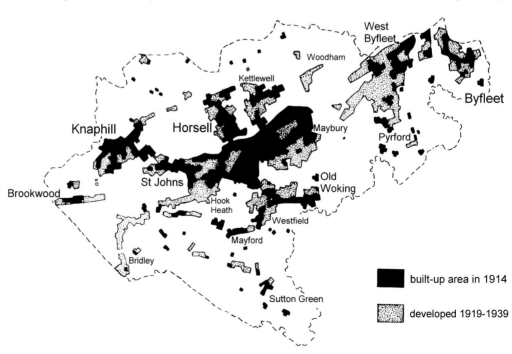

built-up area in 1914

developed 1919-1939

the older communities were changing their character. In 1944 Byfleet, which fifty years before had still been rural, was described as 'a scattered overgrown village with no real centre and a lot of mean development and cheap shop blocks'. Woking had become that complex mixture of architectural meanness and expensive opulence, inadequate public infrastructure and ostentatious private development which was its hallmark for much of the 20th century. To one wartime observer it was 'an expensive London dormitory area for the "managing director" type of resident with a good sprinkling of retired business people occupying large houses with chauffeurs' and gardeners' cottages attached', but that was not how it seemed in Board School Road.

80. Public housing between the wars

In 1910 Woking Urban District Council, aware of the acute problems encountered by lower-income groups as land prices shot up and cheap housing was in increasingly short supply, decided to use its powers to construct 'cottage dwellings'. However, it had one obvious problem – it could not afford to compete on the open land market, as the government enforced restrictions on local government expenditure. The Council wanted to provide houses of a decent standard set in reasonably attractive surroundings, while the Local Government Board told them to 'spend no unnecessary money on appearance or ornamentation'. It was an irreconcilable difference, and almost a century later the problem which underlay it – the exceptionally high cost of land and hence of housing in Woking – is even greater and the solutions even less obvious. But in 1914 the Council went ahead and bought land for housing behind Old Woking High Street. During the First World War, though no building had yet taken place, it was agreed that a large programme of council housing should be implemented as soon as possible. In August 1920 Woking's

Old Woking in 1934: the winding alignment, variable width, and small cottages of the village street contrast sharply with the strict geometry (and notably generous layout) of St Peter's Road and Corrie Road, the first housing estate built by Woking Urban District Council after 1919.

first council house, in St Peter's Road, Old Woking, was occupied, and between then and the summer of 1921 another 99 were completed here and at Westfield, Horsell and Knaphill. They were not what the Council wanted. The ministry, with typically short-sighted parsimony, forbade the provision of hot-water systems, hand basins and electricity. Chertsey Rural District Council had comparable problems. It could not afford land in the Byfleet area at a price low enough to satisfy the ever vigilant and cheese-paring ministry, and two years of hard bargaining passed before sites were purchased in Petersham Avenue (Byfleet) and Engliff Lane (Pyrford). They were developed in 1921, at which point both councils were told to suspend all schemes as an economy measure because Surrey was a 'non-priority area'.

Work did not resume until the end of 1925. The government now required all councils to survey the extent of overcrowding and unfit housing within their areas and to submit figures for rehousing. Woking reported that 34 houses were unacceptable on one or both grounds, noting that the housing shortage was

such that 'there are sheds and harness rooms being used as dwellings', while Chertsey RDC reported a family of four living in a lean-to shed, and three adults and nine children in a two-bedroomed house, both in Byfleet. The problem worsened as the land prices continued to rise and as the town became a magnet for newcomers. In 1927, 193 cases on the Woking Council housing list were defined as 'in dire need of amelioration' and another 81 families needed rehousing 'on the grounds of decency, common modesty, moral and physical health'. Older properties in the district – pre-19th-century agricultural labourers' cottages and the instant slums of the 1870s and 1880s – were identified after 1930 as requiring compulsory purchase and clearance under legislation aimed at tackling the nation's huge legacy of unfit housing. In 1931 Woking UDC listed 55 slum properties in Old Woking, Knaphill and the Walton Road area – the last being an indictment, if one were needed, of the failure of the Necropolis Company to provide even the most basic standards when it developed the town half a century before.

In this 1947 aerial view of Westfield and Mayford the new estates built on flat and relatively cheap agricultural land, just above the floodplain of the Wey, are prominent. This was an area of council housing and modest private houses, contrasting with the opulence of more attractive areas such as White Rose Lane and Hook Heath. The lyre-shaped estate in the centre right is the Woking Council estate at Quartermaine Avenue, Balfour Avenue and Campbell Avenue, where the roads were named after town councillors.

Trying hard to find land at a realistic price, and competing in a free market with developers and landowners who had no intention of selling for public housing, the local authority struggled to fulfil its statutory obligations. Its achievement was creditable, for between 1919 and 1939 a total of 785 council houses were built in Woking UDC. Accomplished in the face of persistent intransigence and exasperating inconsistency on the part of successive governments, the building of so many properties made a real difference by providing affordable dwellings for ordinary people in a district where low income groups were priced out of the housing market. By 1939 the town had a complex and contradictory social and economic structure – a place of very great wealth and acute poverty, of slum housing and large mansions, of overcrowding and three-acre gardens. It was not the bland, uniform dormitory town so often identified by outside observers.

81. *Higher density private building*

While very large houses in very large grounds were crucial to Woking's inter-war image (especially the one promoted by the estate agents) much of the development was more prosaic, with small semi-detached properties and piecemeal housing schemes. Typically these were situated at the edge of the existing built-up area, making use of vacant plots, smallholdings and deteriorating farmland. A firm would buy a couple of fields close to a road or sandwiched between existing properties, and then lay out a cul-de-sac estate road with plots delineated. If the developer was also a builder he would construct houses to a relatively standard design; if not, the plots might be sub-let to one or more local small builders, each with a different house design. Woking UDC and Chertsey RDC did not have planning powers to control such schemes, for as long as the land was zoned for development, and the designs conformed to the minimum building regulations, work could go ahead. As a result there was wasteful duplication of access and services, or roads did not join up or met at awkward junctions. The layout was rarely efficient and often presented an incoherent, untidy and piecemeal appearance. Though time and tree growth have often mellowed and softened the rawness, the

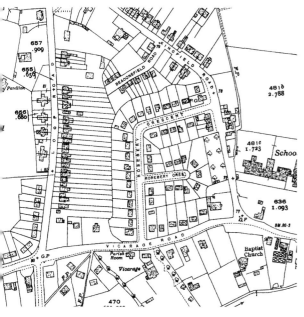

'bitty' character of some of these areas is very apparent.

In Old Woking the first new private development, a single row of semi-detached villas in Hipley Street, was built immediately after the First World War. The land had belonged to Fords Farm and during the 1920s and 1930s the remainder of this property, and most of the land of Kingfield, Shackleford and Howards Farms, was sold off piecemeal in small lots and used for speculative housing. Thus, the builders A. & J. Simmons Ltd of Old Woking bought a part of Shackleford Farm and across its fields built the 42 houses of Shackleford Road and the two flanking parades of shops at its junction with Kingfield Road. The land belonging to Kingfield Farm, an attractive early 19th-century house which still survives, was sold in the mid-1920s and ribbon development followed, with a line of detached houses and bungalows all the way from Kingfield Green to Elmbridge Green and along Tinkers Lane (which in 1928 was widened and rechristened, more marketably, Elmbridge Lane).

The lands of Horsell Grange were sold and broken up, to disappear beneath a sea of speculative housing. Wheatsheaf Close and Orchard Drive were built on its former orchards in 1934-9. Grove Barrs Farm was sold in 1929-32 and Meadway Drive, originally intended to become part of a Woking Western Bypass, was built across the area. In the middle of Horsell Common the large elliptical enclosure known as Roundabouts, carved out of

Kingfield saw rapid growth after 1890 as small farms were sold for development. This map extract (1934) shows that individual plots were sold off piecemeal, giving a typically fragmented plan (note too the way Beaconsfield Road occupies a small patch of former farmland, stopping dead at the edge of the erstwhile field). Rosebery Crescent has medium-sized detached houses of the 1920s but in Loop Road there are tiny detached or semi-detached 'villas' of the Edwardian period.

Making up Russell Road, Horsell, in the early 1930s: the photograph shows how housing estates were pushing out into the agricultural lands surrounding the old village centres.

the heathland sometime in the 16th century, was built over in 1936-8 by E. Hicks of Horsell and stands isolated to this day as the single street of houses called Common Close. Byfleet village, low-lying and near the noise of Brooklands, was not attractive to the developers of expensive housing and was much favoured by speculative builders because prices were correspondingly less. The land between Rectory Lane and Church Road was built over in the 1930s, filling in the formerly somewhat straggling shape of the village and erasing much of its rural and 'antiquated' character. Small estates included that at Clock House (1934), while Foxlake Road, Binfield Road and Hopfield Avenue were built on the land of Foxlake Farm. The names recall a genuine rural past which disappeared just before the Second World War; but that of the 'Summermeades' estate on Church Road, in contrast, was a publicity label dreamed up by a late 1930s estate agent to convey an image of rural tranquillity – ironically, the very quality destroyed by its construction.

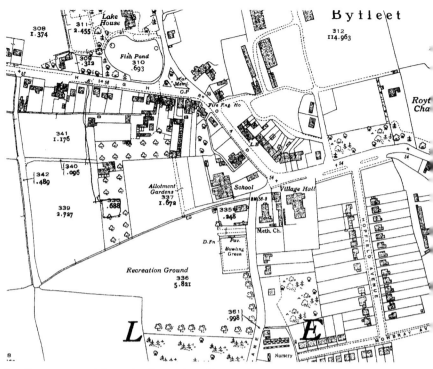

New housing estates and the old centre of Byfleet village, 1934.

During the late 1930s more ambitious projects began to emerge. The electrification of the railway line, the growing demand for relatively affordable housing in the Woking area, the sale of some more substantial farms, and the realisation that higher density building was potentially extremely profitable for the developer, combined to encourage 'estate' development of the sort which was very typical of this part of Surrey between 1935 and 1939 and again from 1952 to the mid-1960s. Such projects could only be undertaken by larger firms and this marks the beginning of the trend whereby housebuilding was increasingly undertaken by major contractors, regional or even national in their scope. In June 1934 Woking Council approved 183 houses and six shops as the first stage in the development of the Hermitage Woods Estate. The Hermitage, an attractive 18th-century mansion, was demolished in 1935 and building started in 1937. It was completed, to a different plan, in the mid-1950s. Davis Estates Limited built a large development of detached houses at a relatively high density in 1932-7 on the site of Woking Lodge, immediately south of the railway in Oriental Road.

The Hermitage, St John's: this watercolour of 1824, by John Hassell, shows the elegant 18th-century house demolished in 1935 to make way for the huge Hermitage estate, one of the largest residential developments of inter-war Woking (though not finished until the early 1960s). The house was on the site of a medieval building said to have belonged to the Dominican friary of Guildford.

The construction of 73 houses in Floyds Lane, Pyrford, was begun in 1936 and in the next year Councillor Griffin received permission to build 93 houses at Winern Glebe in Byfleet. In 1938 Councillor Tarrant, a building contractor who in the 1920s and early 1930s had the contracts for most council housing constructed by Woking UDC, was authorised to develop 12 acres in the Coldharbour area of Pyrford. In the same year the Council gave outline approval for the Pyrford Woods estate, with over 600 houses in total. This, one of Woking's largest housing developments, was not built until the 1950s because of the 13-year break caused by the war and the period of austerity. The largest inter-war scheme to be completed was at Rydens Way, on the site of the medieval Woking Town Field. It included 440 houses and a row of shops, with plans put forward in the mid-1930s for another 250 houses, more shops and a cinema. In a classic instance of what was later regarded as bad 1930s design, the estate was to be built around a new road which was to be part of a dual carriageway from central Woking to the A3 at Ripley. A wide central reservation was left for the new road, with narrow service roads beside it. Today, three quarters of a century later, the road has never been built. At the east end a grassed strip marks its line, while at the west the service roads fade into the unmade track of Stockers Lane – but along Kingfield Road and as far as Turnoak roundabout the wide grass verges still mark the space which was reserved for a dual carriageway back in the early 1930s.

82. The exclusive estates

The image of Woking as a fashionable residential area was developing by the late 1880s, and land speculators and developers were quick to exploit the financial attractions which it offered. The first low-density estates were being developed from the early 1890s and, though the process was abruptly cut short by the outbreak of the First World War, it resumed with even greater effect in the early 1920s. Improvements in rail services added to the attraction of the area and between the wars much of the poor quality agricultural land was sold for building. Paradoxically the reasons why the land was so poor for farming – sandy soil, steep slopes and rough wooded character – were precisely those which made it ideal for expensive housing. Fine views from the edges of Hook Heath and Pyrford across to the Downs, the abundance of heather and pines, and the lack of existing development all contributed to the special atmosphere of these districts. Five main areas attracted low-density development (defined in planning documents of the time as an average of four houses per acre or less): Hook Heath, Bridley and Fox Corner; Pyle Hill and Prey Heath; Heathside-Maybury Hill; Kettlewell and Woodham; and West Byfleet-Pyrford.

The earliest inter-war estate was The Hockering, south of the existing high-quality housing of Park Road and Pembroke Road dating from the 1860s onwards. The Hockering was promoted by the owners of the land, the Smallpeice family of Kingfield House who were prominent local businessmen, politicians, solicitors and farmers throughout the 19th century. The family originated in Norfolk in the 17th century and their new estate was named after the village of the ancestors, Hockering near Norwich. In 1904 they laid out four estate roads with suitably charming 'rural' names: Hockering Road,

A superb aerial view of Woking town centre and Horsell in 1947: at the bottom of the picture is Horsell Common with Common Close, a double row of detached houses, isolated in the middle of the heath. The farmland of Kettlewell and the Wheatsheaf Common area has partly disappeared under new estates of the 1930s (though more development would take place around Woodham Road in the 1950s and '60s). Horsell village is in the top right of the view, fringed by many small residential streets which had been built in the previous half century. In the town the large empty space on the north side of Commercial Road, the first stage in the project for the redevelopment of the centre, is prominent.

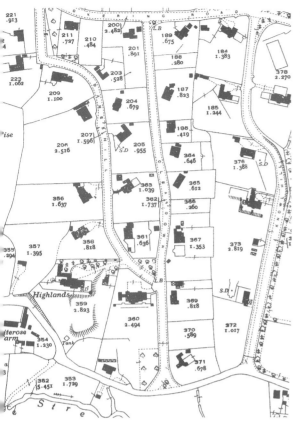

Cleardown, Daneshill and Knowl Hill curved gently down the slope of the Hoe valley towards White Rose Lane. Some 107 plots, totalling 130 acres, were marked out 'for the erection of high class residences' and, though little had been achieved by 1914, every plot had been sold by 1925. Individual purchasers commissioned architects to design houses to their particular specifications and this, together with the lavishly generous landscaping of verges, trees and shrubs, meant that there was no uniformity or predictability. Instead, a secluded and exclusive environment was created. Today the maturing of the landscape during eighty and more years has produced a superb visual impression, perfectly in accord with the original concept.

The 67-acre Woodham Hall estate, on the edge of Horsell Common and conveniently next door to the New Zealand Golf Club, was sold in 1932. Gravelled roads were constructed, curving among the trees and named in an appropriately exclusive fashion – The Gateway and The Riding are typical of the time and place, while the final 'e' of Woodham Waye exemplifies the self-conscious mock-rurality of 1930s' developers. The estate was built up between 1935 and 1955. The remaining plots of Dartnell Park were developed during the 1920s, while north of the railway 54 acres of Sheerwater Farm were sold in 1925 and marketed as the Old Avenue estate, on what had hitherto been useless waterlogged scrub. Trees screened the estate from the railway line, but the developers could never have envisaged that after 1948 the large London County Council overspill estate at Sheerwater would abut their expensive project. The result is that today one of the most deprived wards in southern England, Sheerwater, directly adjoins one of the least deprived, West Byfleet, a contrast among the most dramatic in any English town.

Golf played a prominent part in the marketing of many of these expensive properties. In the western half of Woking, where golf courses are thicker on the ground than in almost any other part of the country (they occupy about 30 per cent of the land area in the south-west quadrant of the borough), the intermingling of housing and 'the links' is especially marked. Hook Heath has its Golf Club Road and close to the Worplesdon boundary the significantly named Fairway estate was developed in the 1930s. Very large houses, set in extensive grounds, are approached by gravelled drives from large iron gates, the shrubberies and pines concealing the houses from the public gaze so that they are well-nigh invisible. John Betjeman, who knew the area intimately, captured the atmosphere perfectly in 'Pot Pourri from a Surrey Garden', with its references to the 'Conifer county of Surrey' in which the gardens were 'approached through remarkable wrought-iron gates'. In his poem the words 'pinewoods' and 'rhododendrons' are powerful symbols for a landscape … while the town achieves its poetic immortality with the reference to the Old Malvernian brother of Pam, the super-healthy tennis-playing heroine. Even he, who plays for Woking, cannot stand up to her backhand drive.

Part of the Hockering estate, 1934: this map can be contrasted with those of Knaphill (p.148) and Kingfield (p.152) to emphasise the exceptionally low densities of building in this exclusive part of the town. The houses were individually designed by qualified architects (in areas such as Kingfield, off-the-peg standard plans were used) and therefore no property has the same layout as any other.

83. Local government since 1920

In 1929 the government instructed every county council to review the pattern of local authorities within its area, the aim being to achieve that ever-elusive goal of 'increased efficiency' by abolishing small councils. Each local authority was asked by Surrey County Council to state its preferred option for the future and the result in north-west Surrey was a scramble for survival and territorial gain. Naturally, no authority wanted to disappear and all sought to extend their boundaries. Chertsey Rural District, with its awkward division into three separate portions, was bound to be the loser and the county had already

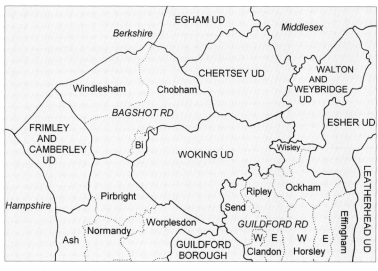

Local government in north-west Surrey, 1933-1974.

made this clear in 1928. Woking Council decided that it would like to annex Bisley, Pirbright, Send, Ripley, Pyrford and the Woodham area (but not Byfleet), while other councils – Weybridge, Walton on Thames, and Chertsey, cast eager eyes upon Byfleet. Only Chertsey wanted Pyrford. In 1930 the county proposed that Chertsey Rural District be shared out among the neighbouring urban districts. Woking would expand to include Bisley, Chobham village, Pyrford and Woodham, while Byfleet would go to a new Walton and Weybridge authority. So strong were the protests from the rural inhabitants of the Chobham area that the county backtracked and in 1931 proposed that Woking Urban District would annex Woodham, Pyrford and West Byfleet, splitting Byfleet parish along the Wey Navigation and giving Byfleet village to Walton and Weybridge.

That, too, caused howls of anguish. When in March 1933 the scheme went ahead Byfleet east of the River Wey was joined to Walton & Weybridge and Woking obtained a small piece of Bisley where the boundary at Knaphill had run through gardens, but most important was the inclusion of the rest of Byfleet and all of Pyrford with Woking. Apart from a minor readjustment at Byfleet in 1936 the boundaries of the urban district as fixed then have remained the same ever since. In 1930 Woking UDC had been granted a coat of arms and a motto, *Fide et Diligentia* (By Faith and Diligence), while generous private donors paid for a badge and chain of office for its chairman. Thus dignified, the next step for the newly enlarged authority was to seek a charter of incorporation as a borough. In 1933 a petition to King George V asked him to grant this privilege, but it was rejected on the grounds that the old and new parts of the district needed to develop closer links – a curious reason, given that a number of newly amalgamated authorities elsewhere in the country were given borough status in these years. The Council was told to try again in 1942, but then there were other things to think about. In 1955, when the population had topped 50,000 (larger than several fully independent county boroughs) a request for incorporation was once again turned down. Woking was unfairly treated. Faith was needed to keep trying, diligence to prepare the case, but it brought no rewards until 1974 when, at local government reorganisation, the Borough of Woking was created. Since then the only significant change to the local government in the borough was the restoration of a parish council for Byfleet in 1990, after an interval of 57 years. This was a recognition of the fact that Byfleet, the easternmost part of the borough, was in a sense semi-detached, the construction of the M25 having given it a degree of separateness which made it a special case. In 2003, though, the future of the parish council is subject to question.

84. *Unworthy meeting places*

The Woking Local Board, formed in 1893, met in any building where there was room for hire – in two months that autumn its members deliberated at the Goldsworth Public Hall, the *Temperance Hotel* and the Masonic Hall. In March 1894, just before it was replaced by the urban district council, it took a longer-term lease on chambers above Ashby's Bank on the corner of Broadway and Chertsey Road. The new Woking UDC decided to build proper council offices – the idea of a town hall, a building which might have had a greater dignity and given some impressive architecture to an indifferent town centre, was never contemplated because financial restraint was the rule. Indeed, although the Council bought a site in Commercial Road for its offices and approved a design in 1897, the scheme was abandoned after public protests – the councillors who had voted for the office scheme had rejected only weeks before the purchase of a fire engine on expenditure grounds. Hypocrisy was said to be in the air … then in 1899 the bank buildings, still in use as a temporary HQ, were burned to the ground and there was no fire engine to save them. 'Nemesis and retribution', cried those who had campaigned for a modern fire brigade, as the Council shifted to cramped rooms over Jobson's shop at 13 Broadway.

The office scheme went ahead, and in March 1906 the Council met for the first time in its new building opposite the junction of High Street and Commercial Road. The cost, £4,500, represented a worthy desire to save the ratepayers' money by constructing a building which, though attractive in appearance, was small and unambitious. Time – a short time – proved that it was in fact excessively small: within a decade much of the work was being conducted from prefabs and sheds erected in the rear yard and less than thirty years after the offices opened a report described their 'inadequacy and inconvenience … their appalling overcrowding … congested, uncomfortable and inefficient'. Chertsey RDC had a local surveyor's office at West Byfleet since 1908, but otherwise was administered from Chertsey town. In 1927 it finally decided to provide offices within its area, and bought Oakfield School, West Byfleet. In July 1928 it opened under its new guise but only five years later the authority was dissolved and the offices closed.

In 1935 Woking UDC, now enlarged to include Byfleet and Pyrford, took a lease on the first floor of the Grand Theatre in Commercial Road to house the Town Planning Department, but by this time it was contemplating a completely new civic centre, with a range of public buildings including a town hall and library. The site was to be in the vicinity of Commercial Road and

The new Woking Urban District Council Offices, in Commercial Road, under construction 8 July 1905.

The Council Offices c.1950, with Sparrow Park on the right: the attractive and modest offices built in the Edwardian period were soon outdated and by the early 1950s several abortive schemes for a replacement had been put forward. The favoured option was a new civic centre in Guildford Road, between York Road and Mount Hermon Road, but eventually new civic buildings were made a visual focus of the town centre redevelopment in the 1970s.

Percy Street. Knowing that this would take some years to come to fruition the Council leased three large detached houses between York Road, Mount Hermon Road and Guildford Road and in 1939 most of the council's departments moved their offices to the new temporary location. Forty years later they were still there, in a motley collection of Edwardian houses, post-war prefabs, timber sheds and 1960s huts. Only in 1982, when the new civic offices were at last built as part of the redevelopment of the central area, did Woking finally acquire an administrative focus which was architecturally worthy and had the dignity and style appropriate to the town.

85. Councillors and officials

The vestries which governed the parishes of Woking until the late 19th century were mostly composed of farmers, landowners, tradesmen and – nominally at least – local worthies such as clergy and members of important families. Only ratepayers could vote or stand for election, so working men had no role in the parish government and a few powerful figures tended to dominate proceedings. Thus, Edward Ryde of Poundfield House, Woking village, was a member of the Woking vestry for over thirty years, exercised a strong influence within the Woking School Board from 1874 to 1888, and chaired *ad hoc* local meetings on subjects ranging from the proposed gasworks, via flooding at Broadmead, to the widening of White Rose Lane and the establishment of a Local Board. As early as 1853 Ryde was advising local people about the proposals of the Necropolis Company, and in 1891 he was petitioning for a proper system of local government in the parish. His close friend, George Smallpeice of Kingfield House, like him a landowner and farmer, was heavily involved in property development, land speculation, commercial schemes such as the first plan for a gas company, and many other public activities. His granddaughter described him as 'a true English yeoman' but in reality he was an up-to-date late Victorian businessman, with an estate agency on Station Approach. He served on the Woking Vestry and School Board, and his brother Mark was clerk to the Board of Guardians of the Guildford Poor Law Union.

After 1893 things began to change. A democratically elected local board and (from 1895) urban district council was divided between the old guard, representing Woking village, Mayford, Sutton and Bridley, and the newcomers who lived in 'New' Woking, Maybury, St Johns and Knaphill. They felt aggrieved that in 1906 the Station and Maybury ward had 48 per cent of the population, contributed 53 per cent of the rate income, but had only 30 per cent of the councillors, who could be outvoted by the minority rural interest. In 1907 this imbalance was decisively altered, when on the amalgamation with Horsell the combined parishes were re-warded on a more equitable basis and thereafter the new elements ruled. Increasingly the leading figures on the Council were those who had business and commercial interests in the town (though they might live in the rural fringes). The first chairman of the Woking Local Board was William Hill Corrie (after whom Corrie Road in Old Woking is named), followed as chairman of the Woking UDC by Gustav Wermig, owner of Egley Nurseries. Of nine chairmen in 1895-1914, two were farmers or landowners, five were tradesmen, one was an architect and surveyor and one was a sanitary engineer. During the 1920s the rural interests gradually waned, though a new element appeared – former military officers who had retired to Woking (lieutenant-colonels chaired the council in 1927-9 and 1934-6). More typical, perhaps, was Henry Quartermaine, who was chairman in 1925-6 and 1930-2 and had a wide range of business activities – garage-owner, plumber, voluntary officer in the town's fire brigade, and entertainments entrepreneur (in 1903 he opened Woking's first cinema).

In 1919 Lady Betty Balfour became Woking's first woman councillor when she was elected for St Johns ward. Thereafter, until the Second World War, there was always one woman on the council but theirs was a quiet voice. Much louder was the vocal Woking Ratepayers Association. In 1928 this new organisation began to campaign in local elections and in 1929 won three seats, defeating a sitting councillor in each. By March 1930 the WRA, which sought to reduce council spending and cut back on expensive projects, had nine out of 22 council seats. After the reorganisation of local government in 1933 its influence waned, but its brief success hastened the politicisation of what had always been a non-political body.

In the parishes of Byfleet and Pyrford the rural interest, not unexpectedly, predominated for much longer. There were fewer controversies and issues which occasioned debate, and individual councillors could exercise greater influence or display greater apathy. One of Byfleet's representatives on the Chertsey Rural Sanitary Authority, Major Collis Browne, attended only one meeting in three years, yet William Shears of Lees Farm, the representative for Pyrford, was present at all but one sitting. When Chertsey Rural District Council was established in 1895 George Barron Holroyd was elected as one of the two Byfleet councillors. The village was already dominated by the Holroyd family, who owned the mill, the brewery, and much of the land. The electoral process increased this role. Holroyd was simultaneously elected to the parish council and in 1897 became its chairman, a position held without a break for the next 22 years during which time he also served several terms as chairman of the rural district council. This might suggest a feudal regime, but in fact Byfleet Parish Council was comparatively progressive, involving itself in street-lighting, sanitary improvements, the provision of recreational facilities and, after 1918, campaigning for housing and environmental improvements.

Councillors were only part of the story. They made the decisions, but the preparation and implementation of policies were the responsibility of the officials, the guiding hands in all local government activity. The driving force behind the agitation to gain urban status for Woking in the 1880s and early 1890s was Robert Mossop, a solicitor of Goldsworth Road who owned land in Kingfield and Woking village. He represented the vestry at public inquiries and acquired an extensive and intimate knowledge of local government in general and Woking and its problems in particular. When his campaigns bore fruit with the creation of the Woking Local Board in 1893 he was appointed as clerk to the board and 18 months later became the first clerk of Woking Urban District Council. He held the post until his death in 1934, a tenure of almost 34 years during which he, more than any other man, was responsible for guiding the town council through its difficult formative years. More importantly, it was he who pursued the policies by which the inadequacies of the Victorian legacy were gradually tackled, striving to raise standards, create the conditions for civilised urban living, and prepare the plans for more substantial improvements which would produce a better town. He has no memorial, and no street is named after him, but the councillors knew his worth, recording on his death 'their deep appreciation of the service which [he] rendered to the town for so long a period; they will remember with gratitude the conspicuous ability with which he, as Chief Administrative Officer, conducted the business of the Council, his guidance, sound judgement and urbanity'.

From the late 1920s some councillors began to use political labels (usually Conservative) and after 1945 this became standard. A few Independents were still being elected in the 1950s and 1960s (though their voting record shows that they had Conservative perspectives), Labour councillors were elected for several wards in the same period, partly because of the development of the overwhelmingly Labour-voting Sheerwater, and at the first post-war election in 1945 there was, remarkably, a Communist victory in Woking Village and Mayford. More recently, Woking's political complexion has altered significantly. The Conservative pre-eminence was gradually eroded during the 1970s as the Liberal party enjoyed a modest revival, and in the 1980s (when they had become the Liberal Democrats) this led to the loss of Conservative control. For over twenty years Woking has had a 'hung' council in which Conservative and Liberal Democrat representation is roughly balanced alongside a small Labour group. After the 2003 borough elections the political make-up was Conservative 17, Liberal Democrat 12, Labour 6 and Independent 1. In parliamentary elections the Conservative candidate has been returned at every general election since Woking became a separate constituency in 1945, and during the 1960s and 1970s Woking was one of the safest Conservative seats in the country. Here, too, the absolute dominance of the Conservative Party has been reduced of late, and in the 1997 general election Woking recorded the greatest percentage fall in the Conservative vote (down by 20.2 per cent) of any English constituency except the special case of Tatton in Cheshire. The Conservatives still won, but compared with the huge surpluses of thirty years ago their majority was but small.

86. Streets and roads

Before 1914 local authorities in the area were already expressing concern about the impact of motor vehicles, which were causing noise, danger and, in dry weather, enormous clouds of dust. Street-watering was used to lay the dust in Horsell and Byfleet villages during the summer months as early as 1905, and in 1906 Chertsey Rural District Council tried unsuccessfully to have a 10 m.p.h. speed limit enforced in Byfleet, 'where the road is very narrow and winding and also [has] a considerable number of people moving about'. After 1910 Woking and Chertsey Councils began tarring road surfaces: the former contracted to buy 15,000 gallons of liquid tar each year from the Woking gasworks and sprayed it onto the roads in the district. The tar mixed with the dust and gravel to form a thin crust which quickly broke up under the weight of larger vehicles but was a good deal better than nothing. In urban areas the councils made concerted efforts to provide decent road surfaces to replace the ruts and dirt and by 1914 most of the roads in Woking town and the villages were comparatively respectable.

In the '20s attention began to turn towards road improvements, as heavier volumes of traffic, higher speeds, and growing congestion produced public demands for 'better' roads. Most schemes were small, but their cumulative effect made a major difference to the appearance of the district as well as to the state of the roads themselves. Pre-1930 photographs show how narrow some of the main roads were, and how tight the bends before improvement.

Woking UDC widened Hermitage Road in St Johns as an unemployment relief project in 1921-2 and the following year culverted the delightful watersplash on Saunders Lane in Crastock. The next stage was to plan for completely new roads and in 1928 a variety of schemes, canvassed over the previous five years, were included in the Regional Planning Scheme for North West Surrey. Some were built, though none for many years. The Byfleet Loop Road was approved in 1928 and land acquisition began at once, but the road was not completed until 1962. The diversion of the main Guildford road from Mayford Green to Pyle Hill was not implemented until 1983 and – largest and most important of all – the plan for a new road between Staines, Chertsey, Byfleet and Leatherhead, the South Orbital Road which eventually became the M25, was drawn up in 1929 and not finished until the mid-1980s. Most other schemes listed in 1928 remained on the drawing board and have now been dropped or postponed so far into the future as to be discountable: for example, the Woking Western Bypass (from Turnoak Corner to Horsell Common), the Old Woking Bypass, and the link from Woking to the A3 at Ripley.

LEFT *The sylvan setting of the watersplash on Saunders Lane, near the junction with Blackhorse Road. The stream, the Corsebrook, was culverted in 1923 as a Council unemployment relief scheme and another bit of historic Woking landscape disappeared.*

BELOW *In the mid-1930s Woking Council began to give serious consideration to town centre redevelopment. At the same time it faced growing demands for the provision of a car park in* the town. Combining these two needs, it bought up properties on the north side of Commercial Road and cleared them to make a temporary car park, anticipating that within a few years redevelopment would begin. This view shows the houses (only about sixty years old) in the course of demolition in the summer of 1936. The car park in fact survived for almost forty years, as war, economic constraints, and planning difficulties led to successive redevelopment schemes being delayed or abandoned.*

By 1939 signs of the modern age were everywhere apparent. Woking UDC completed its first 'traffic circus' at the dangerous staggered Turnoak crossroads in the autumn of 1934 – in some ways, odd though it might seem, Turnoak roundabout is as important historically as the 17th-century house a few hundred yards along Guildford road. The roundabout at the Six Crossroads was not completed until 1963 though planned at the same time. Also in 1934, the first of many one-way systems was introduced in the town centre in an attempt to reduce congestion, and Woking Council's first public car park, between Victoria Arch and Goldsworth Road bus station, was laid out in the same year. Many of us remember it more for its Saturday duty, when it served as a makeshift market place. Just before the Second World War the Council was planning a major remodelling of roads in the town centre, with Commercial Road destined to be widened to a dual carriageway. Many of the properties on the north side of the road had been bought and demolished for this purpose, their sites forming a second 'temporary' car park. After the war the road scheme was dropped and the ugly tarmac car park remained until redevelopment of the centre in the mid-1970s.

87. *Leisure and recreation*

During the 1890s, as Woking town grew rapidly, there was a growing awareness of the need for public open space, because of the loss of common rights, enclosure of heathland, and extensive development of fields and commons. In 1854 the vicar of Woking had fought successfully for the exclusion of St Johns Lye from the enclosure and development plans of the Necropolis Company. This land, though nominally intended for grazing and turf-cutting by the ordinary people of the area, became a public open space. Its management was taken over by the Woking Local Board in 1893 and bye-laws were passed to regulate its use for recreation, though as late as 1928 the council had to threaten legal action after pigs, owned by a nearby 'cottager', had wrought havoc by grubbing and furrowing the grassed area of the Lye, while in 1926 a resident had cut turf on the Lye, allegedly in the belief that the ancient commoners' rights had not been extinguished. In 1901 the death of Queen Victoria prompted calls for the Council to provide a park as a memorial to her late Majesty, but it chose instead to endow the cottage hospital. Rather belatedly in 1904 a

Removing the war memorial from Sparrow Park, 1975: the memorial had been constructed in the little park in 1922, but as part of the central redevelopment scheme it was relocated to the new and much more fitting location as the centrepiece of the new Town Square.

very small garden with trees and shrubs was laid out at the junction of High Street and Commercial Road. Known to generations colloquially as Sparrow Park (perhaps not only for its ornithological life but also for its diminutive size), this still of course exists, though the war memorial which was erected there in 1923 has since been moved to the more appropriate location of Town Square.

In 1902 the Suburban Land Corporation, the development company which had bought most of the Hillview estate, offered to sell the council 23 acres on

Bowls on a summer evening in Woking Park, 1958: the park was laid out between 1905 and 1911 and fifty years later its landscaping had matured splendidly. In the last thirty years it has suffered (as have parks in many other towns) from the loss of original features such as pavilions, and the intrusion of car parks and new leisure facilities, but more recently the tide has turned and there have been welcome improvements and some restoration of older elements of the design.

the southern side of its property as a recreation ground. The sale was completed in December 1904 and the following summer the Council approved a surprisingly ambitious design for an attractive park. The site was excellent, with south-facing hill-slopes giving an interestingly varied topography, the Hoe Stream close to the southern edge, and convenient access from the town centre. The new park was largely completed by 1914, with a formal rose garden, sports ground, tennis courts, bowling green, children's playground and terrace walks. The avenues of horse chestnuts and limes were planted in 1910-11: then they were unimpressive, but today, having matured magnificently, they are among the outstanding features of a particularly good example of a small Edwardian municipal park. Woking Council and its predecessors may not always have had much imagination in the early 20th century but in the design and construction of the park they did an excellent job, a worthy legacy to future generations.

A swimming pool was opened beside the Hoe Stream in 1910, a primitive timber-lined rectangle, 40 by 100 feet, supplied with water direct from the river (health and safety regulations were hardly known then!), but as the adjacent meadows were being used as the town's refuse dump there was always a certain unsavouriness about the locality. In 1920 the first stage of the tip was closed and it was covered over with topsoil and landscaped as an unemployment relief scheme. Rhododendrons, trees and shrubs were given by an anonymous donor and two ponds, with water plants and wildfowl, were created beside the river. They are still there today, one recently cleaned out and improved, the other a wet swampy area which is now a local nature reserve and wildfowl refuge – a nice turn of fate that the former council tip should have been thus transformed. In 1927 the whole area was officially renamed Woking Park. A new open-air swimming pool was built in fashionable ferro-concrete 'lido-style' in 1935, floating on a raft of concrete because fifty years of Woking's household refuse did not provide a solid foundation. This was where several generations of Woking children learned to swim, braving the icy waters at 8 a.m. for lessons … but now all is gone, replaced by the splendours of the Pool in the Park with its warmth, tropical atmosphere and floor to ceiling glass, a far cry from the timber box of 1910. Who in the future, though, will remember the ill-fated Centre Pools, opened in 1975 as the symbol of the brave new world and demolished only 17 years later?

Elsewhere in the district local parks were provided in the years before the First World War. Horsell parish vestry laid out a small recreation ground on the edge of the common opposite the *Wheatsheaf* in 1893 – there had been cricket pitches here since at least 1870. In 1910 Woking Council took over the management of the recreation ground and in 1921, as another of its

unemployment relief schemes designed to benefit the community as a whole, extended the park. At Boundary Road the common alongside the canal was levelled and grassed as a public amenity in stages between 1903 and 1910, providing a much-needed open space for the densely populated Walton Road area. This land was a favoured location for fairs and circuses, recalling its earlier 19th-century reputation as the haunt of gypsies, tinkers and travelling folk. The four-acre Knaphill recreation ground was constructed in 1921-2 and in the following year the Necropolis Company, in a moment of aberration, gave a further acre as a gift. In 1924 Anthony Waterer, of the famous nurserying family, bequeathed almost 15 acres at Lower Knaphill to Woking Council for use as a public open space and over the next three years the Council laid out Waterers Park on the site.

Byfleet recreation ground was constructed by the parish council in 1899-1905, on land leased from the Byfleet United Charities. It was extended in 1921-3 following generous gifts from two local landowners, Henry Locke King and Charles Charrington of Broad Oaks, and in 1936 Woking Council made further improvements. In 1912 the parish council also took a lease of 12 acres in Camphill Road from the United Charities, part of the land allotted to the poor in the early 19th-century enclosure of Byfleet parish. During the First World War it was used for allotments and in 1921, after suggestions that it should remain as such were turned down, a recreation ground was opened. By 1939, therefore, recreational facilities had been provided in all the main built-up areas of the district. The remaining heaths – especially Horsell Common – offered a much more extensive 'natural' open space, and the importance of the parks and recreation grounds was clear ... but Woking Council in 1939 was seriously considering whether, if building on the agricultural areas of the district continued unchecked, it might not have to buy up areas of land along the riversides, the more attractive hillslopes and the woodlands of the area in order to save them from housing development and maintain them as a public amenity.

88. Population in the inter-war years

The population grew steadily between the wars as the tide of building spread across fields and former heaths. The overall rate of increase between 1911 and 1951 was 66 per cent, representing an extra 20,000 inhabitants, but the rate was not evenly spread geographically. By far the fastest growth during this period was in the Woking Village and Mayford ward, where the population increased by 248 per cent. This area not only saw a substantial amount of private housebuilding but, more importantly, the development of the larger inter-war council estates in Westfield and Old Woking. In contrast St Johns grew by only 10 per cent in this period, largely because of a major exodus in population between 1918 and 1930 as occupancy of the barracks and asylum fell. Service families moved out to newer barracks in areas such as Deepcut and Pirbright, beyond the Woking boundary, but the civilian population showed no such reduction and after 1931 St Johns was growing as fast as the town as a whole.

There was, however, an accelerating decline in the population of Chertsey Road and Goldsworth wards, both of which lost over 10 per cent of their inhabitants in 1921-51. These areas accounted for the bulk of the low value working-class housing in the town, and they reached their peak population in 1921. Decline then set in and has continued to the present day, as population was displaced by a combination of slum clearance, voluntary migration from inner urban areas, and the extension of the commercial and retailing area at the expense of housing. Dwellings were being converted to shops, workshops and offices, and piecemeal demolition took place in areas such as Commercial Road, West Street and Church Street. The inner ends of Maybury, Walton, Guildford and Chertsey Roads, which had been residential, were taken over by commercial uses. It is especially striking that this pattern of 'inner city' decline was that found in large industrial and old-established towns across the country, but Woking was only seventy years old when the process got under way. It had been an empty heath in 1840, a booming new town in 1870, and by 1920 was clearly showing signs of inner urban decay and decline – the entire cycle was telescoped into a few decades. Walton Road, indeed, was still being built up only twenty years before its downward spiral began.

The Maybury and Mount Hermon ward also grew slowly between the wars. It had been largely developed by 1925 with expensive low-density housing and there was little scope for continued expansion. That it would eventually become one of the fastest growing parts of the district was the result of what few foresaw – the trend towards high-density redevelopment in the 1960s. Sutton and Bridley ward saw little growth between the wars, because it was relatively remote and had no mains drainage, while areas such as the Sutton Place estate, Bridley Manor and the golf courses were unlikely to be developed in the near future. However, the plans of the late 1920s anticipated that in due course most of this, the most rural and in visual terms the most attractive part of the district, would be developed at low densities. In Horsell, too, substantial areas were excluded from development pressure because they were commonland, but during the 1930s this was the fastest growing ward within the urban district as the rapid sale of smaller farms and building estates on the east side of the village and towards Woodham led to a flood of new housing.

89. Shops and traders 1840-1940

Before the growth of the new town the villages of Woking, Byfleet, Horsell and Knaphill were served by a wide variety of retailers and craftsmen providing for local needs. Of Woking village, with its semi-urban character and larger population, Brayley noted in 1840 that it had 'two good inns, and several respectable shops' (the latter term implying more than just the usual village store) though Edward Ryde recalled that in this period 'the tradesmen's houses and shops were all of the smaller kind'. The village had its weekly market until the late 1830s, and the annual fair survived into the 1870s. The following table shows the numbers employed in trades and crafts in 1851. It is clear that Woking village (including Shackleford and Kingfield) was the main 'shopping centre', serving Send and parts of Pyrford as well as the southern and eastern parts of its own parish. Knaphill was the local centre for Bisley, west Horsell and south Chobham.

Employment in retailing and crafts in 1851					
	Byfleet	Horsell	Pyrford	Woking village	Knaphill	rest of Woking
baker	2	3		5	2	1
butcher	1	1		4	1	2
corn-dealer	4			1	1	
draper				2	1	
general stores				2		
grocer	3	4	3	10	4	4
hotel and inn staff	3	4	1	5	3	5
blacksmith	5	4	2	6	3	3
bricklayer	5	1		4	1	2
carpenter	7	7		9	3	4
cordwainer	3	1		6	3	1
painter/glazier		1		1		
plumber				3		
shoemaker		2		5	2	1
tailor/tailoress	4	1		18	6	3
wheelwright	3	1		6	2	1
TOTAL	**40**	**30**	**6**	**87**	**32**	**27**

There were many specialised trades, flourishing at a time when mass production was not a serious threat. Byfleet had five broom-makers and a whip-maker, there were saddlers in Woking village and Horsell, and Woking had a coach-builder, two milliners, a pump-maker, a rope-spinner, a bookseller and a yeast-dealer. In 1851 an oyster-dealer was living at Kingfield, an unexpected trade so far from the sea but perhaps explained by the fact that discarded oyster-shells were a source of lime for agricultural purposes. By 1871 there is evidence of diversification as the population grew and new fashions appeared: Woking village by then had two chemists, an egg-dealer, a poulterer, a hairdresser and a photographer, together with a basket-maker, two farriers, a staymaker, an upholsterer and a well-digger, while Horsell had an umbrella-

Chobham Road, Woking, in about 1900, looking north from the junction with Commercial Road: on the left is J.F. Gammon's store, for many years a well-known landmark and familiar to those of us 'of a certain age' who lived in Woking before the early 1970s. The view demonstrates the essentially modest and unambitious character of the shopping centre which had grown during the previous thirty years.

maker. Altogether, in 1851 the crafts and trades employed 272 people in the four parishes, or 10.5 per cent of the total workforce. The relative importance of this sector, and the different status of the various communities, had not radically changed since the early 18th century. By the early 1860s, though, the growth of New Woking was dramatically altering the pattern.

The Necropolis Company abdicated any responsibility for the provision of a shopping centre with adequate facilities and amenities. The earliest shops and commercial premises in the new town arose haphazardly and the result was a ramshackle shopping centre, where houses were swiftly and unsatisfactorily converted to shops and with inadequate provision for service yards and storage. The buildings were 'mean and joyless' and there was no possibility, given the lack of effective local government, of building grand and impressive central streets. The first retail premises, apart from the *Railway Hotel* of 1840 and the *Albion* of 1856, was the coal and timber yard owned by Reuben Percy of the *Albion*, but in 1870 the *Surrey Advertiser* noted that

> 66 Mr. Wells, who has recently erected a pretty line of houses near the station, [is] to convert them into shops … [he] has determined to meet the more pressing wants of the district, by erecting in the first place shops for the business of a butcher and a draper … At present railway employees and others have to go to Guildford for meat and other articles of consumption. 99

Thus, houses which had only just been completed were hastily converted into shops. The row in question was in High Street, facing the railway embankment between Church Path and what became Chapel Street. The 1871 census shows that these were occupied by (from the station end) the Post Office, a grocer, a carpenter, a butcher, a draper and milliner, another carpenter and a builder. The emphasis upon construction trades in a place where a town was mushrooming is not unexpected and was repeated elsewhere. Providence

Street (later Church Street) was being developed and its residents included a carpenter and joiner and two blacksmiths, while Ellen Street (West Street) had a bricklayer, a gardener, two smiths, two carpenters and a bootmaker. By the mid-1870s the future of the rising new town was assured and Woking village, hitherto the most important shopping centre, was destined to become a backwater. A sure sign was the move in 1876 of Glosters the corn-merchants from the Market House, Woking village, to new premises near the station in Chertsey Road, grandly styled 'The Corn Exchange'. The firm took a pardonable, though not entirely accurate, pride in advertising itself as 'the oldest business in the trade of Old Woking and the first in New Woking'. Henry Gloster, a prominent local businessman who was Woking's county councillor in the 1890s and chairman of the urban district council in 1904-05, saw the way the future lay.

By the end of the century there was a wide variety of shops and the centre had a genuinely urban character. Many names familiar to older Wokingians had appeared by this time, though the redevelopments after 1970 saw the end of most of these older businesses. In the 1899 directory are listed, among others, Boormans the carriage-builders of Guildford Road; Tylers, the wine merchants of Chertsey Road; Albert Pocock, tobacconist of Chertsey Road; Maxwell's music shop in Maybury Road and Broadway; James Gammon, draper at the corner of Chobham Road and Commercial Road; and Skeet's ironmongery which in 1901 amalgamated with Jeff's to form the well-known partnership. At this time most businesses were small and family-run, and only three shops were owned by chains based outside the area: the International

Chertsey Road, Woking, c.1905: this was the main shopping street of the town until the 1950s, when the increasing commercialisation of Commercial Road began to challenge its supremacy. The upper end of Chertsey Road near the station, and the immediately adjacent length of Broadway, were the only parts of the town centre where substantial purpose-built shops and business premises were constructed.

Commercial Road in 1928, looking east from Church Path: Gammon's store is on the left, beyond the World's Stores, which was shortly to be demolished and replaced by Commercial Buildings (the cleared site for which can be seen behind the gas-lamp). The redevelopment of the site was the first modern element in the shopping centre, a harbinger of more dramatic changes planned for the late 1930s but never brought to fruition, and of small-scale redevelopment schemes in Commercial Road before the Second World War.

In Woking, as in most other towns, names which had been familiar for several generations disappeared in the 1970s as a result of redevelopment, escalating rent levels, and the much greater power of the big name multiples and chains. Even firms which had arrived relatively recently, such as Aerco, succumbed to the pressures of renewal and changing shopping patterns (this advertisement dates from 1968). Instead, today there are giant multiples such as the Virgin Megastore.

Tea Company, the Home & Colonial Stores, and Freeman, Hardy & Willis. More typical was Mrs Gunning's shop at 3 The Pavement, Chertsey Road, which sold 'art needlework of all kinds, fancy goods, plain & fancy stationery in the latest designs, well assorted stock of bibles, prayer books, toys in great variety'. In the villages the old-fashioned all-purpose grocers' shops recalled a vanishing way of life: William Lucas of Byfleet advertised his business as 'grocer, draper & stationer' selling 'books and shoes in great variety; patent medecines [sic] & garden seeds'. There was even a red-light district: in September 1888 Charlotte Goodall was sentenced to three months' hard labour for keeping a brothel in Church Street, Woking.

Chertsey Road became the main shopping street, partly because it was the busiest street in the town and ran directly from the railway station. High Street could never quite live up to its name because it had only one side – the other being the railway embankment – although by 1914 it was entirely given over to shopping and other business uses. The east side of Chertsey Road was not developed until after 1885, by which time it was clear that shops, not housing, was the most appropriate use for the land. There was thus the chance to construct purpose-built shops, banks and offices. It had the few 'multiple' stores as well as Ashby's Bank of 1888 and the Capital and Counties Bank on the prominent corner opposite the station and the Albion. Chobham Road, as another busy thoroughfare, also acquired a range of shops but until 1914 there were very few in either Church Street or (despite its optimistic name) Commercial Road. Although by that date other well-known local names had arrived, such as Elton's the 'Bookseller; Librarian; Stationer; and Printer' at 42 Chertsey Road and Hugh Harris, men's outfitter at the corner of Chapel Street and High Street, there was also further evidence of the rise of the chain store. Timothy White had opened at 24 Chertsey Road, Lipton's at 1 Chobham Road, and the International Tea Company had opened branches in Knaphill and West Byfleet.

The Woking, Horsell and District Co-operative Society was founded by local trade unionists in 1899 and opened a shop at the junction of Percy Street and Church Street in 1902. Between then and 1920 it flourished, with the

original shop trebling in size and branches being opened at Kingfield (1910), Knaphill (1913), Maybury (1919) and Pirbright (1920). The number of members rose from 168 to 3,700 so that for a time this was a significant force in retailing in the Woking area. In 1935 it opened the first department store in the town, on the site of its Percy Street shop. Built in a typical 1930s style, with curving façade and flat roof, the store, which had considerable architectural interest, was demolished in the early 1970s. Today the Co-op is a forgotten element in the history of shopping in Woking and, even then, it was an exception in a town dominated by small shops and small traders.

The scruffy end of Chertsey Road, photographed in 1977 as the massive town centre redevelopment (Mark I) was approaching completion. In the background is the Albion development of 1962, the first element in the post-war replanning of central Woking.

Even so, some national names did come. Sainsbury's opened their first shop at 19 Chertsey Road in 1920 and moved to the wonderful High Street premises in 1934 – with its mosaic floors, mahogany and brass counters, marble slabs, glorious smell of bacon, cheese and coffee, and cashier's window at the far end, it was a place of delight for me in the early 1960s. Sainsbury's also opened a West Byfleet branch, in 1932. Chertsey Road multiples included MacFisheries (with a West Byfleet branch in 1923) and Boots the Chemist, which was so successful that within two years it had moved to larger premises. And most symbolic of all, Woolworth's opened their store at the lower end of Chertsey Road in 1926 and ten years later had to rebuild it to cope with massive growth in business. The inter-war years thus saw a change to the old order. Country ways and country styles vanished, and the modern age arrived.

Yet Woking, by 1939 a medium-sized town, had a shopping centre which

High Street, Woking, in the mid-1960s: shops still had awnings, though Sainsbury's had redone its shopfront with 'state of the art' early '60s lettering. The different rooflines emphasise the piecemeal development of the street a hundred years before, the blank wall of the railway embankment occupies the whole of the south side of the street, the traffic is congested, the pavements narrow, and it is hard to imagine that this is one of the two main shopping streets in a town with over 60,000 people.

was smaller and less attractive than might have been expected of a place with 40,000 people. The town's small traders, who were a powerful interest on the council, were unwilling and unprepared to tackle the legacy of inadequacy, and were hostile to change. This is most famously illustrated by the universal belief that it was Woking Council which in the mid-1930s actively refused to help Marks & Spencer find a site for a store in the town. Woking, though equivalent in size to places such as Guildford and substantially larger than

most other towns in the region, had levels of retail sales far below those of its many competitors. Not until the completion of the second redevelopment of the town centre, in the 1990s, was it possible to claim that it had finally achieved a shopping centre, and commensurate levels of commercial and business activity, which its size of population warranted.

90. *Industry, employment and commuting*

At the end of the 19th century the only important industry was Unwins printing works at Old Woking. There had been minor industrial development in the Chertsey Road and Goldsworth wards. For example, the Electric Accumulator Supply Company had opened in a small workshop in North Road in 1894 (it quickly became a nuisance, producing fumes and allowing acids and other chemicals to flow into the Rive Ditch nearby) and in 1910, having outgrown its original premises, it moved to Maybury and took over some of the buildings of the former Oriental Institute. But when in 1902 Woking Urban District council had to register industrial premises under the Factories and Workshops Act, only five businesses – the printing works, the Accumulator Company, the gasworks, the electricity power station and the Woking and Maybury Electric Laundry – were large enough to come within its scope. Given its size, Woking was exceptionally lacking in industrial employment.

The First World War was a catalyst to industrial development throughout west Surrey. At the pioneering airfield at Brooklands, H.P. Martin and G.H. Handasyde had been building small planes since 1910, and in 1914 they formed the Martinsyde Aircraft Company to produce them on a commercial basis. The outbreak of war brought an urgent new demand for aircraft. Production had to be expanded as rapidly as possible but Brooklands had no facilities. A large weatherproof building was required and the lofty central hall of the Oriental Institute was available. It was quickly converted, production lines were set up, and at Christmas 1914 the first aircraft was built there. Throughout the war the Maybury factory supplied government contracts for warplanes, making a major contribution to the resources of the new RAF (by 1919 over 600 Buzzard fighter aircraft had been built there). The end of the war, though, resulted in an equally rapid fall in demand, and in 1924 the firm went into liquidation.

The Italia Automobile Company had built cars at Brooklands until 1913. In 1915 Vickers, the armaments group, acquired its works for aircraft production, having been given a key role in developing this side of the war effort. The small plant dating from the 'idyllic Edwardian springtime of motor racing' was transformed into a major industrial complex, especially after 1916 when the government concentrated the production of the SE5a fighter plane at Brooklands. By the end of 1917, 10 per cent of all British aircraft production was accounted for by the Vickers works and after the war the factory was expanded, because Vickers developed Weybridge/Brooklands in preference to its other sites. During 1930s, as rearmament for another war gathered pace, this became one of the largest UK aircraft factories. All this had a profound effect upon the area, for the works employed large numbers of local people and the population influx and new housing, together with the factory itself, dramatically changed the peaceful lower Wey valley and its villages.

In 1926 the again-vacant Oriental Institute was bought by James Walker Limited, founded in 1882 in London and specialising in the production of packaging materials. The Woking site was spacious, accessible and ideally placed for the markets in the south-east, for much of the output of the company went into the packing of new consumer goods. Much of the old collegiate complex was demolished to make way for factory buildings, and by 1939 James Walker was the largest single employer in the Woking area, with about 400 people. By 1955, when

there was a workforce of 1700, it accounted for eight per cent of the total employment in the town. Other industries, catering for new demands and using recent technology, also appeared in the 1920s and '30s. The Sorbo Rubber Sponge Products Ltd. opened in the redundant buildings of the Maybury Laundry in 1920. It produced, among other 'rubber substitute' products, the Sorbo Balls which were a favourite toy for children in the inter-war years. In 1922 the company moved to a new factory at the eastern end of Arnold Road, just over the border in Chertsey Rural District – Woking's desire to obtain the rate income from the works was responsible for several attempts in the later 1920s to change the boundary, an ambition finally achieved in 1933.

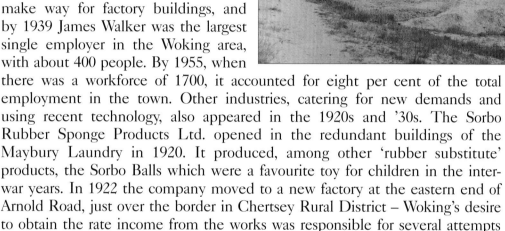

Spanton's wharf and timber yard on the Basingstoke Canal, photographed from Chertsey Road canal bridge in 1927. The main gasholder at Woking Gasworks can be seen in the distance above the rooftops of Boundary Road. The timber wharf and the gasworks were by this date the source of the only freight traffic regularly carried on the canal, and within a decade both had ceased to use the waterway.

In 1944 a planning report was able to declare that 'in Woking are manufactured rubber products, wire nails, accumulators, wireless products and aeroplane equipment, and there are packing specialists, printers and timber stores' while Byfleet was 'associated with the Brooklands aero-engineering works'. The area had shared fully in the national trend of the inter-war years whereby new industries located on greenfield sites in the south-east rather than the old industrial areas of the north. Woking had become a significant industrial centre, in turn leading to a more diverse social and economic structure and more jobs for lower- and middle-income groups.

Paralleling the expansion of local employment opportunities was the very rapid growth of commuting. Throughout south-east England the inter-war years saw the transformation of the railway network as the Southern Railway (formed in 1923) continued the policies of its constituent companies in electrifying the suburban network. The London and South Western Railway was actively developing electrification at the outbreak of the First World War and had prepared plans for the line through Woking. In 1925 its successor electrified the route to Guildford via Cobham and in 1933 the Brighton line, the first fully-electrified main line in the world. The results were triumphantly successful in terms of passenger numbers, and it was decided to extend electrification to most routes in Surrey, Kent and Sussex. At the same time, expanding suburban areas and growing villages were provided with new stations as another component of a strategy to boost passenger figures. In 1927, therefore, the Southern Railway opened a station at Oyster Lane, Byfleet. Its name was a source of controversy: local people variously wanted Oyster Lane, New Haw, or Byfleet. The railway company perversely chose the nonsensical West Weybridge and the station was not renamed Byfleet & New Haw until the 1950s.

In 1933 the Southern Railway began work on electrifying the main line to Alton and Portsmouth via Woking, with the help of large government grants designed to contribute to unemployment relief during the depression. Full public services were inaugurated on 4 July 1937 and Woking's rail service, already excellent, was henceforth outstanding. The speed and frequency of trains to Waterloo, with an almost unequalled peak service, immediately generated a great deal of new commuter business. The pre-1937 'city gentleman' commuter, who could stroll into the office in the middle of the morning, was joined by much larger numbers of ordinary workers for whom an early arrival in London was now feasible. The real cost of rail travel fell sharply in the late 1930s and into the 1950s, as season ticket bargains became available, and by 1939 2,300 people commuted daily from Woking Urban District to London – about ten per cent of the employed population of the district. Woking station was reconstructed to coincide with electrification, in what has been described as 'the Southern Railway's best "Odeon" style'. Its red brick and white concrete weathered badly, and by the 1970s the station had a peculiarly drab and dirty appearance, but recent improvements have made it more cheerful and restored something of the sense of clean, smooth lines and minimalist design which the Southern intended. There are, as there have been for half a century, plans to rebuild the station as a major new transport interchange with offices above, plans which are regularly dusted down as schemes for direct rail links to Heathrow Airport are put forward and then just as regularly deferred. Time will tell if they ever materialise!

A very fine aerial view of James Walker's Lion Works, taken in April 1936: the long brick building in the centre, with the clock tower, is the former Royal Dramatic College and Oriental Institute. By 1939 James Walker's was Woking's largest industrial concern and during the 1950s it employed a substantial proportion of the town's industrial workforce. Nonetheless, this view shows how constricted the site was – there was no room at all for expansion and every available square yard was put to use.

YESTERDAY, TODAY AND TOMORROW

91. The post-war context

After the Second World War the circumstances of Woking, in common with those of the rest of Surrey, changed in one crucial and fundamental fashion. All building stopped with the outbreak of war, so that proposals for further low-density housing development were suspended. For six years after 1945 most non-essential building was in abeyance while efforts were directed to reconstruction work. The national economy, still geared to rationing, could not yet permit a resumption of private housebuilding. During this period the new Labour government introduced a series of key planning controls which imposed tight restrictions on development in the south-east. The 1947 Town and Country Planning Act gave local authorities compulsory powers and statutory duties to exercise detailed planning policies, in contrast to the limited, voluntary, and ineffectual powers they had had before 1939. Essential to the government's strategy was the definition of a green belt around metropolitan London and most of the self-contained towns and villages within a thirty-mile radius of the capital, specifically intended to prevent uncontrolled growth and to act as a restrictive cordon.

Other elements within the planning system which has, for the past sixty years, guided development in the region were also put in place. Decentralisation of population from London was to be achieved by creating new towns, expanded towns and overspill estates. After 1949 a national highways policy led to the planning and construction of a motorway network and the major upgrading of trunk roads. Other far-reaching social and economic changes took place. The massive growth in car ownership in the 1950s and 1960s and continuously thereafter altered for ever the nature and scale of house-building, by freeing development from reliance on public transport and the need to be close to the workplace. The shifting balance between industrial employment and the service industries, including the post-1965 office boom, ensured that the economic structure of every town was destined to change. New patterns and demands in retailing and shopping habits spelled the end of the old order in town centres, while the growth in disposable incomes and free time produced new demands in the leisure sector. More recently, the themes of conservation, protection of the landscape, ecology and environment altered the perceptions of society towards open land, historic places, important wildlife habitats and local history. In all these dimensions the history of Woking has been shaped by trends in society, and by the ever more complex legislative framework within which we must all build our lives.

92. Overspill

Woking emerged from the Second World War largely unscathed and, in contrast to the capital and the inner London suburbs, no major reconstruction effort was required. The town was designated as a reception area for metropolitan overspill, following the recommendations of the 1944 Greater London Plan, the blueprint for post-war rebuilding. Woking was chosen because it had excellent communications and spare land for new building. It was proposed that about 3,250 Londoners should be housed in the urban

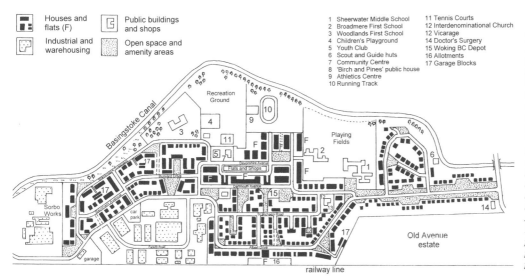

The Sheerwater estate in 1976, when the construction had long since been completed, the landscaping had matured, and industrial decline and redevelopment had not yet begun. The estate was designed as a 'neighbourhood unit' on the most advanced late 1940s principles, and the layout, range of community facilities and amenities, and self-contained nature of the site are typical of the London County Council's progressive housing policies of the immediate post-war period.

district, mostly in Byfleet and Pyrford, to give a total population by 1950 of about 46,000. That figure was already exceeded in 1947, by which time Woking Council was planning for a population of 75,000 in the early 1960s. Targets were revised and in 1948, in conjunction with the Ministry of Housing and Local Government, London County Council selected Sheerwater as the site of a new 'out county' overspill estate. Woking Council, which wanted the land for its own building programme, was strongly opposed, while Surrey County Council, which simply did not want to see lots of Londoners moving into the county, was equally hostile. The government overruled both authorities and the LCC purchased the entire 230-acre Sheerwater estate.

Construction began in November 1948, but formidable physical obstacles were encountered. The site had been a lake until the 1820s and it was still waterlogged. Before any housing could be built the Rive Ditch had to be diverted and culverted for 2½ miles, a system of flood-drains and pumping stations installed, and new mains sewers constructed. The first of the 1,279 houses and flats was handed over to its tenants in September 1951, almost three years after the start of the project. The estate was designed in the contemporary mode, with 272 flats in high-density blocks close to the centre, and terraced and semi-detached houses elsewhere. It was intended as a 'neighbourhood unit, with a careful and integrated design which would allow a sense of community to develop. To a considerable extent', it was said in the 1960s, 'this aim was realised.' The estate was provided with community facilities, a recognition of the lamentable failure of many inter-war estates where no amenities were built and social problems were acute. There was a district shopping centre, churches, public houses, and sports and social facilities, together with three schools and a 30-acre industrial complex, for another theme had been that industry would decentralise alongside its workforce. Visually the estate could be counted, by the standards of austerity and early 1950s planning and architecture, a success. Nairn dismissed it as 'a poor effort, with interminable vistas of cottage units and most of the original trees grubbed up' (he did not apparently realise the nature of the earlier landscape), but others were more charitable: 'a sylvan setting and scrupulous landscaping, and a worthy architectural effort has resulted in a successful blend of natural and built environments'.

The population peaked at about 5,500 in the early 1960s as the 'baby boom' generation grew up, and then began to fall – today there are fewer than 4,000 people in Sheerwater. There were many initial problems in integrating the large influx of Londoners with the existing population and some would argue that this was never satisfactorily resolved (any more than it was in other new and expanded communities). In April 1980 the ownership of the estate was transferred to Woking Council, against the wishes of the majority of the residents, because the Greater London Council, successor to the LCC, was abandoning its housing role. But Sheerwater remains an area with major problems. The decline or closure of many of its industries, which forty years after their arrival had become old-fashioned or obsolete, produced levels of unemployment far higher than those prevailing in the rest of Woking. Like so many large estates, social problems have grown over the years, exacerbated by economic difficulties. In physical terms Sheerwater is still an island, the railway and the canal acting as unbridged barriers to north and south. The 2001 census, in its 'index of deprivation', revealed that Sheerwater was by a considerable margin the deprived electoral ward in Woking borough, and was among the 20 per cent most deprived in England. The building of the estate had a deep impact upon the Woking area, for the influx of 5,000 new residents in just three years ended the lingering sense of a sleepy conservative country town, while its strongly Labour politics altered the town's political complexion. Sheerwater also marked the final coalescing of the two main parts of the built-up area, linking Woking-Horsell and West Byfleet-Pyrford. Lord King, when he drained the lake and planted the pines in the 1820s, can scarcely have anticipated the eventual destiny of what he expected, wrongly, would become good agricultural land.

93. *The green belt*

The Greater London Plan of 1944 proposed a green belt around the capital, as a way of avoiding further urban sprawl, and the government accepted the idea. In the early 1950s, therefore, the planning authorities, including Surrey County Council, made the green belt the central feature of the new county development plans. The Minister of Housing and Local Government approved the Surrey green belt in 1958. In Woking most of the undeveloped land east of Carthouse Lane, Horsell, and the Old Woking Road was designated as green belt and excluded from future development. In the north the edge of the green belt followed the existing built-up area closely, along Shores Road and Woodham Lane, but on the south side of the town substantial amounts of land, already scheduled for building, were left for development in the Pyrford Woods and Byfleet areas. Surrey County Council then submitted plans for the extension of the green belt as a second phase, covering most of the open land to the west of the existing boundary in the Woking, Guildford and Camberley areas. The local authorities, correctly believing that this would greatly impede their own plans to build new peripheral council estates, pressed for substantial areas to be excluded, and at

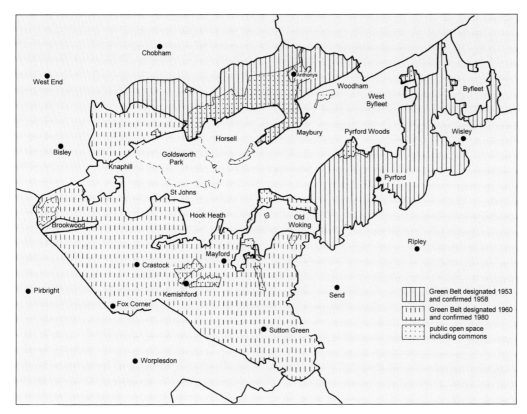

The Green Belt in Woking Borough.

a 1960 public inquiry the county conceded that significant amounts of development land would still be needed. For twenty years an 'interim' solution operated, whereby in Woking the western half of the district was outside the formal green belt but subject to a substantial level of planning restraint. This meant, though, that on occasion the rules could be relaxed and it was comparatively easy to permit certain types of building on undeveloped land on the urban fringe. In 1980 the government finally approved a new outer green belt which, though less extensive than that proposed by the county, nevertheless brought the great majority of undeveloped land within a line from Windlesham to Tongham via Knaphill and Worplesdon under tight development controls. The crucial period, though, was between 1960 and 1980, for during those decades the development of Goldsworth Park (which after 1980 would certainly have been included in the green belt) was possible, as were a number of smaller 'rounding off' schemes such as Stanley Farm, Knaphill.

The green belt has been the single most important contributor to shaping the post-1945 growth of Woking. Without it, there would now be almost no open land in the borough apart from Brookwood Cemetery, Horsell Common and the other minor patches of heathland, and some – but certainly not all – of the golf courses. A few strips of wetland and floodland along the riversides and streams would have survived, but all the rest would have been built over with low and medium density private housing. As already noted, pre-war estimates of Woking's eventual population were in the region of 150,000 and, while we might quibble at the details, there is no doubt that this order of magnitude was plausible. Today the population is 90,000. But there has, of

How it might have been? This map shows the likely growth of Woking had the Green Belt not been imposed from 1953 onwards. It plots all the planning applications for residential development which were rejected by Woking Council or Surrey County Council from 1953 to 1974, the dots being proportional to the size of the proposed scheme. Large areas of Mayford, Bridley, West Heath and the fringes of Knaphill would have been developed, together with parts of Byfleet, Pyrford, Woodham, Brookwood and Westfield.

course, been a downside. The green belt has been a major, though by no means the only, factor contributing to the startlingly high price of land and property in the Woking area and has thus, indirectly, generated considerable social and economic problems for some sections of the community.

Its future, in general terms, is assured. Though every government and many individuals press for relaxation of green-belt policies in specific areas, few challenge the wisdom of the principle of the green belt. Today most people place a high value on the open land and pleasant rural landscapes which it has protected. But pressure for change has never been greater, as the combination of rapidly increasing numbers of households and the difficulties created by exceptionally high prices lead to demands for large-scale house-building in the south-east. Surrey is already the most densely populated shire county in England and Wales, but current government strategies mean that towns such as Woking will be expected to find room for yet more housing and this in turn implies that chewing away at the green belt is inevitable. In 2001 Surrey County Council proposed that Guildford and Woking should each accommodate another 6,000 houses, of which roughly half would be within the existing built-up areas. The balance, another 6,000 houses, would be achieved by the development of three new 'communities' in the green belt, one of which, with about 2,000 houses, would be in south Woking. There was very widespread opposition to the plan, from local organisations, individuals and Woking Borough Council which, while recognising that new homes are needed and that there is a special urgency about the provision of affordable housing for key workers, viewed the loss of green belt, the overloading of the infrastructure (and the cost and disruption involved in adding to it), and the environmental damage which would follow as unacceptable. In August 2003 a revised proposal was put forward by the County Council. Woking is now required to find room for 3,350 homes between now and 2016, a much more realistic target which can be met from more high density building in the central area, redevelopment of brownfield sites, and infilling. Thus the green belt seems, for the time being, to have avoided a major intrusive development. It can never be regarded as entirely sacrosanct, but the recent strength of opposition to development suggests that its benefits to the town and surrounding areas are clearly appreciated by the community as a whole.

94. *Council housing*

From the late 1940s Woking Council pursued an active house-building policy. In the first decade after the war, in accordance with the exhortations of government, the council boosted its housing completion rate to a level four times that of the 1930s, and by 1956 had built 1,688 houses and 101 prefabs. The next ten years saw a fall in output, but in the late 1960s the final major phase of council building saw the highest ever rates of completion, with 1,152 homes in 1968-76 to give a total of 3,309 between 1947 and 1977. This represented, by the standards of the Home Counties, a very high level of local authority involvement and it had a substantial impact on the supply of affordable housing. The sites chosen varied and, inevitably, much depended on the council's willingness and ability to compete on the open market for land. In the first ten years much use was made of derelict or deteriorating farmland on the edge of the existing built-up area. Such sites were ideal because they were within easy reach of services such as water and sewerage, they were large enough to permit economies of scale in building, and – above all – they were sites which in the unique circumstances of the late 1940s the council could buy without serious competition from the private sector. Thus the large estates at Maybury, Barnsbury, Elmbridge and St Mary's (Byfleet) were all bought and developed before a vigorous and revived private sector once again used its superior spending power to acquire land. Equally important was the Council's ability to buy these sites before the 1958 approval of the Surrey green belt – after that each would have been subject to stringent planning controls. These estates were laid out in generous fashion, with curving roads (always too narrow because nobody anticipated the levels of car ownership just a decade or so in the future) and predominantly semi-detached or terraced houses. The landscaping was relatively austere but these estates wore well and when the time came for council house sales to be the policy of government they were popular with would-be purchasers.

From 1955 to 1967 the Council found that it could no longer buy land readily or cheaply. In one period of only four years no fewer than 37 different sites were investigated. Of these, 19 were rejected and building on most of the remainder was impossible because of government financial restrictions. Despite endless argument, deputations to the minister (Conservative, just as the council was Conservative), and a lot of time and effort wasted, nothing could be done. In 1961 the Council decided that it needed a single very large site to permit a longer-term sustained programme of building. This decision coincided with the first outline schemes for the development of 'Slocock's land', the large tract of nursery gardens and damp fields between Horsell and Knaphill. Once the principle of building on this land had been accepted

German prisoners of war labouring on the Woking Urban District Council housing site at Eden Grove, Byfleet, in 1947. This was one of the earliest post-war schemes, and the prisoners are laying the foundations of pre-fabs which provided emergency housing to meet the pressing local demand.

Woking Council bought a large area at the eastern side and there, in 1970-5, built what was at first known as Bullbeggars estate, a development with a high proportion of flats and maisonettes. It immediately acquired a poor reputation and was renamed Lakeview in an attempt to improve its image. This was followed by a mixed local authority and housing association development of 440 houses on the site of the former Inkerman Barracks, and another 60 houses on Goldsworth Park, many of them being low cost starter homes and shared ownership dwellings.

Thus, right into the early 1980s, the Council continued to build on a large scale, but changing government policy then forced a wholesale retreat. Woking has serious housing problems. Prices are so high that affordable housing hardly exists, while land supplies are so limited that such housing could not readily be provided even if the mechanism for public or semi-public building still existed. The Council's current strategies emphasise the desperate shortage of affordable housing, noting that key workers find it increasingly difficult to find somewhere to live. While direct building by the Council is largely finished, the development of low-cost homes in areas such as Brookwood Farm remains crucial to Woking's plans, together with a major reshaping and extension of the rented and private landlord sector of the market. Although the borough has a very high standard of housing, there are pockets of severe deprivation and low housing quality. The worst is, as it has been for well over a century, the east end of the Victorian town, in the Maybury Road and Walton Road area. Here the instant slums of the 1870s and 1880s have produced a legacy of poor housing which has never been eradicated. In the 1950s and '60s Woking Council undertook a programme of slum clearance in this part of the town, using compulsory purchase and declaring clearance areas for comprehensive redevelopment. The replacement housing was in the form of flats using 'industrialised building techniques', the only type the government would countenance. These were soon discredited and produced their own legacy of unfitness. This area has very high levels of multiple occupancy and overcrowding and performs badly on just about every indicator of housing standards. In every index of housing deprivation published by the county council and the Department of the Environment during the 1990s, Central and Maybury ranked as the most deprived of the 208 electoral wards in Surrey, while Sheerwater consistently came second. Indeed, the 2001 census analysis placed Central and Maybury among the worst hundred electoral wards in England in terms of housing quality (91st out of 8,414, placing it on a par with much of Manchester and Liverpool). Equally striking, though, is that the ward adjoins Horsell East & Woodham and Pyrford, which are among the two hundred *least* deprived wards in England. It is a town of extremes.

95. Mount Hermon and Goldsworth Park

The 1953 plan for Surrey, intended to operate for twenty years, envisaged that the population of Woking would stabilise in the mid-1970s at about 67,000. The 1961 census showed that this figure had already been exceeded, as a result of extremely rapid growth in the late 1950s when areas such as Pyrford Woods were being developed, together with the arrival of 5,000 Londoners in the Sheerwater scheme. In 1965 the Council drastically revised the estimates upwards, anticipating a population of 97,000 by 1981. The exercise demonstrates the futility of such projections, since the population in 2001 was just under 90,000. The increase of about 30,000 people which was predicted for 1965-81 was to be accommodated by three very large new developments. One was later abandoned – the construction of public and private housing on the West Byfleet Golf Course, today the only really large area of undeveloped land within the built-up area of the town.

The second project was to be the extensive redevelopment of the Mount Hermon area, together with a smaller but similar scheme in the centre of West Byfleet. Redevelopment in these areas was already under way. As land and property prices increased during the later 1950s the large and under-used grounds of the big Victorian and Edwardian houses south of Woking station and in central West Byfleet became a prime target for developers. Some were falling into disrepair, their size no longer an attraction in the servantless modern age; others were being subdivided and multiple occupancy was spreading; and the maintenance of extensive grounds was an ever-greater problem for their often elderly owners. There was pressure for conversion to business uses such as doctors' surgeries and offices for small firms. But the sudden rise in the value of the land itself meant that full-scale redevelopment was now an attractive proposition. Owners could capitalise on the land values, developers on the new housing prospects.

In 1958 the first serious proposals were made for redevelopment along Guildford Road and in January 1959 the Council approved a scheme for 68 flats to replace three large houses north of Hillview Road. The scheme

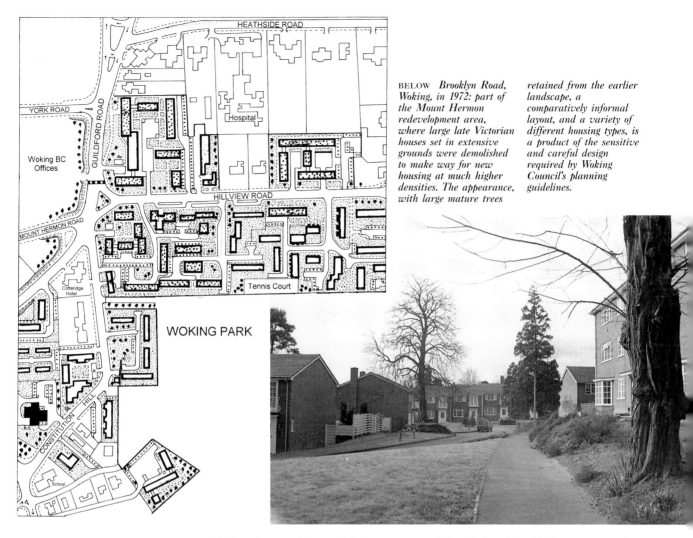

HEATHSIDE ROAD
YORK ROAD
Woking BC Offices
GUILDFORD ROAD
Hospital
MOUNT HERMON ROAD
HILLVIEW ROAD
Cotteridge Hotel
CONSTITUTION HILL
Tennis Court
WOKING PARK
School

BELOW *Brooklyn Road, Woking, in 1972: part of the Mount Hermon redevelopment area, where large late Victorian houses set in extensive grounds were demolished to make way for new housing at much higher densities. The appearance, with large mature trees retained from the earlier landscape, a comparatively informal layout, and a variety of different housing types, is a product of the sensitive and careful design required by Woking Council's planning guidelines.*

ABOVE *The Hillview Road and Constitution Hill area in 1976: the redevelopment of this area with high-density private housing was a major element in the town's growth in the 1960s and early 1970s. Much of the housing is of the 'Span' type, with blocks arranged around landscaped courtyards and parking areas and garage blocks provided on short cul-de-sac roads. At the bottom left is the 10-storey Craigmore Tower, Woking's only high rise scheme of the post-war period.*

contravened density zonings which were enshrined in the 1953 county plan and in April 1962 Surrey County Council, after a public inquiry, agreed to rezone 70 acres between White Rose Lane, Woking Park, Brooklyn Road and Heathside Road. The Mount Hermon High Density Area, as it was officially known, was extended in 1966 to include another 55 acres north to the railway line and south-west to Wych Hill Lane and Turnoak roundabout. A smaller zone was defined in West Byfleet, covering the area between Old Woking Road, Sheerwater Road and the railway station. Within these areas redevelopment by private building firms was to be actively encouraged, there being a stated preference for flats, maisonettes and terraced housing and permission for building at up to ten storeys. The policy, a considerable success in every sense, was designed to encourage renewal while imposing a clear planning framework to avoid a disorderly free for all. There were, for example, to be strict limitations on the removal of the mature trees of the existing properties. The other aim was to focus development pressure on a designated area and thereby to make better use of the land, while diverting attention away from adjacent districts of special character such as The Hockering and the Victorian residential roads east of White Rose Lane (some of which were later designated as conservation areas).

Mount Hermon and central West Byfleet have been steadily rebuilt since the mid-1960s, the greatest period of activity being between 1965 and 1975 when, for example, all the land on both sides of Hillview Road was redeveloped. There was never any possibility of council building in these areas so a variety of private developers implemented individual projects, often buying a single large property and constructing a cul-de-sac or blocks of flats. In the first decade the 'Span' concept, invented and popularised by Eric Lyons of Walton on Thames, was much favoured, with long low blocks of flats and maisonettes around landscaped lawns and courts, but more recently terraces of tall 'town houses', with open fronts and small rear gardens were preferred. The maximum height reached was in the ten-storey Craigmore Tower, the only high-rise block of flats in Woking but, as a private development, a far cry from the municipal blocks built in other towns and cities at the same time. Today the Mount Hermon area has lost much of the rawness of redevelopment and the softening effect of the mature trees and the generous landscaping adds to its attraction. There are still many older houses, with the white-painted wooden balconies, overhanging eaves and varied window and rooflines which were characteristic of Edwardian Woking. These are now highly valued for architectural and historical reasons and it is perhaps ironic that parts of York Road and Mount Hermon Road are now themselves conservation areas. Neither is it too far-fetched to suppose that within a few decades some, at least, of the 1960s housing will itself be protected as representative of good quality urban design and architecture of the mid-20th century.

The third and most important element in the expansion of Woking from the mid-1960s was the construction of a 'mini-town' on the low-lying nurseries between Horsell and Knaphill. The gradual decline of nurserying, and obvious potential of this land for development, prompted the decision in the early 1960s to exclude it from the green belt, and in February 1967 Woking Council produced an outline plan for the creation of the new community. In June 1970 New Ideal Homes Ltd., then one of the largest private housebuilders in Britain, entered into partnership with the Council to build the scheme according to a detailed master plan, the Council undertaking to guide the provision of infrastructure and amenities so that the development was properly phased. The government approved the scheme in June 1973 and development began in the autumn of that year.

Goldsworth Park, as the project was christened, was built in stages during the next fifteen years, involving over 4,500 houses and accommodating a population of about 15,000. This meant that it was equivalent in size to a substantial town such as Haslemere or Alton, and its impact on Woking was thus dramatic. It was by far the largest building project in the town's history and is destined to remain so. Its design was based on a framework of roads forming a rough square: Littlewick Road, already existed but the others were new and one, the eastern side from Goldsworth to Littlewick and Horsell Birch, has not been built. The roads were intended to link with the West End and Bisley bypass which would provide a direct route from Woking to the M3 at Lightwater: that, too, remains on the drawing board. From these main roads a series of distributor routes were to carry traffic to individual housing areas, themselves arranged around estate roads, courts and cul-de-sacs. The original

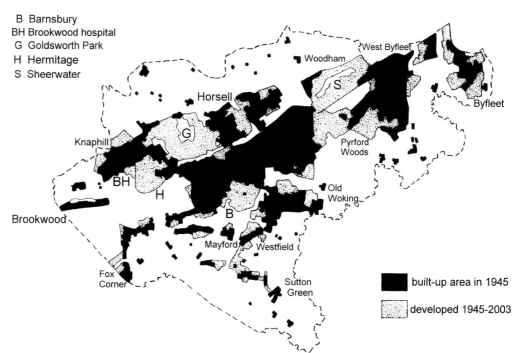

B Barnsbury
BH Brookwood hospital
G Goldsworth Park
H Hermitage
S Sheerwater

built-up area in 1945

developed 1945-2003

The growth of the built-up area 1945-2003.

ambitious plan for a fully-segregated footpath network was scaled down, although some sections were constructed.

At the heart of the estate was a new lake, required for drainage purposes but with a major landscape and recreational value, and north of this a large area was reserved for public open space to form a new park. On the south side of the lake a district shopping centre with superstore was built, together with a church and other community facilities. The Basingstoke Canal, reopened when the new project was nearing completion, is another valuable asset, a linear country park with walks and open space running along the southern edge of Goldsworth Park. The intention was always that there would be a full range of local amenities, but it is perhaps inevitable that to some extent those aims were reduced in reality, simply because in the age of the car people will travel longer distances and local facilities cannot necessarily compete with larger attractions elsewhere. The other key theme of the plan was to avoid any feeling that Goldsworth Park was an 'estate', by encouraging a variety of building styles and layouts, and making sure that each housing development had a distinctive character. The new properties were to be arranged in closes, small groups and clusters, with no long rows or serried ranks of identical houses and with a diversity of materials and shapes. The landscaping, including existing trees and field hedges, together with extensive new planting, would break up the schemes visually to prevent a feeling of monotony, which might easily have been a problem. To a considerable extent these laudable aims have been achieved.

96. *Population changes since 1945*

The basic population statistics clearly demonstrate the extent of change in the Woking area. In 1941, it was estimated, there were 42,000 people in Woking, by 1971 that had risen to 75,000, and in 2001 to 90,000. The trend has been ever upwards, but the fastest rate of growth and the largest increase in population in Woking's history took place during the 1950s, when the post-war housing boom was under way and before green-belt restrictions really began to bite. In the 1960s growth slackened appreciably as the supply of building land dried up, only to accelerate once more in the late 1970s and through the '80s when Goldsworth Park was being developed and the high density redevelopments south of the town centre were coming on stream. In the early 1990s the rate of increase dropped sharply, because although new housing continued to be built the large projects, with the exception of the former Brookwood Hospital site, were completed. Growth has not been evenly spread across the borough – in the Central and Maybury ward the decline continued while conversely and predictably the growth in Goldsworth Park, Knaphill and (from 1955 to 1975) Pyrford and West Byfleet was exceptionally fast.

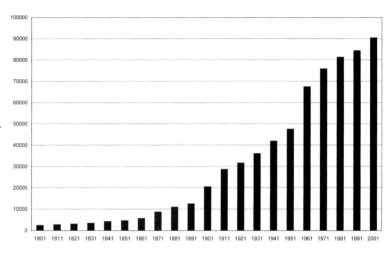

The overall growth in population, 1801-2001: relatively modest expansion in the first half of the 19th century was followed by rapid population increase after the 1860s. During the 20th century particularly high growth rates were recorded in the years before the First World War, and in the 1950s and 1960s. The four small villages in 1801 have grown into a town of almost 100,000 people today.

Woking is likely to experience static population figures a few years hence, unless the county's plan for a substantial new housing development in the rural south of the borough materialises. If it does, the population will probably exceed 100,000 in the years after 2010. However, the town has an ageing population. Its age profile in the 2001 census demonstrated that the percentage in the 25-44 age group was substantially above the national average, as a result of large numbers of young families moving to the town in the 1980s, but that in the 10-24 age group the town was significantly below the national percentage. In other words, unless circumstances change, the next twenty years will see a growing proportion of older people and relatively few children, and the population may therefore not grow by natural increase. Only renewed large-scale in-migration would change that, and such a development would be dependent upon more sizeable housing schemes.

One of the other profound changes of the last sixty years has been the creation of a multi-ethnic and culturally very diverse community within Woking. In the immediate post-war years the town received a large influx of migrants from southern Europe, especially from Spain and Italy, and also of Irish people who participated in the large-scale post-war migration from the Republic to Great Britain. Woking's Spanish and Italian community was one of the largest in the region. Initially many of the Italians worked on the land, while Spanish migrants were employed in, for example, local hospitals, but very quickly this pattern began to change and by the 1960s many from both communities had started small businesses or were working in existing industrial and commercial concerns in the town. The distinctive culture of southern Europe remained strong, with Italian-run coffee bars and cafes, for example, providing a welcome improvement in the town's hitherto less than shining reputation as a centre for quality refreshment.

The European migrants were soon followed by those from south and south-east Asia, and Woking was a leading destination for Indian, Pakistani and Hong Kong Chinese newcomers. Like the earlier generation of Italians and Spaniards, these groups settled particularly in the town's east end, around Maybury Road and Walton Road, which had been an area of poor housing and environmental problems since the 1870s. Over one-third of the population of Central and Maybury ward is non-white, a proportion three times higher than that of any other ward in Surrey. It was of course the case that Woking had a special connection with the Muslim community because of its mosque, already sixty years old when the first post-war migrants came, but, whereas before the Second World War most of those who attended the mosque were prosperous and long-standing residents of southern England, the post-war migrants were poor and experienced considerable social and economic difficulties on arrival and long afterwards.

Today the population of Woking includes over 40 different nationalities, far more than any other town in Surrey, and it is one of the most ethnically diverse places in south-east England. Over 10 per cent of its population was born outside the United Kingdom, the majority being, in descending order, from Pakistan, India, Italy, Spain, China and the Irish Republic. Out of 376 administrative districts in England and Wales, Woking ranks 24th in terms of the proportion of residents born outside the UK. Another way of looking at the same statistic is to take the data on religious adherence which are available from the 2001 census. The town is 44th in the UK in terms of the percentage of Muslims and 3rd in south-east England. The Jewish, Hindu and Buddhist faiths are also strongly represented. At the same census, 8.8 per cent of the borough's residents described themselves as being other than 'white', compared with a national figure of 9.2 per cent.

97. *Employment in Woking since 1945*

During the post-war decades Woking seemed to be developing as an industrial centre of some importance. The industries which came in the inter-war years were associated with new materials and modern processes, and in common with the rest of the south-east there appeared to be a secure future in light industrial output. The expansion of these industries during the '50s and '60s confirmed that trend, so that the Woking economy was diversified and manufacturing employment grew steadily. But by the late 1970s the trend had been halted and then reversed. Manufacturing employment remained steady but its share of the Woking job market began to fall rapidly as the tertiary sector (services, such as office jobs, retailing and banking and finance) expanded. Woking began to emerge as a major centre for such businesses, a status reinforced by the central area redevelopment of the late 1970s and the construction of new office complexes on the fringe of the town centre and south of West Byfleet station.

The last decades of the 20th century saw closure of major firms, most notably James Walker Limited, and the loss of many of the larger industrial employers in the district. What had been new and modern in the 1930s and 1950s was by now obsolete. Woking's light industries were bypassed by changing technology or lost their competitive position as labour costs rose.

Statistics for the 1990s demonstrate the trend very clearly. In just five years, 1991 to 1996, the borough lost 12.4 per cent of its manufacturing jobs, and by 1999 only 11 per cent of the workforce was engaged in industry, the lowest percentage for over seventy years. Other significant losses were recorded by the construction sector, where the end of large-scale development in Goldsworth Park and the town centre was largely responsible. Public services such as education, administration and health also declined, the closure of Brookwood Hospital and other institutions being a major factor.

In contrast, dramatic growth was recorded in the service trades. In only five years the numbers employed in distribution, retailing, hotels, and restaurants increased by 21 per cent, but the most spectacular increase was in banking, finance, insurance and office work, which grew by a remarkable 76 per cent in the same five-year period and is now the largest single employment category in the borough. It accounts for roughly 35 per cent of all jobs in Woking and reflects the town's emergence as one of the most important office centres in southern England outside the London conurbation. During this period unemployment levels shrank rapidly. This was a national trend but in Woking's case the results were spectacular. In 1993 Woking had a 7.3 per cent unemployment rate, which was high though substantially below the national average. In summer 1999 the rate had fallen to just 0.9 per cent, one of the lowest levels in the country.

We can look at this picture from a different perspective. Despite the major loss of manufacturing employment, the number of jobs in Woking rose from 28,000 in 1971 to 38,000 in 1991 and over 41,000 today. Woking is a very important employment centre in its own right and the old view of the town as a dormitory suburb where everybody leaves on the 8.05 to Waterloo is manifest nonsense. Perhaps the most revealing statistics of all in that respect are those relating to commuting. In 1971 some 9,000 people travelled into Woking to work each day but almost 16,000 travelled out, mainly to London and Guildford (that is, there was a net daily outflow of nearly 7,000 commuters). Twenty years later the 1991 census showed that out-commuting had grown substantially, to almost 20,000, but the number of people commuting into Woking from other places had increased much faster, to 15,500: the net outflow had been reduced to 4,500. Today, remarkably given Woking's history and its popular image, the flows are evenly balanced and by 2007 more people will commute *to* Woking than will travel daily *from* the borough. Its meteoric rise as an employment centre over the last thirty years has been the direct consequence of its enviable geographical location close to London, Heathrow Airport and other key commercial centres, its excellent communications and accessibility, and its pleasant, clean and attractive environment.

This fundamental change in Woking's role has now been confirmed by the decision of Surrey County Council to relocate from Kingston, its home since 1895, and to make Woking the administrative headquarters of the county. The development of a new county hall in the town centre not only has dramatic psychological implications for the town, but will also have major practical consequences for employment and enterprise in Woking. As the county's spokesman said in announcing the news, 'Woking is a dynamic forward-looking place, with excellent transport links ... right in the heart of Surrey'.

98. Roads, traffic and railways

The reshaping of the town's communications has never been as comprehensive as the planners – and maybe the inhabitants – would have wished. Since the 1930s Woking Council has repeatedly sought to upgrade the road network, but its own powers have been limited and it has had to rely upon the enthusiasm, financial capacity and planning policies of Surrey County Council and central government. Since the 1920s a series of plans, reports and proposals have urged the construction of new roads and the improvement of existing ones, with comparatively little result. The Byfleet bypass (1962), the realignment of the A320 Guildford road at Whitmoor Common (1969), the first version of the town centre relief road, Victoria Way (1973) and the diversion of the Guildford road south of Mayford (1983) were all longstanding projects. Other vital new links were associated with the development of Goldsworth Park in the mid-1980s, including the Goldsworth Road relief road, Lockfield Drive, and the St Johns bypass.

These projects, each modest by the standards of the expensive schemes implemented elsewhere, have contributed to better vehicle flow or relieved congested residential areas of through traffic, but the perceived requirement for more substantial new roads to link Woking with the outside world, an aim of highway policies since the 1920s, has never been fulfilled. The construction of the M3 through Lightwater (1973) and the M25 (1983), together with the conversion of the A3 to motorway standard between Esher and Guildford, meant that Woking was close to three key national trunk routes, but its direct access to them still depended on narrow, built-up roads within the urban area. New links between Woking and the M3 at Lightwater and the A3 at Ripley, the upgrading of the A322 between Lightwater and Guildford, and the improvement of the A320 between Ottershaw and Woking, were standard

An aerial view of the new roundabout at the Six Cross Roads, photographed in 1964: the roundabout was one of the most important road schemes undertaken by Woking Council before the mid-1970s, but it was one of the very few projects on a long 'wish list' which ever came to fruition.

items in Surrey County Council road programmes but, with the exception of the Lightwater bypass, none has been built. Today the local roads through Knaphill, Brookwood, Ottershaw, Old Woking and Send carry a volume of traffic for which they are manifestly inadequate – these roads evolved as country lanes centuries ago, but are now key links from a very large town to the national highway network.

The issues of safety, congestion, environmental damage and amenity loss are ever-present in these and other communities, but the trend in recent years has been for the planned road schemes either to be dropped altogether or deferred more or less indefinitely. Woking Council is currently pinning its hopes on traffic management studies which might produce solutions for at least some of these problems. Equally uncertain is the future of the schemes, repeatedly proposed since the mid-1980s, to widen the M25. The motorway, eventually built sixty years after it was first planned, was designed with capacity for thirty years' growth of traffic according to early 1970s' projections. In fact it reached design capacity within three years. The possibility of widening it to 14 lanes, by adding three lanes to each side and (in most schemes) parallel lanes for local traffic has been bitterly fought by local authorities and residents of the area between the M4 and the A3, including Byfleet and New Haw. The cost would be prodigious, the disruption traumatic.

Rail access continued to improve during the 1960s and 1970s, the most important change being the electrification of the line from Woking via Southampton to Bournemouth in 1967. At that point the timetable was further enhanced and an unprecedented intensity and speed of service to Waterloo and other key centres was possible. Later, the Portsmouth line was relatively downgraded, so that most trains on that route stopped at Woking. This may not have pleased Portsmouthians but further benefited Woking travellers. Local services were also augmented and the growth of commuting in the 1970s and 1980s gave stations such as West Byfleet a greater importance. For many years Woking has been by far the busiest station in Surrey, while West Byfleet is now the fifth busiest. The troubles of the national rail network since the early 1990s have left the lines through Woking comparatively unscathed, but a succession of abortive plans have foundered on the rocks of politics and money. The most important has been the repeated suggestion that a direct rail link should be created between Woking and Heathrow airport, the so-called 'AirTrack' project. This would make the station into a transport hub of international importance, and would dramatically alter the orientation of Woking's rail links. The expansion of Heathrow which is now under way, after years of planning and public protest, is likely to reinforce the case for such a link, but whether it is built will depend on government and private finance and a willingness to take action. If it *does* materialise, Woking is likely to undergo another commercial and economic boom, and the effects on the town and its development will be profound.

99. Redeveloping the town centre

Central to Woking's economic and commercial renaissance in the last quarter of the 20th century was the redevelopment of the town centre. After 1945 the

Council belatedly recognised the need for a concerted policy to tackle the legacy of poor architecture, inadequate facilities, an unsatisfactory road network and those 'mean and joyless shops and public buildings'. Tentative schemes had been put forward in the 1930s but by the late 1950s, when central area redevelopment was beginning to become a fashionable element in government thinking and in the planning policies of local authorities, it was appreciated that something more substantial was required. A plan prepared in 1948 was based on the assumption that a new town hall or civic centre would be built in Guildford Road and that the area between the railway and the canal would then be given over to retail and commercial uses. The Council began to acquire land and bought up properties piecemeal across the area likely to be redeveloped. In 1960 a new outline plan was approved, based on three key principles: reorganisation of the traffic system; improvement of the visual and architectural quality of the centre; and major expansion of shopping and office facilities. As experience eventually showed, while the three aims remained applicable, perceptions of what was architecturally attractive and what was effective in traffic terms swiftly altered. In the spring of 1962 the first piece in the redevelopment jigsaw was put in place when the old (and by Woking standards historic) *Albion Hotel*, red-brick and creeper-clad, was demolished and in its place a complex of shops, offices and a public house was constructed.

In 1965 the Council modified its outline design to incorporate the latest idea in traffic planning – segregation of people from vehicles and the introduction of a considerable element of pedestrianisation – and in December of that year the formal plan was adopted. The Council bought up the remaining land in the centre and in 1968 large-scale demolition began. About 150 people were displaced and rehoused, although over the previous thirty years several hundred residents had left the area voluntarily, so that the only significant areas of residential property left were in Clarence Avenue, West Street and parts of Church Street. In 1970 the Council reached agreement with Norwich Union for the funding and development of the project and building work began in 1971, the crucial first stage being the construction of Victoria Way which would take all the through traffic out of the town centre.

When the first edition of this book was published in 1982 the work was just completed. An eight-acre shopping centre had been built, the new Town Square laid out, and on its north side a group of public buildings – the library, Christ Church and the Civic Offices – formed a small civic area. The redevelopment included multi-storey car parks, two department stores, a new market place, an indoor heated swimming pool, and a fire station. A police headquarters and courts were planned as part of a later phase. The whole project was dominated by the 18-storey office slab, Woking's tallest building, which was completed in 1976 and had been leased to British American Tobacco as its European headquarters. Already a rash of other new office buildings had sprung up along the roads around the new centre, including Victoria Way and Goldsworth Road. Woking had the foundations of a major collection of later 20th-century corporate architecture.

With the completion of this scheme Woking had a much improved shopping centre, though I noted, in a modest understatement, that 'there are still some deficiencies'. Much of the public disquiet stemmed from the loss of

An aerial view of Woking town centre, 1958: the high quality of this image, taken on a cloudless summer afternoon, shows the detail of the area before redevelopment. The alignments of Chertsey Road and Station Approach (originally a track across the heath) and Church Path (once a footpath across the common from Wheatsheaf canal bridge to the station) are very clear. In the centre is the large car park on Commercial Road, the result of the abortive town centre redevelopment of the late 1930s. There are many houses, with long back gardens, in Church Street and Clarence Avenue. Conspicuous by their absence are any tall buildings or large commercial developments. Trinity Methodist church has not been built and there are allotments where Brewery Road car park is today.

small shops in areas such as Chertsey Road and Broadway, although that was a ubiquitous problem of the 1970s. A great deal of antagonism was also caused by the pedestrian arrangements, including the notorious subway where Chobham Road joined Victoria Way and the even more celebrated, and short-lived, 'Bridge of Sighs' footbridge next to the new market place. The expansion of the shopping facilities in the town had been dramatic. In 1973 there had been 67,000ft^2 of retail space and by 1981 there was almost exactly twice as much. But the shops themselves were not necessarily what was needed. There were two foodstores (Sainsbury's and International), major branches of Boots and Fine Fare, a Co-operative department store and a British Home Stores. Conspicuous by its continued absence was the Great Name, Marks & Spencer. Woking had an early 1960s design, built in the mid-1970s just before a wholesale transformation of the British retailing structure, shopping habits and planning world. Soon the weaknesses of the scheme became all too apparent.

Several of the main businesses – the Co-op, Fine Fare, International – folded, and the limited range of small and medium-sized shops was manifestly incapable of competing with the glamour of Guildford and the increasingly powerful attraction of the new out-of-town superstores. Further, the traffic circulation system proved to be far less effective than anticipated, with clumsy design and too little capacity to cope with the very rapid growth in general traffic levels. The architecture, which had looked so modern on architects' drawings and artists' impressions in the late 1960s, so 'big town' compared with the semi-derelict properties and windswept car parks of the pre-redevelopment town, now seemed ugly, indifferent and weathered badly. The new centre was too small, too unambitious and too uninteresting to exert a major attraction. With it, Woking was better served than it had been, but it still could not act as a retailing attraction for a wider area.

Despite a great deal of expense and ten years' disruption, not to mention a gestation period of over forty years, it was sent back to the drawing board. In the mid-1980s, only six years after the project was completed, Woking Council initiated a review of its success or failure and the first outline plans for a redevelopment of the redevelopment were aired. These gradually took shape over the next five years, focusing on a major expansion of the scale, range and attractiveness of the shopping centre; revision of the road and traffic arrangements and further pedestrianisation; and the refurbishment of the existing (that is, newly-built) shopping precinct. A new dimension, which received relatively little attention in the earlier redevelopment, was the ambition for Woking to become a cultural and arts centre of regional stature, so that a large theatre and concert hall was included in the 'wish list'. In 1990, little more than a decade after the redevelopment was completed, demolition work began.

Brave New World! The artist's impressions of the new town centre, painted in 1971, have the unreal pristine quality typical of the genre. There is no litter, hardly any traffic, the buildings shine and so does the sun, and people have become stylised figures. This view shows a perspective based on the first stage of the design, looking eastwards from what became Victoria Way towards the new shopping precinct of Wolsey Walk and the BAT office block.

A superb aerial view of the town centre redevelopment in progress, 1978: it can be compared with the earlier (1958) image. Victoria Way and its associated gyratory systems have been built alongside the canal, the new office blocks, library and Centre Halls, multi-storey car parks, shopping precinct and Centre Pools have been completed, and work is in progress on the civic buildings and landscaping. Beyond, Duke Street is about to be redeveloped (it is a giant temporary car park), the area south of the station has seen the building of the new telephone exchange, the grammar school is about to be converted into the police headquarters, and Hillview Road has been totally transformed by redevelopment with high-density housing.

The existing precinct was retained, though given a major overhaul, fully roofed and enclosed to eliminate the wind tunnel effect which had been a glaring fault in the earlier version. The library and the indoor heated swimming pool were demolished (the former to be replaced on site, the latter to be replaced by the Pool in the Park) and from their ashes rose a glittering temple

of retail therapy, The Peacocks. With its associated cultural and other amenities, including the 1,300-seat New Victoria Theatre and 1,000 seat cinema, The Peacocks marked Woking's belated coming of age. Its aims were summarised by a borough council press release: 'a place where people will want to be, whether they are shopping, going to the theatre or simply passing the time of day … to create an attractive environment, not only through walkways, malls and galleries, but also through the use of "public" art.' When the new complex was opened by the Duke of Kent in November 1992 Woking at last, 120 years after the first buildings arose on the empty heath, had a centre of which it could be justifiably proud.

The effects of the second rebuilding have been dramatic. Woking is now the second largest town centre shopping area in the county, having overtaken Camberley and Staines and closed the gap somewhat on Guildford. The shopping space in the town centre (excluding all other parts of the borough) grew by 48 per cent in the 1990s and has continued to expand subsequently. It will never outstrip Guildford, because the county town has the centuries of history, wealth of architectural quality, natural advantages of steep slopes and fine vistas, and indefinable qualities which Woking cannot replicate. Nonetheless, the commercial results of the second reconstruction have been amply justified and it has made a major contribution to a changed atmosphere in the town itself. The revitalised streets around the central area bear witness to this – who, in the grim days of the mid-1960s, when the town centre was a windy wasteland, could have imagined a Woking of wine bars and bistros?

TOP *The scale of the first redevelopment of the town centre is apparent from this dramatic view of work under way in May 1974, with the new 18-storey office block rising high above the shopping centre and multi-storey car parks taking shape. The alignment of Church Street was preserved within the new design but its appearance was altered quite beyond recognition.*

ABOVE *The wraps were coming off the almost-finished new town centre when this view was taken in 1979: nobody could have realised that only twenty years later the scene would have been transformed again, as the inadequacies of the late 1960s design became apparent and commercial and planning pressures drove forward the implementation of town centre redevelopment Mark II.*

100. *Planning, environment and conservation*

Maturity and coming of age have brought new perceptions of Woking's historical and environmental assets. During the past quarter of a century

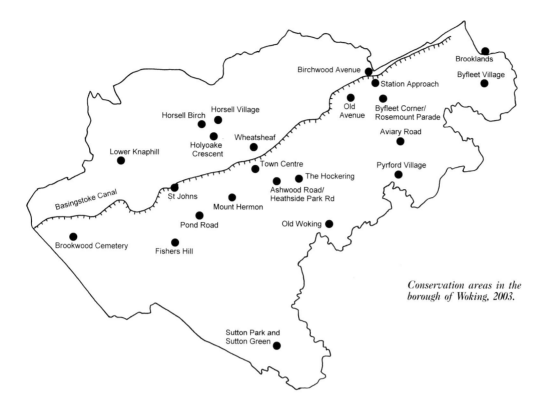

Conservation areas in the borough of Woking, 2003.

The labels on the map read:

Brooklands · Byfleet Village · Birchwood Avenue · Station Approach · Old Avenue · Byfleet Corner/Rosemount Parade · Aviary Road · Horsell Village · Horsell Birch · Wheatsheaf · Holyoake Crescent · Pyrford Village · Lower Knaphill · Town Centre · The Hockering · St Johns · Ashwood Road/Heathside Park Rd · Mount Hermon · Pond Road · Old Woking · Basingstoke Canal · Brookwood Cemetery · Fishers Hill · Sutton Park and Sutton Green

appreciation of these qualities has grown steadily, while the planning framework has increasingly emphasised the need to protect, conserve and enhance the countryside and rural landscapes, the ecological richness of the district, and the areas and buildings of historical significance. Woking has much which deserves protection and appreciation. In the low-density suburbs of the Victorian and Edwardian periods, it has townscapes which are of national importance, textbook examples of the type. Its rural surroundings are attractive and, given the wholesale loss of countryside which affected north-west Surrey during the 20th century, they have now a special value which reflects the scarcity of such areas. Woking Council has, for the past thirty years, paid increasing attention to conservation and heritage issues.

When the first edition of this book was published there were three conservation areas in the borough – Old Woking village, Horsell village and the area around Pyrford church. Now there are 24, the longer list reflecting a growing awareness of the value of more recent development, especially of the period from 1880 to 1930. It includes Pond Road and Fishers Hill in Hook Heath; Aviary Road in Pyrford; Byfleet Corner and Rosemount Parade, Old Avenue, Birchwood Road and Station Approach in West Byfleet; Ashwood Road and Heathside Park Road; The Hockering; Mount Hermon; and Holyoake Crescent and the Wheatsheaf area of Horsell. A much longer schedule of buildings listed as being of historical and architectural interest gives specific protection. Not only the best surviving examples of houses and other properties from the pre-railway age, but also a substantial number of buildings of the 19th and 20th centuries are included, and the Council's planning policies draw particular attention to the need to protect and enhance the setting and surroundings of listed buildings even outside conservation areas. An important development in the raising of Woking's awareness of history was the opening in 1998 of the Surrey History Centre in Goldsworth Road, bringing together the county's superb archive collections, its local studies library and the archaeology unit in one outstanding modern building. Soon, too, Woking will have a museum, and at that point the work of local history societies and others who have campaigned over the years to raise the profile of the town's heritage will be rewarded with success.

The county planning strategies now provide a framework for enhancing the rural landscapes. Surrey has large areas which are designated as being of outstanding natural beauty, most importantly the Surrey Downs which extend from east to west across the county, but it is now recognised that the other rural areas such as the Wey valley, the Surrey heaths and the middle Thames fully deserve protection. In the late 1990s the county singled out these for future improvement and proposed to designate Special Protection Areas which included the heaths of the Woking and Camberley area. The lower Wey, with its distinctive pattern of small and medium-sized fields; extensive areas of riverside meadow; characteristic lines of willows and poplars and on riverbanks and beside drainage channels; historic parks; and ancient churches, was acknowledged to be a landscape of great beauty, a precious resource which had been badly treated over the years but could now be upgraded and cherished.

Woking's more detailed plans and strategies include the continued upgrading of the degraded landscape on the southern urban fringe, around Westfield and Old Woking, with its declining farmland and growing recreational pressures. The completion of long-standing schemes to create a linear park along the Hoe Stream from Mayford to Old Woking, with local nature reserves being established in the Mayford Meadows and White Rose

Bluegate Cottage, Boltons Lane, Pyrford, photographed in May 1898 when it was still part of a working farm: the survival of the domestic architecture of earlier centuries has been very haphazard in the Woking district, and many buildings of considerable architectural and historical merit were demolished with hardly a thought in the 1950s and 1960s More recently, listed building status has been taken seriously, and conservation areas have helped to protect the surviving legacy, as in the case of Bluegate Cottage (which dates in part from the 15th century).

Lane areas, is just one of many specific projects. The most important historic site in the borough, the remains of the great riverside palace of the Tudor monarchs at Old Woking, is scheduled to be opened to the public as part of a major project for a country park with associated landscape and environmental improvements. Surrey lost 85 per cent of its heathland between 1800 and 2000, and Woking's remaining 380 hectares form a landscape and ecological asset of European importance. Environmental work on the commons has centred on the need to retain the very distinctive vegetation of the open heaths. It is essential to prevent them being encroached upon by scrub and eventually being turned into full woodland, as has happened widely across the area. To this end, regular scrub clearance and tree-felling have been accompanied by the reintroduction of grazing by cattle and horses, the most efficient and environmentally sound way of dealing with the problem. Within the Woking area over 70 per cent of all ponds have been drained since 1870, as housing and commercial development has sprawled across the fields and farms, and in the urban area only 10 per cent survive. They, too, are of major ecological and landscape value and the restoration of existing examples and creation of new ponds and wetlands is actively in progress.

The most impressive example of all, achieved by a determined and persistent effort on the part of local authorities spurred on and assisted by the efforts of volunteers and enthusiasts, has been the total restoration of the Basingstoke Canal. Work began in earnest in 1973, after years of campaigning and lobbying by the Surrey & Hampshire Canal Society. Hampshire County Council bought the stretch within its borders in 1970, and in 1976 Surrey County Council purchased the rest of the canal between Woking and Frimley. The enormous task of clearing and dredging, and rebuilding every lock, took over fifteen years, supported by armies of volunteer labourers and publicised by boat rallies and public events. The final stretch, from Woodham to New Haw, was completed in 1989 and the canal was formally reopened in May 1991, the culmination of a quarter of a century of intensive activity and single-

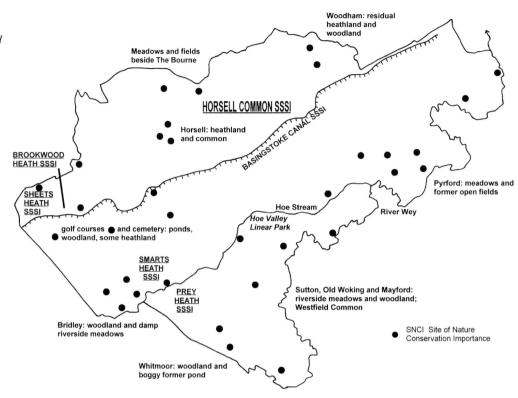

Nature conservation in Woking, 2003: this book has spanned two thousand years of history, but throughout that time the landscape was the backdrop against which the human activity took place. It suffered badly as a result, but in the past twenty years the borough and county councils, and voluntary organisations, have made strenuous efforts to protect and enhance the landscape and environment of Woking. The signs for the future of the natural history and scenic areas of the borough are more encouraging than they have been for two hundred years.

Labels on map: Woodham: residual heathland and woodland · Meadows and fields beside The Bourne · HORSELL COMMON SSSI · Horsell: heathland and common · BROOKWOOD HEATH SSSI · SHEETS HEATH SSSI · BASINGSTOKE CANAL SSSI · Pyrford: meadows and former open fields · Hoe Stream · Hoe Valley Linear Park · River Wey · golf courses and cemetery: ponds, woodland, some heathland · SMARTS HEATH SSSI · PREY HEATH SSSI · Sutton, Old Woking and Mayford: riverside meadows and woodland; Westfield Common · Bridley: woodland and damp riverside meadows · SNCI Site of Nature Conservation Importance · Whitmoor: woodland and boggy former pond

minded dedication by the visionaries who saw that this could one day be a reality. The Basingstoke Canal is a working waterway once more, much lauded for its scenic beauty and the high quality of the work which was done, and benefiting from its closeness to so many large centres of population. The purchase of the Wey Navigation by the National Trust in 1965 guaranteed the future of Woking's other canal and, when the efforts to reopen the Wey and Arun Canal down to Sussex come to fruition, the town will be ideally placed on the national leisure waterway network.

Endnote

Twenty years ago, writing the first edition of this book and referring to the Basingstoke Canal restoration, then slowly approaching completion, I doubted if Woking would ever attract tourists – now I think I will eat my words. The canal's success has been obvious and the town does indeed attract visitors in increasing numbers. Not long before I wrote the book, back at the beginning of the 1980s, Surrey County Council had been thinking about moving its headquarters from Kingston, which since 1965 had been outside the administrative county. Sites in Guildford, Leatherhead, Dorking and Woking were contemplated, but in the end nothing was done. Now, just in time for *this* edition of the book to be revised at the very last minute, came the news that in 2007 Woking will become, in effect (though Guildford will never cede the formal honour), the county town. This, I think, will be seen by historians in the future, with the opening of the railway in 1838, as one of the two most important dates in Woking's story. Another chapter is going to be opened in the long, complex and highly unusual history of this town.

SOURCES AND BIBLIOGRAPHY

The history of Woking was scarcely covered in print until the publication of the first edition of this book, *A History of Woking* (Phillimore, 1982). This second edition has been extensively revised, extended and updated, but more information on certain subjects (such as local government services) may be found in the 1982 edition, where full references for all source material are given. The bibliography below includes all published works used in the preparation of the 1982 original and this 2003 edition:

P. Abercrombie, *The Greater London Plan* (HMSO, 1944)

Adams, Thompson and Fry Ltd., *The North West Surrey Regional Planning Scheme* (1928)

P. Arnold and S. Dyer, *Woking Palace: Henry VIII's Royal Palace – a guide to the Palace with historical notes* (Phillip Arnold, 2001)

F.R. Arnos, *The origins of Christ Church, Woking: a short history* (privately published, 1977)

T. Allen, *A history of the County of Surrey comprising every object of topographical, geological or historical interest*, vol.2 (Isaac Taylor Hinton, London, 1831)

R. Belsey, 'Prehistory and archaeology of the Woking district', *Mayford History Society Newsletter* no.22 (February 1973)

Billing & Sons Ltd., *The story of Billings* (Billings, 1962)

J. Blair, *Early medieval Surrey: landholding, Church and settlement* (Alan Sutton and Surrey Archaeological Society, 1991)

A.J. Blowers, 'London's out county estates', *Town Planning Magazine*, vol.41 (1973) pp.409-14

G. Bourne, *Change in the village* (Duckworth, 1912)

E.W. Brayley, *Topographical history of Surrey* (E.B. Ede, 2 vols., 1841)

V. Brittain, *Testament of Experience* (Virago edition, 1957)

G. Clark and W.H. Thompson, *The Surrey Landscape* (A. and C. Black, 1934)

D.W. Clewley, 'Woking's first public electricity supply', *SEEBoard Staff Newsletter* (December 1975)

C.C. Colbourne, *A brief history of Horsell Common Baptist Church* (C.J. Farncombe, 1914)

A. Conan Doyle, *The Naval Treaty* (John Murray, 1894)

E.A. Course, *The railways of southern England: the main lines* (Batsford, 1975)

B. Cox, 'Place names of the earliest English records', *Journal of the English Place-Name Society* vol.5 (1975-6) pp.12-66

A. Crocker, 'The paper mills of Surrey 1' (*Surrey History* vol.4 no.1 1989-90) pp.49-64 and 'The paper mills of Surrey 3' (*SH* vol.5 no.1, 1994) pp.2-23

A.G. Crosby, *Housing in Woking since 1945* (unpublished BA dissertation, University of Oxford, 1977: Woking Library)

Curl, J. Stevens, *A celebration of Death* (Constable, 1980)

C.K. Currie, *A historical and archaeological assessment of the Wey and Godalming Navigations and their visual envelopes* (unpublished report for National Trust, 1996: copy in Surrey History Centre)

J.R. Daniel-Tysson (ed), *Inventories of the goods and ornaments in the churches of Surrey in the reign of King Edward VI* (Wyman, 1869) [separately published edition of article in *Surrey Archaeological Collections*]

D. Defoe, *A tour through the whole island of Great Britain* (Everyman edition, 1962)

C.F. Dendy Marshall and R.W. Kidner, *A History of the Southern Railway* (Ian Allan, revised edition 1968)

H.G. Dines and F.H. Edmunds, *The geology of the country around Aldershot and Guildford* (Geological Survey, 1929)

M. Dutt, *The agricultural labourers' revolt of 1830 in Kent, Surrey and Sussex* (unpublished PhD thesis, University of London, 1966)

M. de G. Eedle, 'Street cleaning and refuse collection from the sixteenth to the nineteenth centuries', *Surrey Archaeological Collections* (vol.68, 1971) pp.161-81

M. de G. Eedle, *A history of Bagshot and Windlesham* (Phillimore, 1977)

J. Francis, *History of the English Railway* (1851)

E. Gardner, 'Weybridge and Byfleet: traces of old ironworks', *Surrey Archaeological Collections* (vol.34, 1921) pp.115-6

M. Gelling, *Signposts to the past* (Phillimore, 1988)

M. Gelling and A. Cole, *The landscape of place-names* (Shaun Tyas, 2000)

J.E.B. Gover *et al*, *The place names of Surrey* (Cambridge University Press, 1934)

H.L. Gray, *The English field systems* (1915: Merlin Press edition, 1962)

G.B. Greenwood, *Woking and district: a dictionary of local history* (Martin & Greenwood Publications, 1972)

D. Grenfell, 'The Jackmans and their plants: a history of the Woking Nursery 1810-1972' (*Surrey History* vol.3 no.1 1984-5) pp.29-40

P. Holmes, *Aldershot's Buses 1906-1992* (Waterfront Publications, 1992)

D. Hudson, *Munby: man of two worlds* (John Murray, 1972)

R. Hunt (with D. Graham, G. Pattison and R. Poulton), *Hidden depths: an archaeological exploration of Surrey's past* (Surrey Archaeological Society, 2002)

W. James and J. Malcolm, *General view of the agriculture of the County of Surrey* (Board of Agriculture, 1794)

K. Jones, *A history of the mental health services* (Routledge and Kegan Paul, 1972)

J. Karim, *Rapiers and battleaxes: the Women's Movement and its aftermath* (George Allen and Unwin, 1966)

M.D. Lister, 'Via Necropolis Junction', *Railway Magazine* (vol.119, no.862, 1973) pp.74-76

A. Locke, *A short history of Woking* (1924: originally published in the *Woking Review* but reprinted 1980 by Nancy Leigh Bookshop)

O. Manning and W. Bray, *The history and antiquities of the County of Surrey* vol.1 (1804)

Ministry of Health, *National Survey of Overcrowding* (HMSO, 1936)

E. Mogg (ed), *Paterson's Roads* (1822)

G.T. Moody, *Southern Electric* (Ian Allan, 1968)

I. Nairn and N. Pevsner, *The buildings of England: Surrey* (revised edition by Bridget Cherry, Penguin, 1971)

E. Pankhurst, *The Suffragette Movement* (Longmans, 1931)

E. Parker, *Highways and Byways in Surrey* (Macmillan, 1908) pp.217-18 and 229

A.G. Parton, 'The 1801 crop returns for the County of Surrey', *Surrey Archaeological Collections* (vol.64, 1967) pp.113-23

D. Robinson and C. Webb (eds), *The 1851 Religious Census: Surrey* (Surrey Record Society vol.35, 1997)

W.K. Robinson, *Some notes on the history of Quakerism in Woking and district* (unpublished typescript, 1969: Woking Library)

J.D. Scott, *Vickers: a history* (Weidenfeld, 1962)

L.R. Stevens, *Byfleet: a village of England* (Woking Review Ltd, 1953)

W. Stevenson, *A general view of the agriculture of the County of Surrey* (Board of Agriculture, 1809)

A.H. Stockwell, *The Baptist churches of Surrey* (privately published, undated: circa 1910)

F. Street, *A history of Goldsworth Nursery 1760-1960* (Walter Slocock Ltd, 1960)

Surrey County Council, *Antiquities and Conservation Areas of Surrey* (1976)

Surrey County Council, *The future of Surrey's landscape and woodlands* (3 vols, 1997)

W.E. Tate, 'Enclosure Acts and Awards relating to the County of Surrey', *Surrey Archaeological Collections* (vol.48, 1943) pp.118-49

P. Unwin, *The Printing Unwins: a short history of Unwin Brothers* (George Allen and Unwin, 1976)

D. Upcott, 'Notes on The Grange and some of its occupants', *Woking History Society Newsletter* no.170 (October 1999)

Victoria County History of Surrey, volumes 1 (1905); 2 (1907) and 3 (1911)

P.A.L. Vine, *London's lost route to the sea* (David and Charles, 1963 and subsequent editions)

P.A.L. Vine, *London's lost route to Basingstoke* (David and Charles, 1968 and Alan Sutton, 1994)

W.R. Ward (ed), *Parson and parish in eighteenth-century Surrey: replies to Bishops' Visitations* (Surrey Record Society vol.34, 1994)

C. Webb (editor/transcriber), Abstracts of wills proved in the Archdeaconry Court of Surrey 15-18th centuries (series of typescript volumes in the Surrey History Centre)

R. Wells, 'Popular protest and social crime: the evidence of criminal gangs in rural southern England 1700-1860', *Southern History* no.13 (1991) pp.32-81

West Surrey Family History Society, *The Woking Collection* (CD-ROM, 2002): parish registers for Byfleet, Horsell, Pyrford and Woking; census indexes; other parish records; and photographs

A. Whiteman (ed), *The Compton Census of 1676: a critical edition* (British Academy: Records of Social and Economic History, new series 10, 1986)

E.J. Wilson, *Nurserymen to the world: the nursery gardens of Woking and north-west Surrey and plants introduced by them* (privately published, author, 1989)

Woking and District Co-operative Society, *Pictorial Souvenir of Twenty-One Years work of the W.C.S.* (1920)

V. Woolf, *Night and Day* (1919: Penguin edition, 1969)

PRIMARY SOURCES

The archives held at the Surrey History Centre are the most important source for historians investigating the four parishes. Those used for the 1982 volume (which were then at Surrey Record Office in Kingston, Guildford Muniment Room, and Woking Council offices) are now at the SHC together with much material deposited subsequently. The following summarises the main categories of archive material which has been used in my research and writing:

Parish records

Byfleet St Mary [BY] including the vestry minute books from 1795 and overseers' records; Horsell St Mary [HORS] including registers from 1653, churchwardens' and constables' accounts 1600 onwards, poor law papers inc. settlement and removal orders; Pyrford St Nicholas [PYR] including records of the National School 1848 onwards; Woking St Peter [P52] including churchwardens' accounts from 1617, the 1818-1830 vestry minute book, overseers' accounts from 1611, settlement certificates and removal orders, lists of paupers, and parish registers 1653 onwards.

Local government records

The Woking Borough Council records [6198] are exceptionally important and comprehensive – a particularly fine example of a local authority collection. They include the records of predecessor authorities and I have used them very extensively in researching this book. Among the main categories used are the minutes of the council from 1897 onwards and of its committees from 1893 (including separate committees for all key aspects of local government such as fire brigade, housing, planning, sanitation and health, lighting, amalgamation with other authorities, highways, drainage and sewerage, and swimming baths). Other essential categories include yearbooks, papers and title deeds relating to slum clearance, a very good photograph collection, building plans, annual reports of the Medical Officer of Health, and files on subjects such as town centre redevelopment. The collection includes the surviving records of Byfleet, Horsell and Pyrford Parish Councils, which are of variable quality – the Byfleet collection is reasonably complete, that for Horsell much less so. The records of Chertsey Rural District Council are scattered among the collections of its successor authorities, including Bagshot Rural District Council and Chertsey Urban District Council. It is more difficult to track down this material. The SHC also holds the records of the Guildford and Chertsey Rural Sanitary Authorities and Highway Districts.

Private collections and other archive material

Original wills for Woking people 1483-1858 are held at the London Metropolitan Archives but most are available on microfilm at the Surrey History Centre. Cliff Webb's calendars and abstracts of these probate records (see above) are invaluable to any researcher. The Surrey quarter sessions records (QS), which are indexed, include many petitions, certifications and statements of evidence in civil and criminal cases for all four parishes. Among the more important private papers consulted were:

2158 and 2284	Byfleet and Weybridge enclosure records
LM/865/1/2	Byfleet and Pyrford park survey 1568
G165	Locke King family and estate records
SP/9/53/13	York estate sale particulars 1895
6003/161-166	Sale particulars of properties: Kingfield and St Johns 1930s
G65/1/1-35	Records of the manor of Sutton 1506-1830
1482	Bridley or Crastock manorial records
CEB 10/1-8	Woking School Board records
1216	Records of the Jackman family and nurseries
Z 113/3	1709 map of Brookwood and surrounding areas
3167	Suburban Land Company records
G97 [RB670]	Onslow collection including Woking manor court records and extensive material relating to estates in the area; the collection also includes a large quantity of correspondence and legal papers concerning the sale of land to the London Necropolis Company and the development of the cemetery
1216/6/1-19	material relating to Goldsworth brickfields 1877-1888
1244	diaries and other personal papers of Edward Ryde
864	tithe records (including maps and apportionments) for Woking, Byfleet, Horsell, Pyrford and Sutton 1838-1854

INDEX

A & J Simmons Ltd, 152
Abbey Road, 101
Abraham, Henry, 75, 79
administrative history, 5-8, 61-4, 117-30
Aerco Records, 172
agriculture, 3-4, 11, 15-18, 29-32, 35-39, 41, 43-5, 51, 53, 55-9, 83, 90, 105, 112, 114, 131, 136, 200-1
air raids, 129-30
aircraft industry, 174
Albert, Prince Consort, 86-7
Albion Hotel, 79, 170, 173, 194
Anchor Hill, 2, 28, 34, 133-4
Anne of Denmark, 15
Anthony's, 140
archaeology, 3-4, 9
architecture, 9, 11-12, 15-16, 19-21, 24-7, 45, 68, 75-6, 78, 80-8, 91, 93-5, 101, 103-4, 107, 133, 137-9, 148-9, 153, 156-8, 170, 172-3, 176, 185-7, 193-201
Arnold Road, 84, 175
Arthurs Bridge, 52, 123-4
Arthurs Bridge Road, 102
Ashwood Road, 199
assarting, 17-18
asylum, 71, 74, 93, 96-8, 100, 114, 131, 133
Atlee, William, 45
Aviary Road, 199
aviation, 105

Baker, Thomas, 47
Balfour Avenue, 150-1
Balfour, Hon. Gerald, 110
Balfour, Lady Betty, 110, 160
banks, 172
Barley Mow, 38, 133
Barnsbury, 183
Barrack Path, 100
Basingstoke Canal, 29, 46-7, 50, 53, 66-7, 107, 119, 121-3, 126, 133-4, 175, 188, 201-2
Bassett family, 9, 11-12
Bath Road, 81, 122, 144
Beacon, the, 10
Beaufort, Lady Margaret, 9
Betjeman, John, 156
Bicker, William, 62
Birchwood Road, 199
Bird in Hand, 61, 111
Bisley, 4, 7-8, 14, 16, 22, 28, 96, 120, 127, 133, 157
Blackdown, 59
Blackhorse Road, 74-5, 122
Blackness Farmhouse, 45
blacksmiths, 42, 111

Blair, John, 6-7, 17
Blomfield, Arthur, 94
Blue Anchor, 104
Bluegate Cottage, 200
Board School Road, 84-5, 127, 142, 149
Bolton, Susannah, 60
Boltons Lane, 200
Bonsey Lane, 141
Bonsey, Richard, 47
Boots the Chemist, 173, 196
borough status, 157-8
Boughton, John, 47
boundaries, 5-8, 10, 29-30, 58, 84, 99, 157
Boundary Road, 84-5, 126, 167, 175
Bowles, Rev. Charles, 141
Brewery Road, 137, 194
brewing, 136-7
brick-making, 18, 28, 46-7, 52, 98, 100, 133-4
bridges, 29, 52, 67, 69, 121-3
Bridley, 4, 12, 14, 18, 28, 33, 42, 132, 147, 155, 160, 168, 182
British Home Stores, 196
Broad Mead, 37, 160
Broadway, 78, 80-1, 158, 172, 196
Bronze Age, 4
Brooklands, 29, 39, 104-5, 129, 146, 153, 174
Brooklyn Road, 121, 186
Brookwood, 2, 14, 18, 40, 47-8, 52, 60, 67-68, 73, 76, 98-9, 138, 142, 147, 182, 193
Brookwood Cemetery, 33, 54, 71, 72-6, 181
Brookwood Farm, 184
Brookwood Hospital, 71, 96-8, 189, 191
Brown, John, 125
Brown, Major Collis, 161
Browne, Sir Anthony, 15
Bulbeck, John, 42, 44
Bullbeggars (Lakeview), 36, 184
Bunkers Hill, 34, 111, 132, 134
Burdenshott, 18
Byfleet, 5-7, 18, 30, 41, 43, 50-1, 54, 103, 119, 126, 147, 149, 153, 162, 172, 179-83, 193
Byfleet brewery, 137, 161
Byfleet bypass, 163, 192
Byfleet church, 20, 22, 137
Byfleet common fields, 35-6
Byfleet enclosure, 55-8
Byfleet fire brigade, 129-30
Byfleet Lodge, 104
Byfleet manor, 14-15, 116
Byfleet Mill, 4, 28, 30, 45-6, 161

Byfleet Parish Council, 105, 119-20, 127, 129, 146, 158, 161
Byfleet Park, 14-15, 30
Byfleet recreation ground, 167
Byfleet refuse collection, 125
Byfleet sanitation, 124
Byfleet schools, 140-2
Byfleet stations, 68, 105, 176, 193
Byfleet street lighting, 127-8
Byfleet union with Woking, 157
Byfleet water supply, 120
Byfleet workhouse, 61-2

Calne, Ruald de, 7
Camphill Road, 56, 62, 105, 167
canals and navigations, 24, 29, 32, 38-40, 46, 50-4, 66-7, 100, 107, 121-3, 126, 133-4, 175, 188, 201-2
Candlerush Grove, 31
Cartbridge, 40, 45
Carthouse Lane, 180
Catherine of Aragon, 14
Cemetery Pales, 75
Chapel Street, 81, 170
charity, 61, 167
Charles II, 11, 14, 24
Charrington, Charles, 167
Charrington, Henry, 137
charters, 23-4
Cheapside, 34
Chertsey, 6-7, 48, 50, 64, 68, 115, 119-20, 128, 147, 157
Chertsey Abbey, 6-8, 14-15, 22
Chertsey Highway District, 117
Chertsey Road (Woking), 79, 81, 122-3, 128, 137, 168, 171-5, 194
Chertsey Rural District Council, 103, 119-25, 146, 149, 157-8, 161-2
Chertsey Rural Sanitary Authority, 118
Chobham, 7, 43, 96, 120, 129, 157, 169
Chobham Road (Woking), 52, 80, 123, 170
cholera, 123
Church Path, 170, 194
Church Road (Byfleet), 153
Church Street (Woking village), 23-5, 135
Church Street (Woking), 80, 121-2, 129, 137, 168, 171-2, 194-5
Church Street school, 141-2
churches and chapels, 4, 7-8, 19-23, 38, 71, 74, 78, 80-1, 83, 100, 137-40, 179
Chylde, John, 45
civil unrest, 63
Clandon, East and West, 120
Claremont Avenue, 91

Claremont Road, 105
Clarence Avenue, 82, 194
Clematis Jackmanii, 54
Cleveland, Barbara, duchess of, 11
Clock House, 153
coach services, 50, 67
Cobbett, Henry, 54
Cobham, 46, 66
Coldharbour, 4, 34, 58, 107
College Road, 111
Commercial Road [Way], 69, 79, 81, 117, 158, 164-5, 168, 172, 194
Common Close, 152-5
commons, see heaths and commons
commuting, 68, 98-9, 101-2, 105-6, 109, 116, 146, 149, 175-6, 191, 193
Conan Doyle, Arthur, 110
Connaught Road, 98-9
conservation, 26, 77, 91, 103, 107, 178, 186-8, 199-202
Conservative Club, 81
Constitution Hill, 91, 126-7, 186
Cooke, John, 44
Cooke, Thomas P., 86
Copse Road, 100
Corrie Road, 149, 160
Corrie, William Hill, 160
Corsebrook, 2
council offices, 158-9, 194
councillors, 128-9, 160-1
county hall, 191, 202
Courtenay Road, 84
Craigmore Tower, 186-7
Crastock, see Bridley
crematorium, 100-1
Cricketers Inn, 35, 62
crime, 47-8, 63, 94, 104, 127, 139, 172
Cross Lanes Farm/Estate, 90-2

Dartnell Park, 55, 106
Davis, James, 47
Deepcut, 52, 168
deer parks, 11, 15-16, 24
Defoe, Daniel, 16, 30, 48-9
Dennett, Henry, 137
Despenser family, 9
Dilke, Sir Charles, 109
Domesday Book/Survey, 6, 9, 14, 16-18, 28, 45
Donald, Robert, 31, 54
Dover, Robert, 49
Drummond, Henry, 63, 71, 73
Duke Street, 142, 196
Dunford Bridge, 4, 15, 62, 122
Dydleston, Hugh, 22

East Hill, 58-9
ecology, 3-4, 30, 167, 200
economic history, 18, 23-4, 30, 38-40, 43-5, 47, 49-53, 59, 63, 100, 114, 126, 130-6, 169-72, 174-6, 189-91, 193, 196-7
Eden Grove, 35, 184
Edmund, duke of Somerset, 23
education, 74, 78, 139-43
Edward II, 9, 14
Egham, 7, 69, 115
Egley Road, 27

Electric Accumulator Supply Company, 174
electricity, 25, 85, 111, 126-8, 174
Elizabeth I, 10, 15, 22
Ellis, Sir James Whittaker, 129
Elmbridge, 37-8, 90, 122, 124, 126, 152
Elton's, booksellers, 172
employment and occupations, 41-2, 63, 93, 97, 100, 114, 116, 130-6, 146, 163-6, 169-70, 174-6, 179, 189-91, 196
enclosure, 15, 17-18, 29, 32-5, 51, 55-60, 71-4, 109
Engliff Lane, 149
environmental history, 3, 4, 126, 174, 178, 200-1
essential oils distillery, 106, 136
ethnic minorities, 189-90
Eve Road, 84

Fairway estate, 156
Farley, Marcy, 48
Fenn, Abraham, 47
fire services, 128-30, 158
fires, 45, 129-30, 158
Fishers Hill, 93, 110, 199
Fladgate family, 36, 47, 90
Flowing Ditch, 44
Floyds Lane, 155
football, 36, 38, 167
fords, 28-9, 163-4
Fords Farm, 152
forest law, 17
Fox Corner, 155
Foxlake Farm, 153
Frailey Heath, 34
Frederick, Duke of York, 14, 57
Freeman, Hardy and Willis, 172
Frimley, 7, 96
Frog Lane Farm, 109
fuel, 30-2, 50, 56, 126, 134, 165

Gaddiston, John, 21
Gammon's store, 170, 172
garden suburb, 103
gas supplies and gasworks, 25, 53, 83, 85, 96, 126-8, 134, 160, 162, 174-5
Gaveston, Piers, 14
Getty, John Paul, 11
Gloster, Henry, 139
Glosters, corn merchant, 171
Godalming, 18, 45, 67, 69, 136
Godley, hundred of, 6, 15-16
Goldsworth, 14, 28, 40, 52, 54, 69, 82-3, 93, 100, 133, 141, 144, 168, 174
Goldsworth brickworks, 134
Goldsworth Farm, 144
Goldsworth Green, 38
Goldsworth Nurseries, 31, 54, 75
Goldsworth Park, 2, 16, 181, 183-4, 187-9, 191-2
Goldsworth Road, 69, 83, 124, 161, 165, 194
Goldsworth Road School, 117, 142
Golf Club Road, 93, 156
golf clubs and courses, 60, 71, 93, 156, 168, 185
Gongers Lane, 108
Goodall, Charlotte, 172

grammar schools, 143
Grand Theatre, 158
green belt, 178, 180-3, 187
greens, 27, 29-30, 35, 37-8, 108
Grove Barrs, 152
Guildford, 18, 22, 38, 45, 48, 50, 66-9, 115, 126, 128, 139, 147, 175, 198
Guildford Highway District, 117, 121
Guildford Road (Woking), 69, 90, 159, 185, 194
Guildford Rural Sanitary Authority, 118, 123, 144
Guinness family, 110
Gybbs, Edward, 22

Hale End, 13, 42
Hamilton, James, 48
Hammerton, William, 47
Harland, Mary, 48
Harris, Hugh, 172
Hart, James and Hannah, 47
Hassell, John, 20, 23
Hathewell, John, 45
Havering Farm, 33
health and disease, see public health
Heathrow Airport, 191-3
heaths and commons, 3-4, 17-18, 30-4, 45, 51, 55-8, 66-73, 84-6, 92, 94, 105, 165, 167, 181, 194, 200-1
Heathside, 13, 83, 155
Heathside Farm, 90
Heathside Park Road, 199
Heathside Road, 68, 79, 89, 91, 144, 186
Henry I, 11
Henry II, 17
Henry VI, 23
Henry VII, 9-10
Henry VIII, 9-10, 14
Henry Virtue Bayley & Co., 134
Hermitage, 18, 47, 52, 67, 74, 100, 133, 153
Hermitage Road, 163
High Road, 30, 46, 103-4, 129
High Street (Horsell), 101-2
High Street (Woking village), 25, 107
High Street (Woking), 78, 80-1, 136, 165, 170, 172-3
highway districts, 117
Hill Place, 16
Hillier, John, 21
Hillview Road [estate], 89, 91, 165, 185-7
Hipley [Bridge], 3, 18, 135
Hipley Street, 152
Hockering, The, 155-6, 186, 199
Hodd, Robert, 36
Hoe Bridge, 36-7, 59, 61
Hoe Bridge estate, 116, 124
Hoe Place, 10, 20
Hoe Stream, 2, 36-7, 91, 124, 126, 166, 200
Hollands, 13
Holly Bank Road, 93
Holroyd family, 126, 137, 161
Holyoake Crescent, 103, 199
Home and Colonial Stores, 172
Hone, Robert, 22
Hook Heath, 2, 13, 48, 52, 67-8, 71, 74,

92-3, 100, 110, 115, 124, 126, 132, 136, 147, 155, 199

Horsell, 2, 5-6, 17-18, 28, 34, 41, 43, 45, 50-1, 54, 64, 101, 114-15, 117, 126, 147, 149, 152, 162, 166, 169, 199

Horsell Birch, 36

Horsell brewery, 137

Horsell church, 8, 20-3, 68, 102, 137

Horsell Common, 3-4, 36, 60, 69, 139-40, 152, 154-5, 163, 167, 181

Horsell common fields, 36

Horsell fire service, 129

Horsell Grange, 103, 152

Horsell manor, 15

Horsell Parish Council, 119-20

Horsell refuse collection, 125

Horsell schools, 140-1

Horsell union with Woking, 119-20, 124, 160

Horsell water supply, 120

Horsell workhouse, 62

Horsley, East and West, 6, 120

hospitals, 52, 144, 165

housing, 28, 33-4, 59-60, 62, 78, 83-5, 88-93, 96, 98-100, 102-3, 106-9, 111, 126, 132-3, 146-7, 149, 151-2, 155-6, 168, 178-90, 194

industrial decline, 190-1

industries, 45, 51, 85, 114, 126, 136, 146, 174-6, 179, 190-1

industries, aircraft, 146, 174

industries, brewing, 136-7

industries, brick, 18, 28, 46-7, 52, 98, 100, 133-4

industries, iron, 28, 41, 46

industries, lime, 46, 51

industries, milling, 45-6

industries, packaging, 175

industries, paper, 28, 46, 114, 134

industries, printing, 114, 135-6, 174

industries, rubber, 175

industries, textile, 45

industries, wire, 41, 46

Inkerman Barracks, 95-6, 163, 168

institutions, 85-6, 93-8, 114, 131, 146

International Stores, 172-3

iron-making, 28, 41, 46

Jackman family, 54, 100, 134

Jackman, George, 54

Jackman's Nurseries, 54-5

James Walker Limited, 146, 175, 190

James, William, 30, 37, 43

Jebb, Sir Joshua, 94

Jekyll, Gertrude, 93, 132

Kettlewell, 69, 102-3, 144, 154-5

Kiln Bridge, 18, 47, 100, 133, 137

King [Locke King] family, 14-15, 58, 103, 116, 180

Kingfield, 13, 26, 36-8, 45, 63, 108-9, 124, 132, 139, 152, 155-6, 161, 169, 173

Kingfield Farm, 152

Kingfield forge, 111

Kinton, Henry, 12

Kittredge, Councillor, 128-9

Knaphill, 2, 4, 14, 16, 18, 28, 32, 34, 38, 41, 47, 50, 52, 54, 69, 71, 74, 83, 96, 98, 115, 124, 127-8, 133, 138, 141, 147-9, 157, 160, 167, 181-2, 189, 193

Knaphill Common, 32, 34, 94, 99

Knaphill schools, 142

Knaphill shops, 169, 173

landscape history, 11, 16-18, 24, 30-8, 44, 51, 55-60, 72-7, 93, 107, 109, 112, 124, 155, 166, 200-1

Lane, Sarah, 50

lavender-growing, 105-6, 136

leisure and sport, 52, 60, 73, 93, 104, 107, 126, 156, 160, 165-7, 188, 198, 201-2

Leitner, Wilhelm Gottlieb, 87-8

libraries, 158, 194

Lightwater, 192-3

lime-burning, 46

liquorice, 136

literature and poetry, 57, 109-12, 156

Littlewick, 16, 69, 187

Loampits Farm, 44

local government, 6-7, 10, 13-14, 16, 29, 61-4, 81, 85, 97, 110, 117-31, 142-4, 147-9, 157-62

Locke King, Henry, 103, 167

London County Council, 156, 179-80

London Necropolis Company, 60, 70-80, 82-4, 89, 92-3, 94, 96, 98, 101, 117, 120, 123, 137, 142, 151, 160, 165, 170

Loop Road, 108, 152

Loudon, John Claudius, 54

Lovibond, John & Co., 137

Lucas, William, 172

Lutyens, Sir Edwin, 93, 110

Macfisheries, 173

Malcolm, Jacob, 30, 37, 43

Malet, Robert, 11

Mangles, James, 72

manorial history, 6, 8-12, 14-16, 24, 31, 33, 37, 60, 72-3

markets and fairs, 23-4, 45, 121, 165, 167, 169

Marks & Spencer, 173, 196

Martinsyde Aircraft Company, 174

Mary I, 10, 22

Maxwell, music shop, 172

Maybury, 13, 32, 34, 74, 85-6, 115, 124-6, 132, 134, 138, 155, 168, 173-4, 183

Maybury Board Schools, 142

Maybury Inn, 59, 90, 111

Maybury Road, 84-5, 110, 122, 172, 184, 190

Mayford, 5, 12, 27, 38, 40-2, 46-7, 49, 54, 60, 67, 75, 109, 111, 126, 147, 150, 160, 163, 168, 182, 192, 200

meadows, common, 15, 28, 35, 37

Meadway Drive, 152

medical services, 62, 85, 94, 143-4

mental health, 96-8

Mesolithic sites, 4

migration, 50, 93, 115-17, 132, 156, 168, 179-80, 189

military history, 51, 75, 95-6, 129-30, 168

mills (water), 28-30, 40, 45-6, 134-5

Mimbridge, 15, 122

Mizen's Farm, 4

monasteries, 6-7, 14-15, 19-20, 22, 153

mosque, 83, 88, 190

Mossop, Robert, 128, 161

motorways, 147, 158, 163, 178, 187, 192-3

Mount Hermon, 91, 110, 115, 168, 185-7, 199

Mount Hermon Road, 121, 159, 187

Munby, Arthur, 20, 109, 131-2, 134

Nairn, Ian, 82, 103, 137-9, 179

National Land Company, 102

Necropolis, *see* London Necropolis Company; Brookwood Cemetery

Neolithic sites, 4

New & Maynes Limited, 126

New Haw, 3

New Ideal Homes Ltd, 187

Newark Mill, 45, 122

Newark Priory, 4, 7-8, 22, 25

Newland, John, 136

nonconformity, 139-40

Norfolk Farm, 59

North Road, 174

North Surrey Water Company, 120

Norwood, Thomas, 22

nurserying, 31, 43, 53-5, 75, 92, 100, 114, 131-4, 160, 167, 183, 187

occupations, *see* employment and occupations

Offa, King of Mercia, 7

office development, 83, 178, 190-1, 194, 198

Old Avenue, 105, 156, 199

Old Brew House, 26

Old Woking, *see* Woking village

Omega Road, 84

Onslow, earls of, 11, 47, 61, 72, 101, 110, 124

open fields, 35-8

Orchard Drive, 152

Oriental Institute, 85, 87-8, 174, 176

Oriental Road, 79, 89, 127, 153

Ottershaw, 64, 144, 193

overspill, 156, 178-80

Oyster Lane, 30, 46, 105, 176

packaging production, 175

Page, Richard, 21

Palmer, John, 33

Pankhurst, Emmeline, 110

paper-making, 28, 46, 114, 134

parish records, 40, 50, 61

Park Road, 155

Parker, Eric, 29, 112

parks and open spaces, 73, 81, 91, 126, 159, 165-7, 188, 199-201

Parley Brook, 52

parliamentary constituency, 162

party politics, 162

Parvis Road, 30

Peacocks, The, 82, 198

pedestrianisation, 79, 194, 196

Pembroke Road, 155

Percy Street, 121, 159, 173

Percy, Reuben, 79, 170
Peterborough abbey, 7
Petersham Avenue, 149
Pirbright, 7-8, 33, 51, 67, 74, 96, 116, 127, 129, 134, 139, 157, 168, 173
place names, 2, 5, 13, 15, 18, 28
planning, town planning, 24, 26, 58-60, 67, 69-71, 73-85, 89-92, 98-9, 101, 103, 146-7, 149, 151-6, 163, 166-8, 173, 176-202
Plough Bridge, Byfleet, 29-30, 122
Pocock, Albert, 171
political history, 63, 110, 128-9, 142, 160-2
pollution, 126, 174
Pond Road, 199
ponds, 27, 38, 108, 201
poor law unions, 64, 160
population, 17-18, 33, 40-1, 49-50, 93, 114-17, 134, 144, 146-7, 156-7, 168, 179-82, 185, 187-9
poverty and the poor, 27-8, 30, 34, 50, 56-7, 61-4, 76, 92, 132-3, 151, 156
prehistory, 3
Prey Heath, 58-9, 73, 155
printing, 114, 135-6, 174
prisons, 74, 93-6, 98, 100, 114, 133
probate records, 21, 44
public buildings, 81
public health, 62, 70, 85, 97, 118, 123, 143-4, 151
public houses and hotels, 26-7, 35, 47, 52, 61, 68, 78
Purdam, Robert, 23
Pyle [Pile] Hill, 3, 36, 58, 109, 155, 163
Pyrford, 2-6, 14, 18, 28, 34, 40-1, 43, 60, 64, 107, 114-15, 122, 124, 126, 128, 132, 147, 149, 155, 179, 182, 199
Pyrford church, 8, 19-21, 28, 137
Pyrford common fields, 35-6
Pyrford Court, 108, 110, 133
Pyrford enclosure, 55-6, 58
Pyrford Green, 15, 29, 44, 62
Pyrford Heath, 58
Pyrford manor, 15-16
Pyrford Parish Council, 119, 129, 161
Pyrford School Board, 142-3
Pyrford schools, 141, 143
Pyrford union with Woking, 157
Pyrford wall paintings, 19
Pyrford water supply, 120
Pyrford Woods, 155, 180, 185
Pyrford workhouse, 62

Quakers, 139
Quartermaine Avenue, 150-1
Quartermaine, Henry, 160

Railway Hotel, 68, 78, 90, 170
railways, 51, 66-70, 72-3, 75-8, 80-1, 86, 98, 103, 105, 111-12, 114, 116, 122, 136, 146, 153, 163, 175-6, 191, 193
Raistrick family, 78-9, 83
rates and taxes, 18, 61-2, 118-20, 123-4, 128, 160, 175
Rectory Lane, 153
Red House Hotel, 124
refuse collection, 119, 125-6, 133

religion, 5-8, 14, 19-23, 74-5, 81-2, 100, 137-40, 190
retailing, 81-3, 98, 106, 121, 131, 169-74, 189, 194-8
Ripley, 7-8, 66-7, 120, 126-7, 135, 155, 157, 163
Rive Ditch, 2, 52, 59, 119, 124, 174, 179
river traffic, 39, 42, 45, 52
roads and highways, 4, 25-6, 28-9, 34, 38, 49-50, 58-9, 63, 66-9, 72, 74, 78-80, 83-5, 96, 104, 108, 117, 121-3, 147, 151, 155, 162-5, 187-8, 192-4
Robin Hood Road, 94, 134
Roman Catholicism, 139
Roman period, 4
Rooke, Thomas, 21
Rosebery Crescent, 152
Rosehill Avenue, 54
Rosemount Parade, 105-6, 199
Rowbarge public house, 134
Royal Dramatic College, 85-7, 89, 176
Rudehall, 13
Runtley, 12-13, 18, 47
Russell Road, 102
Ryde, Edward, 32, 44, 66, 160, 169
Rydens Way, 36, 155

Sainsbury's, 173, 196
St George's Hill, 6, 29-30, 46, 55-6, 66, 103
St Johns, 18, 47, 52, 67-8, 74, 99, 110, 115, 123-4, 127-8, 136, 142, 160, 163, 168
St John's church, 137
St Johns Hill, 54, 100
St Johns Lye, 31, 73, 165
St Johns schools, 141
St Peter's Hospital, 144
St Peter's Road, 149
Sanders, Thomas, 62
sanitation, 85, 103, 118, 123-6, 144
Saunders Lane, 38, 46, 75, 163-4
Saxon period, 5
school boards, 142-3
schools, 74, 78, 80, 117, 134, 139-3
schools, secondary, 143
Scott, George Gilbert, 137
Send, 7-8, 26, 37, 39-40, 45, 47, 120, 126, 134-5, 157, 193
settlement history, 4-5, 16-17, 23-8, 33, 52, 56-7
sewers and sewerage, 53, 85, 118-20, 123-4, 179
Shackleford, 13, 27, 40, 42, 109, 139, 152, 169
Shaftesbury Road, 89
Shears, William, 161
Sheepwalks, 124
Sheerwater, 2, 58-9, 147, 155, 162, 179-80, 185
Sheerwater Court, 105
Sherlock, Charles, 128-9
shops, 81-3, 98, 106, 136, 149, 155, 168-74, 188-9, 194-8
Shores Road, 180
Shrapnells, 103
Sithwood, 16
Six Crossroads, 165, 192

Skeet and Jeff, ironmonger, 172
slum clearance, 85, 99, 149, 151, 184-5
Smallpeice family, 155
Smallpeice, George, 126, 160
Smarts Heath, 3, 27, 46, 73, 111
Smyth, Dame Ethel, 110
soils, 3, 16, 44, 46, 53
Sorbo Rubber Company, 146, 175
South West Suburban Water Company, 120
Spanton's timberyard, 53, 100, 175
Sparrow Park, 81, 159, 165
sport, *see* leisure and sport
squatter housing, 28, 33-4, 99, 111, 132
Stanley Farm, 181
Stanley Road, 80
Station Approach (West Byfleet), 199
Station Approach (Woking), 69, 160, 194
Station Road (West Byfleet), 105
Stedman, John, 137
Stevenson, William, 30
Stockers Lane, 37, 155
Stoke next Guildford, 6, 44, 64
Stream Close, 61
street lighting, 25, 118-19, 127-8, 172
Suburban Land Company, 91, 165
Sun Inn, 136
Sundridge, 27
Surrey County Council, 179-80, 191-2, 202
Sutton [Green], 3, 11-12, 14, 18, 27, 32-3, 39-40, 42, 45, 57-8, 109, 139, 141-2, 160, 168
Sutton enclosure, 55, 57-9
Sutton Place, 11-13, 39, 43-4, 47, 109, 139, 201
swimming pool, 126, 166, 196-7

Tarbox, Rev. E.W., 140
Tegg, William, 60
Teylar, Thomas, 22
Thorpe, 7
timber trade, 53
Timothy White, 172
Tite, Sir William, 75
tithings, 10, 13, 16
topography, 2, 3
town centre redevelopment, 138, 147, 158-9, 164-6, 168, 172-3, 190-1, 193-8
Town Square, 194
Town Street, 13, 26, 45
Townsley, 15
Townsley Mead, 37, 58
traffic problems, 162, 164-5, 173, 192-4, 196
tramways, 69
Trevet, Thomas, 21
Triggs Lane, 38, 74
Trigg's Lock, 39
Turner, Jacob, 54
Turnoak, 155, 163, 165, 186
Twichen in Horsell, 15
Tylers, wine merchants, 172
typhoid, 123

Ulwin, 14
United Land Company, 84
Unsworth, William, 138

Unwin Brothers [Limited], 135, 174
urban deprivation, 156, 168, 180, 184-5, 190

vagrancy and itinerants, 49-50, 132, 167
vermin, catching, 61
Vicarage Road, 27
Vickers aircraft works, 174
Victoria Arch, 69, 83, 121-2, 165
Victoria Road, 133-4
Victoria Way, 192-6

Walden, Joan, 22
Waldens Farm, 101
Waldens Park Estate, 102
Walsham Mead, 37, 58
Walton on Thames, 18, 119, 157
Walton Road, 13, 69, 82, 84, 86, 122, 168, 184, 190
Wapshott, 18
war, 43, 46, 51, 76, 95, 123, 128-30, 134, 146, 174, 178, 184
war memorial, 165
War of the Worlds, The, 110-11
wards, 118-19, 160
waste, the, *see* heaths and commons
water supplies, 120, 123
Waterer family, 54
Waterer, Anthony, 54, 167
Waterers Park, 167
weaving, 45
Webster, Mr and Mrs, 86
Wells, Daniel, 47
Wells, H.G., 110-11
Wells, James, 47
Wermig, Gustav, 160
West Byfleet, 3, 33, 56, 58, 60, 105-6, 115, 124, 126, 138, 155, 158, 173, 189
West Byfleet redevelopment, 106, 185-6, 190-1
West Heath, 182
West Street, 168, 171, 194
West Surrey Mutual Benefit Building Society, 80
West, Richard, 32
West, William, 42
Westfield, 13, 27, 35, 44, 60, 62, 73, 132, 147, 149, 150, 168, 182
Westfield common fields, 36
Westfield Road, 108
Westfield schools, 134, 141-2

Westminster Abbey, 15, 19
Weston, John Webb, 13, 47, 57-8
Weston, Sir Richard, 11, 39-40, 43-4
Wey Navigation, 24, 38, 40, 42, 45, 51-2, 157
Weybridge, 7, 56, 66, 68, 119, 136, 157
Weymede, 103
Wheatsheaf Bridge, 52, 69, 119, 121, 123, 144
Wheatsheaf Close, 152
Wheatsheaf Common, 101, 154-5, 166, 189
Wheeler, William, 23
White Horse Inn, 26
White Rose Lane, 80, 89-90, 112, 121, 139, 148, 160, 186, 201
Whitmoor [Common], 3, 33, 36, 42, 47, 58-9, 192
William I, 9, 11, 15
Williams, James, 47
Windlesham, 7-8, 119-20, 181
Windsor Great Forest, 17
Winern Glebe, 35, 155
Wintersells, 29, 104
wire-making, 41, 46
Wisley, 7-8, 46, 116, 124-5
Wocc/Wocca, 5-6
Woking and Maybury Electric Laundry, 174
Woking brewery, 137
Woking Broad Mead, 37
Woking Christ Church, 81, 137-8
Woking church (St Peter), 6-8, 20-3, 38
Woking common fields, 35-7, 155
Woking Community Hospital, 144
Woking Co-operative Society, 103
Woking Crematorium, 100-1
Woking District Gas Co., 53
Woking Electricity Supply Company, 126, 128
Woking enclosure, 60, 72
Woking Gas and Water Company, 120, 126
Woking hundred, 6, 16
Woking Local Board, 85, 118-19, 121, 124-5, 127-8, 143, 158, 160-1, 165
Woking Lodge, 79, 83, 153
Woking manor, 9, 72
Woking manor house, 24, 26
Woking market house, 23-4, 171
Woking mills, 40, 45, 134

Woking monastery, 7-8, 20
Woking Mutual Improvement Society, 143
Woking palace, 9, 12, 39, 201
Woking Park, 38, 45, 91, 126, 166, 186
Woking Park Farm, 4, 10, 124
Woking population, 114-15
Woking projected university, 87-8
Woking Public Halls, 81, 117
Woking Ratepayers Association, 161
Woking School Board, 142-3, 160
Woking station, 67-8, 74, 78-80, 89, 101, 112, 114, 121, 134, 136, 193
Woking town centre, 68-9, 74, 77-83, 137, 147; *see also* town centre redevelopment
Woking, treaty of, 10
Woking Urban District Council, 53, 79, 81, 91, 96, 119, 121-7, 129, 146, 149, 151, 157-63, 167, 174, 193-5
Woking Victoria Hospital, 144, 165
Woking village, 4, 13, 23-6, 40-2, 107-8, 112, 124, 127-8, 134-5, 141-2, 147, 152, 159, 160-2, 168-9, 199
Woking workhouse, 62
Woking, Horsell and District Cooperative Society, 173
Wolsey, Thomas, 10
Woodham, 14-15, 39, 51, 59, 134, 147, 155, 157, 182, 201
Woodham Hall estate, 156
Woodham Heath, 58
Woodham Lane, 59, 138, 183
Woodham Road, 154-5
Woodham Waye, 156
woodland, 3, 5, 16-18, 30, 45, 47, 59-60, 77, 106, 201
Woods, Edward, 68
Woods, James, 121
Woods, William, 47
Woodward & Co., 136
Woolf, Virginia, 109
workhouses, 29, 61-4
Worplesdon, 50, 68, 139, 181
Wych Hill [Street], 71, 92, 121, 132, 186

Ynwood, John, 22
York Road, 91, 138, 159, 187

Zouch, Sir Edward, 9-11
Zouch, Sir James, 23